COP!

Also by L. H. Whittemore
**The Man Who
Ran the Subways:**
The Story of Mike Quill

COP!

A CLOSEUP OF VIOLENCE AND TRAGEDY
by L. H. WHITTEMORE

37910

HOLT, RINEHART AND WINSTON
NEW YORK • CHICAGO • SAN FRANCISCO

A portion of this book has appeared in somewhat different
form in *Life* magazine.

Published simultaneously in Canada by Holt, Rinehart
and Winston of Canada, Limited.

Library of Congress Catalog Card Number: 68-12216

Published, July, 1969
Fourth Printing, November, 1969

Designer: Robert Reed

SBN: 03-076475-0

Printed in the United States of America

to
GLORIA

Contents

Introduction

I have written this book not as an editorial but in the hope that the reader will be able to share my experiences of following a few American policemen on their jobs. For many months I spent extended periods of time with individual cops in Harlem, the South Side of Chicago, and Haight-Ashbury, San Francisco. I followed the policemen everywhere, experienced their jobs, and listened to what was on their minds as they worked for eight hours of day or night in situations boiling with violence and tragedy.

The cop's world allows him little time for working out reasonable conclusions about his work. If he is lucky enough to return home physically unharmed, at the end of his daily tour of duty, he still must repair his emotional equipment to be able to go through the ordeal the following day. In the social turbulence of our time the cop is often simplified—labeled the villain or the victim of individual events. Yet, in the personal view I had, I found complex and sometimes confused individuals grappling firsthand with the sickness of society while the rest of us theorize about prevention and cure. The cop flays instinctively at the social cancer around him, using his night-stick and his gun—inadequate, primitive tools—as it spreads under his feet until he, too, becomes both a sufferer and a carrier of the disease.

In collecting this material, I feel reasonably certain that my presence did not influence the cops' behavior because of the great amount of time I spent with them. In time, I became just an ordinary companion, as if I were a shadow they had learned to live with and, occasionally, ceased to notice. As my presence grew less awkward for them, the individual men seemed to grow more determined to say whatever came into their minds. In one sense, I became almost invisible. On the other hand, I gave them an everpresent audience for their thoughts, a chance to get their own viewpoint on the record.

I used written notes and a portable tape recorder. At first, the recorder attracted a lot of attention, but eventually it too was accepted as an unbiased, routine companion. Once the men understood my job, they did not seem overly conscious of the machine though, of course, they knew its purpose.

Prisoners and occasionally other passengers rode with me in the back seats of patrol cars, but most of the time I was alone, as if in a taxicab. I accompanied the cops outside the car, on the streets, and inside the buildings. I was often uncomfortable, a journalist among policemen, a white man in the ghetto, a "square" in hippieville. I was aware of people staring, first at me and then at my tape recorder. However, my identity was construed at different times as that of a police inspector, an insurance salesman, a government-subcommittee member, a narcotics agent, and, a few times, a criminal suspect.

I was not afraid in any of the situations we confronted, mainly because I felt that the policemen I was with would protect me. However, it was understood that if we encountered any serious trouble, I would be left to my own devices and would not get in their way. At times, therefore, I did find myself thinking about various methods of self-defense. I learned for myself that in police work, even as I experienced it, there is always an underlying element of fear.

Yet, there was only one incident in which I was affected physically. A cute little boy in Harlem walked up to the window of the patrol car and said, "Hi, police." I patted him on the head and he playfully socked me in the face.

The little boy's action was solid evidence of what was, for me, the "background sound" of the ghetto. In Harlem and in the South Side, and in ghettos everywhere, I imagine, there is a constant hum of children. My tape recorder demonstrated this vividly. Children's voices perpetually clamored in accompaniment to the dialogue as I played it back. In reality, you eventually screen the youngsters out, in the same way that you become used to the sounds of a factory. But the tape recorder is not so selective and the tapes insistently remind me that our slums are filled, not with flowers and trees, but with new generations.

Another part of the "atmosphere" in which I worked was the police radio. In the narrative, I have cut its babbling for the sake of clarity, but, for the cops, the radio never lets up. With one ear they listen continually to its crude, unconnected reactions to the day's misfortunes. At any moment, the announcement may directly concern them, and their listening is a ceaseless, tension-filled act of anticipation.

Putting the material together for each of the three sections of the book was a process of distillation. The result is a selective reality as true to the total experience as I could make it. Manipulating the timing and sequence of some of the events was necessary in order to spare the reader the weeks and months I spent on the scene. For example, many of the situations in the book were repeated in various forms, several times over. I selected those which I felt served best to express each cop's character as well as his environment.

I have also disguised all names and identities, and on occasion have merged two or three cops into one character for the sake of a unified narrative. In many cases I had the feeling that although I was listening to a particular cop, it might as well have been any of his companions speaking. In addition, specific addresses and locations have been disguised.

Originally, I wanted to keep myself out of the book, in order to present the cops as they normally go about their work. However, to keep faith with the reader, I was compelled to indicate where the dialogue was directed at me, or where I thought it was spoken for my benefit. I knew from the start that I would not see cops taking bribes or beating people up. Yet, I am fully aware that those subjects, and perhaps others, deserve separate treatment in another kind of book.

In fact, if there were any thesis in the pages to follow, it might be simply that policemen are individual men who work on the cutting edge of social conditions. The cops' moral behavior is as reflective of our values as of theirs. If they become corrupt or criminally brutal, then we should not only correct their conduct, but also examine our own consciences.

I am grateful to the police departments of New York, Chicago, and San Francisco for having extended the courtesy and cooperation without which I could not have done the research for this book. I am especially in debt to those officers who let me tag along and who spoke their minds freely. To my knowledge, they are still going through the kind of situations which I have recorded. I do not envy them.

—L. H. Whittemore
June, 1969

I

**Patrolman Joseph Minelli
Harlem, New York**

The two cops slid from the radio car and walked in the sunlight to the door of the five-story tenement building, leaving behind them the whistles and screams of black-brown children and the sound of Spanish music. They moved into the smell of urine and vomit of the dark hall and walked slowly up the creaking stairs, side-stepping the overflowing bags of garbage on each floor, glancing at the writings on the paint-cracked walls, and nodding to the curious, terrified people who first peeked and then, as the officers continued upward, spilled out of their doors to see what the trouble was this time.

Sounds followed them up the stairwell: mothers shouting, babies wailing, dogs barking. Kettle, the larger cop, opened the top three buttons of his uniform, uncovering a red-plaid shirt and a thick neck with rolls of dirt in its creases, formed there by the sweat pouring down from the flesh of his baby face. At the beginning of the final, narrow flight of stairs, he turned to his partner: "Shit."

As they plodded to the top floor they could hear a long, deep moaning and the words "Oh, Lawd, oh, Lawd, oh, Lawd!" Patrolman Joe Minelli, Kettle's partner, knocked on the door to apartment 5-C and after a moment pushed it open. An old Negro woman, her face a mass of black wrinkles and her hair white as if from shock, was swaying back and forth on a small chair in the center of a kitchen torn apart by a victorious burglar. The cops walked inside but the old woman continued to rock and hold her breast, moaning, "Oh, Lawd, oh, Lawd, oh, *Lawd*," without once indicating that she was aware of their presence. Minelli walked closer, taking out his memo book and pen.

"How'd he break in?" he asked, but the woman could not hear him. Beyond her was a window whose black iron gate had been broken and twisted, apparently enabling the burglar to slip into the apartment from the fire escape. Minelli inspected the gate, then turned to the woman: "There's good and bad kinds of gates. I can show you where to get a good, strong gate."

The old woman, her eyes closed and her face slanted upward as if she were praying, cried softly, making some indistinguishable sounds. The patrolmen stood on either side of her, waiting to get the information necessary to make out a report. "What'd they take?" Minelli asked. To his colleague he muttered, "What did she have worth taking?"

Suddenly a cockroach crawled from a pile of empty cans and dishes onto the table next to the woman, and instinctively her hand shot out, squashed the cockroach and rubbed it off the table. Then the woman's hand moved back to her face to wipe the tears. "How old are you, Momma?" asked Kettle, the burly cop. No answer. "Listen, Momma, we'll send someone over, if they're not too busy, to get the information. When you collect yourself just make a list of the things that were taken and their value."

"Oh, Lawd!"

The two cops backed out of the room, closed the door, listening to the black woman moaning, and trudged down the stairs again while the doors of the curious tenants were slowly swinging shut. "Hey!" shouted Minelli. "Anybody seen the *boig*lar?" There was no response and the cops began laughing and walking faster, moving downward and away from the misery on the top floor.

In a baritone voice that filled the depressing tenement building with a brief refrain of loud absurdity, the larger cop sang, "Ohhh, the *mon*key wraps his tail around the *lamp*post!"

"C'mon," said Minelli, "let's go fight some more crime."

On the sidewalk again, the glare of the sun ripped into the cops' eyes, a sudden contrast to the darkness of the building. They returned to the shelter of the radio car, which had been double-parked, and Minelli took the wheel. The police radio splashed out its stream of staccato reports while the car moved through the street under a barrage of familiar sights and sounds. Minelli, gliding into a world of rubble, bricks, old tires, and broken glass, turned onto a wider street whose sidewalks were thick with displays of limp dresses and shirts. They moved past liquor stores and groceries and between taxis, trucks, and buses whose gasoline fumes mingled with an aroma of fried foods and the sound of bongo drums and children. They crept past old men playing dominoes; past peddlers with oranges, cabbage, and bananas; and past storefront social clubs and churches. The cops continued over cobblestone and concrete bordered by slums, housing projects, and burned-out stores. A subway rumbled beneath the street, a train thundered on the elevated tracks; and ambulance, fire, and police sirens shrieked the sound of East Harlem, filled the air, echoed and pounded into the brain, assaulting the senses and leaving the mind and muscles uncertain and tense on this lazy summer afternoon.

On Minelli's mind this day was a young rookie, Paul, who was out walking the beat in Harlem for the first time. The captain had told Minelli to keep an eye out for the rookie, just in case he should get into some trouble he could not handle.

"Of course," said Minelli, "he's on his own. It's a strange world here, to a boy twenty-one years old. Let's say that he comes from a middle-class family, he's lived in Queens all his life, and let's say that now he lives in a suburb. Let's also assume that he's never been in the service, which today is common. Twenty-one years old, and they come into this job, a young rookie, and he comes up here, and this is another world. And up here you have junkies, you have your winos and your queers, your pimps and whores and whatnot, and he comes up here and he looks around, and this is another world. He's seeing things here that he's never seen before in his life.

"Now, he's probably been out in the car with some of his friends, and he's gone into an area—maybe he's gone with a whore or something like that—but he's still not seeing it like *now* he's gonna see it. Now he's gonna see it five days a week, eight hours a day, and now he's out here and he has something to *do* with it. He's associated with it. In many forms, out here. And I say, when you get a young fella like that, twenty-one years old, and you put a shield on him and he leaves that Police Academy and he comes up here to this new world, when most of them have never had a piece of ass with their pants off yet. That's what the old-timers used to tell me. He's up here and he's lost, the young kid. He's up here running around like a cock in the pen. He don't know which way to turn, and it's exciting to him, also. It's another world, but he's afraid, too.

"He's afraid, and there's all kinds of things to go with that, and this individual of course isn't going to come up here and perform the lines. Uh, well, let's face it, this whole world is a stage, right? And we're all actors to a degree, and when you go on the job, that's a part of the job, the acting. You act. I mean, every individual is a different personality, and you have a different act that you have to go through, right?

"And this boy comes up here, and he doesn't *know* any of the acts yet, he doesn't know any of the lines. You have to learn the *lines* that go with this job, and with these people here. You don't have to take a course in psychology if you're brought up well in this job, and if you're fortunate enough to associate with the men who know how to deal with the people. You *learn* from them, and you see that a little bit of psychology goes a long way with these people.

"I was born on the job, so to speak. In the beginning it's a little tougher because, as I say, you're in another world. If you've been used to a place for a great length of time, however, you'd hate to leave and start all over again. I wouldn't leave this precinct, myself. It's an education in itself, this job. You learn a great deal. This is the other side of life that the rest of the world never sees, that the rest of the people don't know about. A cop here sees more and hears more than the average individual will in a lifetime. We'll see more things here in one eight-hour tour—people and things that people like to read about. There's always something interesting, something to excite the mind a little bit here. And there's a million laughs. You can't leave those out. A million laughs. That's a part of your job. That's a part of some of the enjoyments of the job. There's funny things.

"But if you work in a shithouse like this for a while, you can go to *any* precinct and it would look great. A guy who's worked twenty years in Staten Island, he ain't even gonna walk the streets up here. I think you'll find in all police forces, and especially in this one here, that a great many patrolmen are a product of their environment within the job, of their associations within the job, their fellow workers and the people they have to deal with . . ."

With a few details rearranged, the young man whom Joe Minelli is talking about might have been himself. At forty-three, Minelli is a seasoned ghetto cop in East Harlem. Physically, he somewhat resembles Frank Sinatra in size and shape of body and even in tone of voice. Joe Minelli's face, however, is more jagged; and his spoken words carry the rough edges of someone who has spent his boyhood and manhood on the streets of the city, away from any need to smooth out his style. Yet style he has. Minelli's style is as inconspicuous as his emotions are unrestrained. The undeliberate, reckless state of confused anger with which he confronts most situations is tempered by the good nature in his dark-brown, sensitive eyes.

"They can't afford to get rid of Minelli," commented one of the cops who works with him. "I would say that Minelli is conscientious about certain parts of his work, and I feel when he does a job he does a good job. Of course, he's very uncouth. He's not one to impress a Harvard graduate. You couldn't put Minelli downtown, for instance, to direct traffic.

He couldn't be a detective either, because he's going to have to deal with all kinds of people, and he's too blunt. But he'd probably make a better detective than many guys who *are* detectives. It's a matter of how he would deal with the public. He's exactly what they need up here."

Minelli was transferred "up here" to Harlem after working for two years as a plainclothes man on vice and gambling. He likes to refer to himself as an "ex-detective" whose major accomplishments include forty-four direct solicitations by prostitutes, out of which he obtained forty-three convictions.

"The forty-fourth was his girlfriend," his partner, Kettle, offered.

"No," countered Minelli. "The judge had lost his judgeship that day and he was so pissed that he threw everything out of court."

On the gambling end of his plainclothes experience, Joe was equally zealous. He once kept a bartender under surveillance for a week on a hunch that the saloon was part of a betting operation. Finally he saw the bartender write something on a slip of paper and Minelli closed in. The bartender quickly seized a wad of slips and crammed them into his mouth. Joe reached in to grab the slips and the bartender bit down—hard. Minelli yanked his hand out, still holding the evidence, and found two of his fingers lacerated.

The sleuthing ended, however, when Minelli had an argument with his boss. Joe apparently had been angry at being unable to make an arrest because of insufficient evidence. "But we *know* the guy's guilty," Minelli screamed. His boss agreed, but Minelli was hustled into a blue uniform and sent to Harlem as a foot patrolman.

"What the hell," he shrugged, "It's better not to be a detective. There's always the chance you'll get bounced back on the street. This way, I'm already *on* the street. At first I thought it was a curse, coming up here. But it's a good place to learn the job. I don't care what it is, we've had it here. It can't get any worse. If they want to punish you they can't do anything to you. They can't send you anyplace worse. You're at the bottom of the pit here. The crime is beyond belief."

Settling down for a career in the ghetto, Minelli walked the beat for 2 years and for the past 10 years he has been driving the same radio car. For those dozen years, he has spent most of his waking hours in the nine-tenths of a square mile that make up his precinct. Within this small area there are nearly 117,000 people, Negroes and Puerto Ricans equally divided among 80 percent of the population. The remainder are Italians and "mixed" whites. The people are crammed together in filthy tenements, overflowing into the hot summer streets, and the less than 200 precinct cops are drowning in a surge of crime that is steadily increasing. Divided into three shifts, the cops make several thousand arrests each year. In this small area there are 2 hospitals, 58 bars, 12 elementary and 9 other schools, plus dozens of churches. There are countless thousands of junkies, pimps, whores, winos, perverts, thieves, looters, muggers, burglars, and psychopaths. There are young children, teen-agers, and young adults who have nothing to do that is of any help to themselves. There are old people who are immobilized by their own infirmities and victimized by the muggers and burglars. The majority of the people are poor, afraid, and angry.

At one edge of the precinct a Temporary Command Post had been set up to deal with riots. Tables were lined up in a small park with rows of boxes on them. In the boxes were helmets, shotguns, bulletproof vests, and various riot paraphernalia; and there were buses ready to transport 200 tactical cops instantly to the scene of an uprising. On normal days, like this one, 9 radio cars patrolled the 25 miles of streets.

"Let's get some coffee," Kettle suggested.

Joe Minelli turned down a side street, past red-brick and dirty-brown walls and yellow-gray tenements blackened with soot. Minelli drove the car slowly through the narrow street toward a group of black people gathered around an ice-cream truck. The faces of the children were wild, expectant, electric; but other faces stared dully. The two cops sneered at a cluster of young black men, especially at one with pink pants. The resentment built up on both sides but the car crept by. Minelli waved at a girl and she smiled back. The cops accepted this brief collision of animosity and friendliness without noticeable change in mood or comment.

Ahead, at the end of the block, there was a commotion and the patrol car crept to it slowly. A fire hydrant was gushing water into the intersection while the kids rolled in and out of the spray. One little boy held an open-ended beer can over the huge volume of water and a thin stream flew across the street.

"All day long," Minelli complained to me, "we'll be shutting off these hydrants. That cop that got hit with a brick the other day was shutting off a hydrant. The kids thought they'd be funny, so they went up on the roof and threw bricks and bottles at the cop. One of them hit him on the head. So now the cop is a vegetable. He don't even know his own family any more."

Minelli stopped the car and watched as an older boy put a garbage can, with the bottom cut out, over the hydrant. The water shot up through the hole in a thick column of foam for three stories, splashed down on parked cars and finally rolled into the doorway of a store advertising "prayer and guidance."

"Get that goddamn can offa there!" screamed Joe Minelli, transforming himself from a member of the audience to a cop on the job. He turned to me and explained, "The bad part about this is if they get a big fire, there's no water pressure. The water won't even reach two floors in this whole area. You gotta run around and shut off the pressure on every hydrant you can, just so the firemen can get enough water to put the fire out."

"We must have shut off thirty hydrants yesterday," Kettle answered.

"Well, shit," Minelli went on, getting out of the car, "it

don't bother me. 'Burn, baby, burn,' that's what *they* say. Let 'em burn their whole neighborhood down, right to the ground."

Walking to the rear of the patrol car, Minelli maintained an impassive expression as a group of Negro boys yelled, "Hey, motherfucker whitey!" Joe found his wrench and walked across the street to the hydrant. He pushed through the crowd and kicked the garbage can off, watching as it rolled on the new thrust of water into the street in front of a moving taxi cab, causing the driver to screech to a stop. Then he stuck his wrench in and turned the hydrant shut.

The crowd followed him back to the car. He pushed past a boy with a transistorized radio, shouting to Kettle and me, "That's the only bath they get for a week." The kids seemed to be crawling over the car as they leaned in the windows and sat on the rear. Minelli made a playful move toward them with his wrench and they slid off the trunk.

"I know you," a Negro boy said as Minelli put his wrench away. "You're the fuzz."

"And you're the good guys, hunh?"

"That's right, man."

"Future Black Muslims," Minelli muttered to himself. "That's what they are."

"Whitey cop!"

Patrolman Minelli returned to the driver's seat and his partner slumped down, muttering, "If this weather holds, we'll be busy tonight."

Suddenly, the same hydrant went off again. This time the water rolled out in big waves across the side street. "All right!" Minelli yelled through his window. "We're mad at you guys. The war is on!" The water kept flowing out and the whistles and chatter made it impossible to hear what the car radio was saying. Two blocks away, a fire truck raced somewhere with its siren blaring. The radio was calling Minelli, whose signal this day was David, and Minelli shouted back, "David here!" The radio dispatcher answered that a child had been hit by a car.

"What about the hydrant?" asked Kettle.

"Burn, baby, burn," Minelli replied, moving the car up the avenue, away from the water and the crowd.

"Hey, Joe, are we gonna get that coffee or what?"

"We will." As he turned down a side street, Minelli waved to a group of Puerto Rican women on a stoop. "Marylyn! You look bee-yoo-tiful!"

"Thank you, Joe."

"Ah, that Marylyn. What a big junkie whore she is. She's got a face only a mother could love."

"Hey, there's the rookie."

Minelli pulled over to greet Paul, the new rookie. The slim, blond-haired young man was standing between two parked cars trying to look casual. "How are things, Paul?"

"Fine."

"You'll soon get used to this horseshit," Kettle offered.

The young rookie smiled and Joe continued down the street. Turning to his partner, he said, "Why do you tell him it's horseshit?"

"Because that's what it is, and you know it, Joe."

"Well, look, I have to agree with you, there are a lot better jobs in the world. Personally, though, I like my job. I always maintain that a good cop is a cop who likes his job. If he likes his job he'll be a good cop, a conscientious cop. You shouldn't tell him it's horseshit."

"Then who's gonna tell him?"

"I just mean that too many cops are born the wrong way in this job. Because when they come into the job, their associations are important. They meet other cops, and they learn from other cops, and sometimes they learn the wrong thing. A guy comes into this job, he's brand-spanking new, and if by perchance he manages to hook up with a couple of guys who may not be conscientious about their jobs, they do a job in a lackadaisical manner, in their attitude about everything, and they use their favorite word, that it's all horseshit, well, believe it or not, this young boy, this is the way he's being groomed in this job, unless somebody gets ahold of him."

"Aw, come off it, Joe."

"Look, everybody has somebody he likes to emulate, or copy. And he can copy the wrong way. That's one thing police departments are gonna have to solve one day, how to keep a kid from learning the wrong way. I mean, they taint the new cops, that it's all horseshit. A lot of guys, like yourself, they've been here two or three years, they tell you it's all horseshit."

"Because it is, Joe."

"Well, I ask you, tell me something, that little kid that's been whacked with the car that we're going to, and they've called on us, and we're gonna get outa the car and walk over —will you feel like horseshit? Or do you feel like you're gonna *do* something there? When all the people step back and say, 'Here comes the officer,' what will you feel like? Horseshit?"

"Well, that's different..."

"No, no, it's not different. That's your *job* right there. Now you're showing you have compassion! You're gonna look at that kid and you'll feel funny, right?"

"Yeah, I'll laugh my balls off."

"Well, that's because *you* are nothing but a product of somebody telling you it's all horseshit. You wanna be one of the boys. You wanna be accepted by your group that you drive in here with from Long Island every day."

"And you, Joe baby, you're a dedicated cop?"

"Me? Hell, no. I got into this job because it was good pay and a twenty-year pension. But the bosses don't want that any more. You take these dedicated guys that never got married, right? They got nothing else to do but be dedicated. With me, it's just a job."

"It's horseshit, right?"

"No, I'm not saying I'm not gonna *do* my job. But dedication, *idealism,* that's bullshit for the Hollywood pictures, you know? I mean with you and me, it's more of looking out for one another than any dedication. At least, when you come onto this job, you *think* you're gonna do a job, you think it's a good job, that you can help people, and *some* of it's dedication. You *try* to help the people, but then when you see the way the people treat *you,* you sort of lose it, you know?"

"I know, Joe. That's what I was tellin' ya."

Minelli turned to the back of the car, trying to make me understand. "It's the Negroes. We used to be able to talk to them, but something happened, and now we don't talk at all. It's the young punks, mostly. Not so much the older people."

Just before the car reached First Avenue, a Negro woman waved at the cops and said, "Hi, you, po-leeceman! Bless you, honey!"

"Hear that?" Minelli asked me. "Very seldom do you hear that, around here. That's the thing. We don't get polite words around here. I'm startled if someone says, 'Good evening.' Last night, remember those groups of kids? They came flying around the precinct like they came from Mars. In ten or twelve groups of from a dozen to fifty kids each. You think they was organized?"

"Maybe."

"And look at these guys, here. Pretty boys." Minelli called our attention to a group of Negro young men on the corner, wearing red, green, and maroon slacks and fancy hats. "Look at the stares they give you. If they had a gun they'd shoot you on the spot."

"Horseshit, horseshit."

"As a kid, I always went to the movies, and I liked to go see the cops. I always remember this one flick, with Paul Muni, where a cop gets shot up in the loft, someplace. I always remembered that thing. I always had a certain *feeling* to be a cop. Also, I used to see the wiseguys. I hated wiseguys. I used to see them beat up somebody and so forth. And I always figured it was a cop's place to straighten guys like that out. And I guess I just always wanted to be a cop. Another thing,

I guess, I just like to deal with people. And there's always something to do out here, one way or another. And, I guess, I like being a cop. You know?"

"You're a bull, Joe. A real bull."

Minelli was brought up in the Bronx and still lives there. The drive from his apartment to Harlem is only eight minutes.

"I went to public school," he said, "but I wish I'd gone to a Catholic school. Might have learned a hell of a lot more. We played stickball in the streets, everybody together. I mean, a lot of white people discriminate against white people, you know? So why is the Negro such a big thing? In the Bronx, we had a Negro family living next door. They were there two years before I even knew they lived there. In one square block we had a League of Nations—Italians, Irish, Jewish, Poles, Finns, maybe a Chinaman thrown in. Of course you had your own club, a gang, and you played ball together, so what was the big thing? You might have had four individual cliques on one block—all in the same age group. But we still didn't go around stabbing each other, like these kids. Fighting, there was. But you had to fight fair. Even kicking was out. But a knife? You kiddin'? Never heard of it. That goes back a ways. Now, up here, without a knife you're lost, you ain't nothing.

"I was poor when I was a kid. I used to go out and get wooden boxes, for the coal stove, because we couldn't afford coal, and we used to eat bean soup three times a week. And my school principal, who liked me, bought me shoes and what not, and I brought 'em home to the family from school. So being poor, when I look around here, and then at the house I used to live in—a tenement, a walk-up, a cold-water flat— well, what can I say? I'll tell you one thing, that building I lived in was clean! Well, that was in a so-called white neighborhood. But everything was clean. And if the people in the early 1930s—and there were more people who were poor then than there are now—I mean, if they ran around the streets and smashed windows, and tore down people's establishments because they thought they were being deprived of the right to live like people with money, what kind of a country would we have today?"

Minelli went on to tell me about his days in the Navy: "I did deep-sea diving, under water, and salvage work, demolition work under water. All over Europe, all the harbors and what not. I blew up docks and piers. And I did a lot of diving. Got some pretty good money. Then, after I got out, I lived in a housing project in the Bronx in 1947 and worked in a jet factory, building aircraft engines. I was always looking for something to do, I didn't care what it was. It ended up that I was making sketches for the engineers. Cutaways of the inside of the plane and all. Just to have something to do. It was interesting work, I liked it."

Now Minelli has two stripes over his badge representing twelve citations for good police work. "They're for nearly everything," he said casually. "From homicide work to stick-ups, all the way down the line. Mostly for good arrests. You write 'em up and the captain checks 'em over, and if he likes 'em then he sends 'em to the division. The division calls you over and you have a hearing. You go down and tell 'em all the facts."

When I went to his apartment in a middle-class white neighborhood near Van Cortlandt Park, Minelli showed me a brown manila envelope he keeps rolled up in a desk drawer. In the folder are a half-dozen newspaper clips, some with pictures of him as an "unidentified" patrolman, a few others with his name mentioned—usually misspelled. One of the photographs shows Minelli in the middle of a Harlem riot, without a helmet, his nightstick clutched tightly in one hand at his side.

He also has in his desk two sheets of thin white paper stapled together and folded to keep them from falling apart. The papers contain reports of his activities, which were called "highly intelligent police performance" and "intelligent observation and interrogation." He is also cited for "exemplary conduct and performance."

A tremendous crowd was standing around the small boy who had been hit by a car. Another patrol car was there also and the policemen were trying to keep the people away from the small Negro boy who lay on his back in the middle of the street, looking up, quiet. His mother was at his side, weeping, and perhaps sixty children were standing around. "What a madhouse," Minelli said as he walked into the crowd. "But what the hell, we get these kids run over all the time." The mother was becoming hysterical. People were leaning out of the tenement windows and the police tried to peel away the crowd, layer by layer. Someone placed a pillow under the boy's head as the ambulance arrived.

"These kids," Minelli said, "they run out in the street all day and the mothers say nothing. They never say nothing until their kids get hit and then they act so worried. You almost get a feeling that they *want* 'em to get hit. Then when the kid gets hit they realize, ooh, there goes the relief check. They don't want 'em to get *killed,* because then they'll lose their welfare. But if the kid just gets hurt bad, then the mother can get to sue the driver."

When the boy had been lifted into the ambulance, his mother asked to get in with him, but she had forgotten her shoes. She raced back into the building to get her shoes, but the ambulance began to move away. "Hey," Minelli shouted to the driver. "Wait for the mother, will ya?" The driver obeyed. Finally the mother returned and the ambulance screamed away from the scene, leaving the cops to dispel the crowd.

"Hey Minelli," called another patrolman. "Remember Hilda? Your girlfriend?"

"What about her?"

"She's a junkie."

"No," said Minelli. "Hilda ain't no junkie."

"Well, I saw her with a bunch of junkies last night."

"So what does that mean? She's got five sisters who are junkies, so she hangs around with 'em a lot. But that don't mean she *is* one."

"Joe, she looked real hooked."

"Go to hell, will ya?"

Angry, Minelli walked back to the car to wait for his partner. I realized that he was upset about this news that Hilda, a Puerto Rican girl he had talked about and apparently cared for, had succumbed to drug addiction.

"What's the matter, Joe?" Kettle asked, bouncing back into the car.

"Nuttin'."

"Then let's go get that coffee, okay? It's almost four-thirty."

The two patrolmen had now been on the job just over an hour. Today, because of the semiriot conditions that had been proclaimed in various parts of the city, they were scheduled to be on duty until about three in the morning. The entire force had been put on twelve-hour shifts for the duration of the trouble.

"I'm gonna pick up the rookie and see how he's doing," Minelli said.

"Ohh," sang Minelli's partner, "the *rook*ie wraps his tail around the *lamp*post."

The car moved only a block when the radio directed them to investigate a lost-child case. "Oh, Christ," complained Minelli. "If they're not gettin' hit by cars they're gettin' lost. If they survive, by the time they're ten they'll be packin' knives a foot long, and by fifteen they're shootin' their veins full of heroin. By twenty-one they're full-time thieves. By twenty-five they—"

"Let me out!" mocked the big cop. "I want coffee!"

"I just hope the kid's not under seven years old. Then we'll have to conduct a search and everything. And you know what burns my ass? You'll be searching for hours and hours, and you know where the kid'll be?"

"Where, Joe baby? Tell me now!"

"At some friend's house. They don't bother to tell nobody, not even the mother. Up on 119th Street, you know where we found the kid?"

"Where?" I asked.

"Sleepin' in a bunk bed. At a friend's house upstairs."

"Well, Joe, speaking intellect-chewally, it's the parental supervision around here," Kettle said. "The kids are their own parents. No father, and the mother's never home."

"A few years ago," Joe told me, "we found a lost kid frozen on a rooftop. He was five years old. I think that's why they make us search so intensely if the kid is under seven. We have to ring every doorbell in the goddamn building, and then in the whole block. If we don't find the kid, we search all the *surrounding* blocks. And there are a couple of thousands of people living on *each block*. One time, a bus trip for underprivileged kids from the housing projects went up to a lake in upstate New York. And they left a kid up there! But they swore up and down that they didn't leave him. They took two busloads of kids upstate to a lake, for an outing, and they came back saying, 'Oh yeah, he got off the bus. He sat next to me on the bus all the way back to the city. Yeah, sure.' This is the grownups talking, the ones that ran the thing. 'He got off the bus. He sat next to me and ran across the street and into his building,' they said. Right? Three hours later, we finally called upstate and there he was.

"They didn't wanna be responsible! They didn't wanna admit the fact that the kid was missing. Imagine that? They lied like a trooper. Imagine that? 'I sat right next to him on the bus. I helped him across the street to his apartment.' And the kid is in upstate New York! And we were searching and searching for him. They didn't know where he was at all. They didn't even know he was missing in the first place. In other words—"

"Whattaya tryin' to say, Joe?" asked Kettle.

"In other words, they left him up there and it's their own fault that they did it, you know? And they didn't want to admit it! I guess they were hoping he'd show up somehow, that maybe he was on the other bus. But you know what it is to search a twenty-one-building set of housing projects? All those buildings, where the kids came from, we searched 'em up and down. About three hours later, they called the sheriff's office upstate and he said, 'Oh, yeah, we got the kid here.'

"If they had *told* us that in the first place, we could have immediately called up there, you know? At least you'd know the kid's there and you don't have to worry any more. At least you'd know he's alive and well. But when they're under seven, you have to do some terrific searching. Because we had one kid turn up dead—not that same kid that was frozen, but another one, also on a roof. Some degenerate, seventeen-year-old guy got the kid up on the roof and strangled him and screwed him in the ass. A five-year-old kid. This was in an Italian block. What a job we had getting that guy outa there and bringing him in the car to the station house! I caught him and the people in the neighborhood wanted to kill him. I had to protect him. He was a psycho. He'd been let out of a nut house."

The cops parked outside a gray tenement building in a Puerto Rican section. "Look," said Minelli. "A live chicken market. We used to have them in the Bronx. When we were kids we always used to buy our chickens in the live market. You pick out your own chicken, feel him up, and the rabbi cuts his throat." Next to the chicken market was another *bodega,* or grocery store, with the word *"carnicería,"* meat market, across the window. The cops walked into the tenement building and small children's voices rang out: *"Policía! Policía!"*

"Top floor again," said Kettle.

The officers plodded up the stairs, at the same time angry at having to get out of the car and spend time in the nauseating, darkened building, yet apparently pleased to be able to keep active. They headed to the top floor out of curiosity as much as duty, knowing that, even now, their job was not to prevent trouble but to pick up the pieces.

Several Puerto Ricans—brothers and sisters and cousins —were in the doorway of their small apartment.

"Where's your mother?" Minelli asked.

"She's outside, looking for Raphael."

"Is Raphael the one who's lost?"

"Yep."

"How old is he?"

"Four years."

"Four! How long's he been gone?"

"Since noon."

The hallway exploded with Spanish phrases. Minelli turned and bumped into a dark-skinned girl who had come from another apartment on the floor to watch. Pregnant and round shouldered, her belly protruding beneath a thin, sack-like dress, she held a young child without pants and fondled his penis as she stared aimlessly at the confusion.

"Oh!" said Minelli, startled. "Why don't you give him a pair of pants, for Chrissake. Hunh? No speaka da English?"

Minelli again turned to the group of arguing Puerto Ricans and shouted, "Where was Raphael when you last saw him?"

"His brother took him to the carnival with Chino. He came back about four o'clock, but not with Chino and Raphael."

"How old is Chino?"

"Three years."

"Is he lost too?"

"No, he came home."

"He made it back here by himself? And the kid is only three years old?"

The people laughed at Minelli's astonishment over little Chino's ability to wander back home for seven blocks in one of the world's most crowded areas. "How old is the brother?" Minelli continued.

"Ten years."

"Ten! You let a ten-year-old kid be in charge of a four-year-old and a three-year-old? Hey—" Minelli motioned to little Chino playfully and shouted, "Where's your brudder and your mudder? I'll give ya the thoid degree."

Suddenly the ten-year-old wandered out of the kitchen and the whole family pounced on him: "Where's Raphael? . . . Why you leave him and Chino? . . . You *took* him, so why you leave him? . . . Where's Raphael?" The boy stood there, mute.

"You oughtta take your mother and throw *her* in jail," offered Minelli. Eventually the policemen ascertained that four-year-old Raphael, who presumably had been wandering over East Harlem for nearly five hours, was about three feet tall, weighed forty pounds, and had black eyes. Also, that he was wearing a white shirt with polka dots and had full-length blue pants.

"Any scars?" asked Minelli.

"No."

"Ah, yes," Joe said to me. "That sounds like about a million little kids around here. Did you people look all around in the street here? You did? Well, we'll alert the other precincts. We'll be back, don't worry about it."

The cops turned from the family, which again had exploded into a highly emotional conversation in Spanish.

"Ohhh, the monkey—"

"Horseshit," interrupted Minelli.

The front seat of the patrol car was hot, burning through the men's pants as they began to creep into the jarring mixture of traffic and people again. They paused for a light, watching a boy with a kite cross in front of them, a strange reminder of carefree youth in this oppressive world of concrete and decay. Not only the seat of the car burned, but the motor too, and the heat waves seemed almost visible. Kettle took off his hat to wipe the sweat from his forehead.

"Louie? Louie! Loo-ee!" called Minelli to an elderly Puerto Rican man who waved back. "What's doin', Louie? Hey, you look straight today. Hunh? What're you doin', working again or what?"

"Hey man, what's happenin'?" said a shirtless Negro man who stepped off the curb and looked into Minelli's window.

"Hello, Sweetwater," Minelli said. "We're working, man. Work, work, work. That's all we do, man, work our ass off!"

As the car moved on, Minelli said to me, "That was Sweetwater. Every once in a while I lock him up, for stealing something. I got him for taking batteries out of a few cars one time."

Minelli took the microphone and reported a description of the lost boy.

"Joe, let's get some iced tea instead of coffee, okay?"

"Cuchifritos! Cuchifritos! Cold beer, fresh meats, hero sandwiches!" Joe read aloud the signs on the storefronts as the car crept by. The garbage cans that lined the streets had spilled over and tiny boys and girls were playing in the midst of the debris. Three boys roller-skated past the patrol car and turned down another street. Men came out of delicatessens and liquor stores with bulging brown paper bags, arming themselves against the stagnant heat of another evening in the ghetto. They went back to the tenement buildings, but some of them paused on stoops or steps or against the railings, joining others who stood there seemingly waiting for something to happen.

"What next, Joe?"

"Ah, you can feel it in the air. Trouble, somewhere. But where? And what?"

The car moved on, but soon its movement became a senseless, endless journey to nowhere; and the sense of purpose of the two men was so numbed that I felt that they *wanted* something to happen. They seemed to need to explain to me the lack of "action" during this period of time and to remind themselves as well of what they were doing there.

"Everything is farfetched until it happens," said Joe. "It's like a fuckin' Vietnam. You don't know if one of these little kids has a cup of acid, just waiting to throw it in your face."

"Just wait till it gets dark," Kettle added.

"Wonder how the Mets are doing," Joe said.

"Losing, probably."

"Did you listen to Long John on the radio last night? Man, did he put those people down! He hangs up on people in midsentence when they call in to sound off. The caller says, 'Hello, I'd like to say—' And bam! Long John slams the phone down on 'em. Laughs. 'Hello, I hate—' Bam!"

"Look at all the stores with gates on 'em. All hit with burglaries. Those gates, they get ripped right down. Now some of them use solid-steel gates. They're just a little harder to break, that's all."

On this block, most of the stores were burned out and boarded up. The gates on the stores were twisted and broken, and on the next block there was a solid wall of plywood covering the broken windows of a large supermarket.

"This joint was burned up the other night," said Minelli, as he pulled to a stop outside a pile of rubble where two Puerto Rican men with a wheelbarrow stood, looking guilty.

"Hello, men," said Kettle. "Anything left?"

"No, nothing. *Nada, nada.*"

"*Nada,* my foot," Minelli yelled. To Kettle he remarked, "Then what the hell are they doing there with a wheelbarrow, I'd like to know."

"All these stores are closing up early now."

"Yeah, well, they ain't safe. That jewelry store there," Joe told me, "the kids picked up a trash can and heaved it through the window. They grabbed all the jewelry they could and ran like hell. That was in broad daylight. That's the same store they ruined back when Martin Luther King was killed. I thought the world was gonna end that day. This guy here has bricked up his whole liquor store. He must figure he's better off without any windows at all. What a country this is gettin' to be—stores without windows." Farther down the block, a woman was struggling with a large piece of plywood to cover her store window in order to close shop. "That men's-wear place got cleaned out recently. And the meat store—out of business. And the wig store, too."

The car turned past "La Marketa" and Spanish groceries advertising *cerveza fría,* cold beer. Peddlers were wrapping up their wares and going home. "They keep their stuff in somebody's cellar," Minelli commented. "You always see the Board of Health catching these guys making ice cream in a cellar. Wow, they mix it all in with the ice cream—cock-roaches, crap—and when they get caught there's a near riot. They just take the stuff and dump it right in the street. Then they lock 'em up or give 'em a summons."

"Joe, how about getting some Italian ices?" said Kettle.

"Maybe. If not we'll go hit Sam's later, if he stays open. Those ices, you can get 'em for a nickel on First Avenue. You should see all the people stopping to get 'em. All night, they got nothing to do, so they go down and get some ices. A big deal."

"David."

"David here."

"Maternity . . ."

"All these stands on the sidewalks are Jewish-owned, but with Spanish names," Minelli told me, changing direction without acknowledging the radio. "They always get robbed. They creep out on the sidewalk with their junk and we give 'em summonses galore. They're allowed to move onto the sidewalk so much distance, but they'd get the whole sidewalk if we didn't crack down. Every day they move out another six inches, another foot, and then they have the whole sidewalk. So we give 'em summonses again and the cycle starts all over. This has been going on for forty years, back and forth. It's endless.

"And these stores too, almost all owned by Jews. The

Jews hire Negroes and Spanish-speaking people. Not that they really want 'em, but it's necessary. They don't want any trouble with the people here.

"All these furniture stores. You see 'em all with the Spanish names, right? They give credit. Everything is on sale, right? About 90 percent of them are owned by Jews. They've been here for years and years. This all used to be a white neighborhood, thirty or forty years ago, and the Jewish business people stayed on. As the Negroes moved in, the whites moved out. And the Puerto Ricans came in by the boatload. Between the Negroes and the Puerto Ricans and the Italians, you gotta be a three-way cop around here."

I asked Minelli if he thought he "had anything against Jews" and he said, "Hell, no—I grew up with Jews." He continued, "Look at the furniture stores. Seventy-eight weeks to pay, *grande venta,* big sale. A dollar deposit on any item, pay two bucks a week for the rest of your life. Buy your furniture direct from the factory and save. Ha! That's a laugh. You couldn't save a nickel around here if you stood on your head. They're the biggest thieves in the world. I believe the people should get a fair shake. Some of the Jewish people have exploited them something terrible. Items end up costing more here than up in the rich suburbs. Look at the sign there: 'As advertised,' right? Where's the price? You got the most misleading advertising in the world here. They'll put a price out in big letters and then, in small print that you need bifocals to look at, it'll say, 'And Up.' You know? The Jews own most all these stores. And the *garbage* they sell! They don't wanna sell nothing for cash, either. They *want* to sell on credit, because when you miss one payment they go right up to your house and take it back. Zoop! Take it right back. And they go and resell it. And if you pay the whole thing off on installments, it ends up three times the fair price. 'Reductions up to 50 percent.' Ha! I've seen reductions up to a *hundred* percent around here. It don't mean a thing. Here's a bedroom set, for a hundred dollars. If you want the *bed* with it, of course, you'll find out it costs *seven* hundred bucks or something. The poor people just sign for two dollars a week. Most of the Jews have Puerto Ricans working for them. So it's the Puerto Ricans that fuck the Puerto Ricans. They sell their own people the worst shit. That's why, when they have a riot around here, it doesn't hurt my heart. I have no pity."

Kettle broke in, "Joe, please, you're corrupting me!"

The rookie was on a side street, and he looked relieved to see the patrol car approaching.

"Hey, Paul, you wanna come with us? We got a maternity case."

Paul the rookie had been patrolling the same block for the past two hours of the afternoon. "Looks like he's got a Puerto Rican mystery on his hands," commented Minelli. Two men were arguing, half in Spanish and half in English, and Paul was trying to intervene.

"Just walk away from 'em, kid," said Kettle.

"They're arguing over some woman."

"Come on, get in the car."

"Hey, Paul, you see a kid that looks lost?"

"They all look lost to me."

"What's with those two winos?"

"They're arguing. Each one wants me to arrest the other one."

"Just walk away and hope they kill each other off," counseled Minelli as the rookie climbed in the back seat next to me. "These people, they don't do much fighting, at least not in the normal course of the day. But like tonight, when they get their welfare and home relief and they start drinking, they're great ones for fighting among themselves. It's unbelievable how they can ever get together, the way the families fight amongst themselves. Brothers-in-law, sisters-in-law, mothers—they all fight each other. The Italians, they fight like hell among each other. But what's the sense of a cop wrestling with 'em in the street? I mean, you go to court and the judge'll throw it out. Otherwise, the Italians have respect for law. It's just that they have their *own* law, know what I mean?"

Minelli went on, as if instructing the young rookie. He said, "In one way, things are better now than they used to be. One thing, the gangs are out now. Gang wars are out of fashion. We had some terrific fights down here between the Italians and the Puerto Ricans. This park we're passing is the scene of where they killed a Cuban one time. They killed him with bench slats. See those wooden benches in the park? They ripped the slats off and crushed his head in. And they busted a gallon jug over his head. And the girl that he was with got her arm half-slashed off. I found her several blocks away, without knowing anything about the Cuban guy. She was walking down the street, half-dead, with her arm hanging out. She had wandered away from the park for five or six blocks at least. Guess she was in shock from the bleeding and from seeing her boyfriend killed.

"That same night, a guy shot another guy. And meanwhile, up in the projects, a girl had a fight with her boyfriend. She pulled out an ax from next to the fire extinguisher and chopped his head in half. Three murders in one night in this precinct. Mostly Italians."

"Like you, Joe," said Kettle.

"That's right."

"What do we do on the maternity case?" the rookie asked. Minelli lit a cigarette and started to drive again.

"Not much. These maternities aren't so tough, really. One thing about 'em, we never have to carry the women down to the ambulance. They could be dying on their feet, but we just say, 'Get up and walk, lady.' No need to carry 'em. There's nothing *wrong* with 'em except the fact that they're having a baby. I delivered nearly a dozen babies in this precinct. Then the ambulance attendant cuts the cord and the woman gets up and walks outside. Only once did I carry a woman down. I delivered the baby but there was a lot of blood lost."

The rookie said nothing, but I felt that he might have been envisioning himself delivering a baby. His face was intent as Minelli continued, for my benefit as well.

"Speaking of carrying people, the other day I carried a blind old colored lady down four flights of her fire escape. The building was burning like crazy, smoke pouring out. Me and Kettle here, at six in the morning, we took this old couple out the front door. Then I look up and see this old colored lady, and she's blind as a bat, eighty-five years old, looking out of the window and screaming. So I go up the fire escape like a burglar and carried her down. Took her to Harlem Hospital. The fire had shot up through the air shaft. Happens all the time around here."

Again the rookie was silent as the car stopped. "Another toilet," said Kettle, looking out at the tenement.

"Come on, Paul, I'll let you deliver the kid," Joe said. "Ha."

After climbing up five flights again, the cops wavered slightly from the heat and the smell. "Stop or I'll shoot," said Minelli to a small girl with a doll. "Where's your sister, or mother, or whoever's having the baby?" The little girl pointed down the hall and Joe tapped her on the head as we went to the door. Again the people spoke Spanish and almost no English.

"I know a little Spanish," Paul offered.

"Yeah? *Bueno* for you." I was not sure whether Minelli had meant to discredit the rookie's academic qualifications, but instead of apologizing he offered some more of his own observations: "It's amazing the woman is here. Soon as the ninth month comes and they're ready to have a baby, it seems like they're always out in New Jersey or someplace all of a sudden. They hardly ever stay by their apartment where they're supposed to be."

The apartment was crowded with brown-skinned people and smelled of perspiration. There was no color in the room except for a pair of red shorts worn by a plump girl with curlers. Minelli asked her if the pregnant girl was suffering from any pain. The girl was unclear and the people in the room turned to Minelli to see what he would do.

"Where is she?"

They pointed to another room and Minelli walked behind a tan curtain to see her. She was sitting in an armchair, heavy with child and staring at the ceiling. Minelli looked at her quickly and returned to the main room.

"Something black came out of her!" someone exclaimed.

"Something *black*?" The cops smiled. There was a sudden burst of chatter as Minelli watched a newsreel of the Vietnam war on the television set, the only thing of any value in the room. "The ambulance'll be here in a minute. They're dispatched the same time we get called. Does she have her clinic card? Good. She's got no pain, I don't think." To the rookie, quite loud, Minelli added, "No husband—no father. Which is usually the case."

The rookie held himself stiffly and did not answer Minelli. I think he felt that the older cop had offended the people in the room.

"How old are you?" Minelli asked a small boy who promptly held up six fingers. "These young kids speak better English than their parents," Minelli informed the rookie, who again looked embarrassed. "Wonder what she means, that something black came out of her?" Minelli continued. "Another Puerto Rican mystery."

The ambulance attendant arrived and quickly spoke to the people in fluent Spanish. The cops greeted him—they had seen him many times before—and we made our exit.

"Another welfare check," Minelli mused as we went down the stairs. "Another kid, another handout."

When we emerged on the sidewalk, Minelli pointed to the ambulance driver and said to me, "See, now, if that driver was ambitious he'd have gone up there with the attendant to help him. But he's not ambitious. So he stays there behind the wheel, like a jerk. He's told that all he has to do is drive the ambulance. But if everybody stuck to their job like that, very little would get done. Like us, we have an hour for a meal, separately, which we never take. We eat in the car, if we get a chance."

"Let's eat now, Joe baby," Kettle complained.

"Okay, but we gotta go back to the station house and see about that lost-child case. We may wind up searching like madmen."

"Then just stop for a coffee."

"Okay, right." Minelli halted the car near the elevated tracks and hopped out to fetch the coffee. "What do you want?" he asked me and the rookie over his shoulder. "Two blacks? Right." He gave his order to the old man behind the counter, which faced the sidewalk. As he put a dollar bill on the counter the man shook his head. "Come on, take it," said Minelli, aware that there were other people watching.

"No, no."

"Yeah, yeah, come on, will ya?"

"No, no."

The man walked away, the dollar bill remaining on the counter. Cursing to himself, Minelli picked it up and returned to the car. "Some guys," he explained to the rookie, "they want to give you coffee and stuff. They won't take your money. You give him the money and he pushes it right back at you. They like a cop. What do you do if they won't take your money? I've known that guy twelve years. You just have to leave the money there a lot of time—just leave it there and walk away." Minelli paused as the noise from an elevated train drowned out his voice. "But they get insulted. If you try to pay for something, a cup of coffee or a piece of pastry or something, they won't let you! According to the rules you're supposed to pay. You're not supposed to take anything for nothing, no gratuities, you know? But they get offended! You tell 'em and they say, 'What'choo mean, if I wanna give you a sandwich I'll give you a sandwich.' Then he gets the impression that he's giving you this for extra protection, but how are you gonna protect him more than you are anybody else? Sure, if you got a one-block post you can stand in front of his store all day. But the radio car, we gotta cover a whole area. If you make it through every block in one tour you're lucky, 'cause you got so many jobs in between. I didn't pay for this coffee we're drinking! But I put my money up!"

"Joe—relax and drink the damn coffee, will ya?" Kettle said impatiently.

Minelli went on talking.

"Now, you can understand that if I put my money up, and he doesn't take it—well, I *know* that man there. I mean, I can't fight that man! What, am I gonna look *stupid* there? I'm gonna *argue* with him, over paying for the lousy coffee? He won't take the money! I gotta fight him? Of course, this is it. I mean, this ain't workin' down by a big hotel or something, where they could be throwing twenty-dollar bills at you."

"Joe, you're a crooked cop," Kettle joked, and laughed when I asked Minelli about police corruption.

"Corruption! Corruption! That's all you hear. Christ, there are a lot of cops assigned just to look into the behavior of other cops. It's what you wanna make of it. I mean, if a cop wants to go out and try to shake down people, well go ahead. But if you get caught, you're gonna pay the price. It's not only that, but the fact that there are a lot of other cops with you. You're bound to get into trouble. But if people can't get a cop for anything else, just accuse him of graft. Around here, that's their famous saying—that cops take graft. People go to the movies, all they see is pictures of cops taking graft and committing murder. So now everyone knows that cops are crooked, right?

"But they crack down every once in a while. Every rule and every infraction, they give you a complaint and everybody suffers. You can't relax! They don't enforce the rules that much, but the rules are there if they're necessary. And if somebody does something that ain't in the rules, they'll *make* a rule for it. Everything they can make a rule for—from going to the shithouse to getting a day off.

"Just like us, we're supposed to get an hour meal apiece. So meanwhile, what happens to the radio car if one of us gets out? I'm not allowed to go on jobs by myself. You can't do it. Nobody I know of leaves the car for a meal. If we got a gun alarm, and I went alone, I'd get myself in trouble with the captain.

"But graft—if a cop takes a five-dollar bill for letting somebody go through a light or something, it's page 1 in the newspapers. A full-page spread. So where's your justice? Because a cop does it, that makes it a thousand times worse than any other crime. Which is not exactly fair. You get these guys, they been locked up twelve and fifteen times—for felonies!— and you go down to court and they're out on a five-hundred-dollar bail. A cop gets locked up, for attempted extortion or something, and it's *ten-thousand* dollars' bail. Where's the equality? Is he any better than me? You take a cop that gets caught one lousy time, and he's gotta suffer? Meanwhile, the *felon* whose got twenty convictions, he gets away with a few-hundred-bucks bail, or parole. Now, if we're gonna be equal, let's be equal!"

I asked Minelli if there weren't some cops who did take advantage of their positions.

He answered, "Sure, I admit it. For instance, some cops keep girls. Well, if they do that, then they're taking a chance. I don't know of any personally, but it's happened. You can get thrown off the job for less. A lot of cops get thrown outa this job that the public don't know about. They're not just demoted, but fired. And we've had inspectors demoted back to captain just because of what their *men* have done. They're responsible for their men. I mean, you think they got a soft job, but if their men do wrong they suffer."

"Police! Police!"

"What the hell—?"

"Police!"

A stout man with a black raincoat and black hat was running toward the patrol car. "What is it, bub?" said Kettle.

"Some boys are robbing my building!"

"What?"

"Burglars!"

"Get in."

The man climbed in the back seat where the rookie and I sat. Minelli and Kettle threw their coffee containers out their windows, but the rookie held on to his; and when Minelli jerked the car into motion, the rookie spilled his last half-inch of coffee onto the man's lap.

"Which way?"

"Down there."

The car raced through a red light, narrowly avoiding a taxi cab, and abruptly stopped in front of a vacant crumbling building halfway down a side street.

"I'm the landlord and I want you to arrest whoever's in there!"

"Is there anything to steal?"

"There's some lumber. I just want them out of there!"

The landlord's building was one of many in the city that are completely vacant and awaiting demolition. As Minelli had told me, "It's a matter of time until these places are torn down. Some guy'll set up his bed in there and live there, and another guy'll open up a little business in there or something, selling ices or something. They squat in there, like they own the place. Especially in the summer when they don't have to worry about heat." Perhaps a hundred such buildings have been torn down in this area in recent years, but the number still standing is amazingly large. "They get condemned and boarded up. The junkies break in and use the place to shoot up. The kids get in and burn 'em, and then the buildings are just a hulk." Even now there were kids walking in and out of the bricks, rubble, and trash in the alley. "The junkies go up on the roof a lot. All these buildings are empty, unfit to live in. I wonder why they keep cleaning them out. They got a crew of guys who cart plastic bags full of garbage and they pile 'em up on the street for Sanitation to pick 'em up. It doesn't make sense."

On the charred walls of this building there were Nazi insignias painted in dark-red paint and also phrases such as "Rip Cops!" and "Fop u cop cop!"

"Looks like they used some patrolman's blood," said

Minelli, observing how the red paint had dripped slightly from each letter of the angry messages.

"I want you to go in there," ordered the pink-faced landlord, "and arrest whoever's in there. I'll be at your headquarters, ready to press charges against them."

Minelli watched as the landlord swiftly walked away from the scene, hailed a taxi on the corner and vanished.

"How d'ya like that?" Minelli screamed. "The bastard is just waiting for the city to buy his lousy building so he can get his cash. They oughta tear down this damn place. I don't know what that landlord's trying to prove, aside from the fact that he's trying to keep the junkies outa the building."

"He really ran out of here," Kettle remarked.

"Sure. He knows the neighborhood don't like him, so he flits in here to watch his sacred slum. When he sees something wrong he finds us and then gets the hell out of here before they kill him."

"Well, who goes in?" Kettle said.

Joe looked at Paul, who was holding his nightstick and tapping it into the palm of his left hand. "You stay here," Joe told him. "Kettle, why don't you stand in the back?"

I walked with Kettle through the alley. We emerged behind the vacant building, where a row of slum structures on each street backed to form a corridor for the length of the block, filled with mattresses, furniture, old and rusted sinks and bathtubs, bottles, beer cans, bricks, cement blocks, litter, and mounds of dirt. A clothesline hung across the corridor, one end attached to the landlord's building. The sun was beginning its descent, making the fire escapes stand out in eerie, jagged form against the pink and white of the sky; young Negro boys jumped and climbed on the fire escapes, their voices echoing between the buildings and reaching us in vague pulsations of shouts and laughter.

I left Kettle and went back to the street, where the rookie, standing on the sidewalk in front, nervously watched the building, ready to call for help on the car radio. Meanwhile, Minelli had disappeared inside and I followed him.

Joe had taken out his silver and red flashlight, and was walking slowly up the stairs of the empty building, pausing now and then to listen. About two floors above, we heard voices.

"All right—come outa there!"

"We're coming!"

Two Negro boys, perhaps fifteen and sixteen years old, emerged from an empty apartment and started to walk down. Minelli aimed his flashlight up at their faces. There was the slightest hesitation on both sides and then a quick recognition that this time there would be no blind violence, no misunderstanding. They came down the stairs quickly, smiling, with a superb look of innocence and nobility. Minelli also was relaxed, affecting a nonchalant pose. "Whatcha doing?"

"We tied a clothesline for my mother."

"What?"

"A clothesline." The boys explained that they had tied a rope to the building, from the back of their apartment to the rear of this one.

"The landlord thinks you're up here stealing something."

"No, man. We ain't stealing nothing."

"Well, I gotta take you into the station house. It's his goddam property. Don't worry though. It'll be routine."

"You don't *believe* us, man?"

"Yeah, yeah, I believe you. But the guy who owns this place, he has the right to keep people out of it. So I gotta take you in to talk to him."

Minelli handcuffed the two boys together before they reached the door. It was still light outside, but something had changed. Minelli looked down at the street, at hundreds of faces, men and women, young boys, children. The rookie was in the front seat of the patrol car and Kettle was walking toward the front of the building. The crowd reacted with a sudden gasp at the sight of the two young boys handcuffed together, and called out as Minelli led them down the steps.

"They're being arrested!"

"They weren't doin' nothing!"

"They're goin' to jail for nothing!"

In one swift movement Minelli hustled the boys down the steps. Kettle grabbed them and pushed them into the back seat of the patrol car, jumping in next to them. I got in on the other side. Minelli began to walk calmly around the car to the driver's seat, but the crowd started to close in. The rookie sat in front, on the passenger side. People ran from each end of the block and poured off the front stoops toward the car. The angry crowd converged upon Minelli, who was flushed but defiantly confident. The sweat washed off his face in waves as he pushed a few people aside and opened the car door, quickly jumping inside; but the car had no room to move, with black faces and frantic bodies completely surrounding the car.

The crowd chanted, "Let them go! Let them go! Let them alone! They didn't do nothing! Let them go!"

The noise became overwhelming. It pounded into the car, which was being rocked from side to side. There was a thundering of sustained anger and hysteria, which the cops let fall around their bodies and brains without twitching a muscle. The two boys were silent, apparently enjoying themselves. Somewhere, beyond the noise, as if those of us inside the car were dreaming it, furious sirens came from all parts of the precinct; and the mass of hatred around the car intensified as the wailing of the sirens came closer.

"I called an assist-patrolman," the rookie said, his voice several notes higher than usual.

Finally, the sirens pierced the yelling as two cars came down the block from the east side and another prowl car screamed in from the west. The crowd instinctively became looser and now there were people running back and forth in the street—some openly formulating strategy for the confrontation—and suddenly rocks, bricks, and bottles were pelting the top and sides of our patrol car.

"This is it," said Minelli. "Put helmets on these two guys." Kettle placed our only pair of riot helmets on the heads of the two Negro boys, who still remained silent observers of the chaos. "As soon as these bastards get off the hood I'm gonna step on the gas. You know what? I'm gonna tell you something now," Minelli said to Kettle. I could not tell whether the cops were angry or, as I was, frightened. "I'm gettin' *married* on Saturday. True! I'm only telling you that now because we might not make it outa here."

"Why didn't you say so, Joe? Married?"

"Yeah. But don't tell anyone, will ya?"

"Why not?"

"Because then everybody'll be on my back."

"Are you *really* getting married?"

"No, I'm only kidding."

Suddenly there was a black face looking at Minelli through the car window, but this one was friendly. Sand, a light-skinned Negro cop, asked what the trouble was about. His eyes seemed to express terror, although his posture remained slack as he leaned on the car. A Negro woman stood next to him, yelling above the confusion and trying to tell the cops that her son, who was in the back seat of the patrol car, had been tying a clothesline; and Minelli nodded his head. Sand spoke to her softly and indicated to Minelli that he should drive away.

"I'll drive you into the station house," Sand told the woman.

The bricks stopped coming—in fact, they had only been thrown in a brief flurry—and somehow the time had past for things to get out of hand on that street. However, even now, according to Minelli's car radio, groups of young boys were gathering in various parts of the precinct. Harlem's unique system of communication had been set into motion—word-of-mouth spreading the news that tonight there was a chance for some action, some dispersion of choked-up energy.

The immediate crisis was over almost before it began, but now there was a feeling in the air, an electricity, which for the cops was intensified by the radio's insistence that in a three-precinct area a rash of troubles had begun: "Disorderly youths"—"Bus driver being held up"—"Looting" (a fire

truck with siren wailing crossed Minelli's path)—"Youths
are starting fire"—"Youths breaking bottles"—"Assist-patrolman"—"Youths ..."

To the young boys in the car, Minelli said, "You guys
don't need the helmets any more."

He turned to me and explained, "Not so long ago we had
no helmets. Then later on they gave us some big steel pots
from World War I, but there was nothing to hold 'em on to
your head. Now, since the riots, we carry these helmets
around in the car."

After a silence, Minelli assured the boys, "Nothing's
gonna go on your records. Just stick to your story. Of course,
all your friends back there probably think we're beatin' ya up
at this moment. Either of you guys on parole?"

"No."

"That damn landlord, him and his rotten old empty
building ..."

The car rolled in front of the station house, with its green
lights flanking the doorway. Minelli double-parked, then
rolled the car onto the sidewalk across the street, which was
so narrow that a large truck would have difficulty passing
through. The headquarters, built in 1870, faced a furniture
warehouse and a small alley.

"Would you believe," Minelli said to me as we walked
around the car, "that we just got AC current for the station
house? We ran on only DC current for about a hundred years.
Anyway, we got a new station being built."

Minelli and Kettle led their "prisoners" up the six steps
from the sidewalk to the main floor of the station house,
where a rope across half of the room held a sign: "PLEASE
STOP. IDENTIFY YOURSELF. STATE YOUR BUSINESS," written
both in English and in Spanish.

A Negro sergeant behind the desk observed the incom-
ing party—Minelli, Kettle, Paul, the two young boys, and me.
Kettle leanded on the brass railing in front of the desk and in

a sarcastic, mocking tone, he sang, "We shall overcome!" The Negro sergeant smiled.

"You see this?" Minelli said to me. "These copper pipes were stolen." Joe pointed to a huge pile of metal, taken from the basement of an elementary school in Harlem. "They stripped the place clean. We picked up the stuff in a store a few blocks away. We caught the guys that did it, too."

"In there," Kettle interrupted. "Let's go." The boys were ushered into the sitting room in the rear, where the landlord sat at one of the two long, low tables placed end to end in the center of the room.

Without the handcuffs, the boys were given seats at the table opposite the landlord and a discussion ensued about the rights of property owners. For the landlord's benefit, Joe censured the boys for breaking into the building. Minelli then drew the landlord into a corner and agreed to watch his tenement more carefully. He brought the landlord into another room, where a patrolman sat at a typewriter.

"Take down this man's name, address, and number," Minelli said, "and keep a file on him, so that we can protect his property better." The landlord, satisfied that justice was done, dropped his charges against the boys.

As Joe turned to reenter the sitting room, a Negro woman named Olga came downstairs from the detectives' office. She was an elderly woman without teeth. Joe told me he had known her for several years. "She's a junkie whore," he said. "She's getting a bit old, but the detectives like to use her for information." Olga was glad to see Joe Minelli. He whispered to her and she smiled, nodding her head, and walked into the sitting room, where Kettle was reading a paperback book. Olga walked to him, bent down and kissed him on the cheek. Kettle stared her briefly in the face, bolted out of his chair, cheeks red and eyes bulging, and cursed at the woman who kept saying over and over, "Joe told me! Joe told me!"

Enraged, Kettle shouted, "You know what, Olga? Joe is getting married! On Saturday!"

"Why, Joe," said a patrolman, "we were just having a discussion of consensual sodomy. What's your fiancée's phone number? We'll be glad to call her up and give her instructions."

"Yeah, yeah," Minelli muttered, his face reddening.

"You really gettin' married, Joe?" said Olga in a sweet, sentimental voice. As the other cops roared with laughter, Joe told her, "Get outa the station house before I lock you up!" Olga hurried away, looking hurt and bewildered.

Now the Negro cop, Sand, came in the door with the mother of the two boys, who were relased in her custody.

"Your own people," Minelli yelled at the cop, "they almost killed you with the bricks."

"Well . . ." Sand replied.

"Well, what?"

"I'm just another uniform to them," Sand answered almost inaudibly. "I mean, you have to understand *why* they're throwing the brick at you."

"I know why," Minelli snapped. "Because they wanna bust my head in!"

Overhearing Kettle tell the rookie that "education is bad for this job," Sand corrected him by saying that "all the education in the world" was good for him. Kettle and Sand looked at each other in silence. The rookie's face seemed thinner. His hat was off and his blond hair was matted against his head with sweat. "I had three years of college," he offered, "and I think I agree that education hurts you on this job. If you're out on the street, you try to apply that psychology bit and it doesn't work all the time. You try it once and you end up dead. I took up math and engineering . . ."

"How can education hurt you?" asked the Negro cop.

"You don't need it," Kettle replied. "You need respect, that's what. Respect! I want respect. I'm out there, I'm supposed to be representing the people! You need a little pride out there."

"And you need to understand the people, too," said Sand.

"Well," Kettle answered, "I treat people the way they treat me. That's fair."

"The bosses wouldn't send us to that antiwar parade," Minelli interrupted. "I think they were afraid of what we'd do to those long-hairs."

"That's the thing," Paul said. "So many kids go to college and they're taught to think more. They start thinking about war and stuff. I mean, I myself started to grow my hair long, but then I looked in the mirror and I said, 'I don't wanna look like a bum,' you know?"

"Name one thing," Kettle said to Sand, "where education helped you to do your job better."

"It's a matter of helping people," Sand replied. Then he told a story about how a girl was hit by a car and taken to the hospital. Three of her front teeth had been knocked out and the doctor told the cops that if the teeth could be replaced within twenty minutes, the girl's face would heal without deformation. Sand jumped into his prowl car and raced back to the scene of the accident and, after a search, found all three teeth and made it back to the hospital in time.

After a silence, Sand said, "I realize I'm just another uniform to the people up here. Like one case I used to go on every week. There was three winos—one woman and two guys. The guys were always fighting over the woman. I went up there so often, to break up their fights, that eventually I knew their names by heart. One was Buster, the other was Harold, and the woman's name was Lucy. So I went up there once and I said, 'How's Harold today? And how're you doing, Lucy?' She said, 'You know my name?' And I said, 'Well, I been up here so many times, I might as well start getting to know you people.' But they didn't realize it had been me always up there on their fights. I was just a uniform coming through the door."

"Well," said Minelli, "I gotta check my gossip box."

The gossip box was attached to the wall near some posters advertising the Holy Name Society, the Emerald Society, and the Guardians Association. The cops were supposed to drop in notes of interesting "news" that Minelli could insert in his monthly column in the departmental magazine. Minelli had just begun his job as gossip columnist for the precinct. His first composition had appeared in the current month's issue. "It takes me about a whole month to scrape up enough dope," he said. "At the end of the column I list guys who made good arrests, like assaults and robberies. This way, a lot of cops get their names in print. That's all they want. No matter what it is, they take it home and show their wives."

"I thought you were going to put in *my* name last month," a sergeant complained.

Minelli was apologetic. There were two notes in the gossip box: "Knowledge is power" and "No news is good news."

"How the hell am I gonna write this column if guys fool around and don't give information?" Minelli asked aloud. "It's like the FBI. Do you guys think the FBI are great Sherlock Holmeses or something?" he asked me. "They're not. They deal strictly on information—*paid* information. Sure! The FBI has quite an expense account. They'll go into an area and they'll spread money all over. And you see how they come up with things? All from information. They *buy* it! It's a matter of knowing people. The FBI has stoolies, and they have a payload . . ."

"I'll let you use my name," a patrolman said. "For ten dollars."

At this point a young Puerto Rican child walked into the sitting room and shot at all the cops with a toy ray gun. The captain, standing at the door, said, "Hey, Minelli, I want you to interrogate this fellow."

Pulling the boy onto his lap, Minelli said, "I know you. You're da kid dat's lost! Raphael, right?" The boy pointed his ray gun at Minelli. "Your name Raphael?"

"No."

"You live on 115th Street?"

"No."

"What's your mommy's name?" No answer. "Your mommy's name Mommy?"

"No."

"This is the lost kid, all right," Minelli told the captain.

"Look at the kid," Minelli continued, this time to Kettle. "He's a gutter child. Can your kids on Long Island compete with this kid?" Apparently, one of the foot patrolmen had found Raphael wandering about Harlem, unconcerned over being lost. "Come on," Minelli told Kettle and the rookie, "let's take him home."

"Let me finish filling out my overtime," Kettle replied.

"Hey," the captain said to Kettle. "You're 1600 on the sergeants' list. Minelli here's been coaching you and you supposedly studied your ass off. We all thought you'd be number *one*."

Kettle muttered an incoherent reply. Minelli had taken the test, landing 913 on the list, which meant that there were that many names ahead of him in line to become sergeants. Every year about 200 patrolmen become sergeants, according to the number of openings. "The list is only for two years," Minelli explained to me. "I got about 20 months to go on the list. If you don't get appointed by that day, you gotta take the test all over again. The citations count points, which helps to move you up on the list."

As the three cops walked across the main room to the door with little Raphael, they gave the impression of football players about to take the field after intermission.

It was not entirely dark outside when Minelli paused on his way down the steps to greet some other patrolmen. Kettle promptly told them of Joe's forthcoming marriage.

"Both me and her are divorced," Joe explained, "so there's no big romantic deal involved."

"He's having a nudist wedding," Kettle said.

"Ah, those are the best kind," a cop replied. "What's nice about nudist weddings is that you can always tell the best man."

A charter bus filled with elderly ladies maneuvered through the side street past the cops. "Here's the wedding party," said Kettle.

"Look at all those old ladies. Must be goin' to a crap game."

"Minelli, are you really getting married?"

"Yeah, what's the big deal?"

"We're holding a bachelor party in the station house," Kettle announced. "At three in the morning."

"What do you mean, a bachelor party?" Minelli snapped.

The cops got into their car, Minelli and Kettle in front and the rookie in the back seat with me and little Raphael, who looked quite pleased. Minelli moved the car slowly for a few blocks and deliberately, as if for the rookie's benefit, stopped outside a dimly lit bar, where on the sidewalk junkies, whores, and pimps mingled together. They leaned on the dark walls next to the tavern and some slumped against each other. They grimly watched our car.

Pointing to the only white girl inside the bar, Minelli said, "She's a junkie whore. She goes with Negroes and Puerto Ricans. The niggers like her. She charges according to how sick she is. They go to anybody's apartment. In this area, they're not the hotel type. Twenty minutes and they're back here. You gotta pay more if you want a long time with her. They all have syphilis, four-plus. Some of it is inactive syphilis. All the girls have the clap, or gonorrhea. It can't get any worse—it'll kill 'em, eventually. That other girl there on the street—they won't even let her *in* the bar. I wonder if Hilda comes around here? You know Hilda?"

"Yeah," said Kettle.

"You get a lot of queers around here," Minelli told the rookie and me. "Dressed as girls—and they look like girls, you know? They'll pick up a guy, you know, and they'll say, 'Come on, you wanna get laid?' or something like that. Plainclothes men get 'em every once in a while. You look at their Adam's apple. If they got an Adam's apple sticking out, you know they're a guy. A girl's apple don't stick out like a man's. Junkies, junkies, junkies, junkies, junkies! I wonder if Hilda became a junkie?

"Look at all the junkies. You can point out who *aren't*

the junkies. The jail is a revolving door, a four-month rest. Most crimes here come from the junkies. They take the heroin in powder form and use a candle to cook it. They make a hole in their vein with a pin. Then they put in the liquid with an eyedropper.

"There's a couple of junkies right there," Minelli continued as he drove the car slowly. "They must have been shooting it up on the roof. They sit on the top-floor landing, by the roof. They sit on the steps and they cap and they cook up their junk and they shoot up."

Minelli pointed from one person on the sidewalk to another, as if we were on a guided tour of dope addicts. He spoke excitedly, sometimes with anger and even with astonishment at what he was telling us.

"Junkies here, every one, like that guy with the brown hat, right there. The heroin peddlers, or pushers, they're usually junkies, too. But they push the stuff to support their own habit. Small-time pushers, that is. They buy a load of junk, or half-a-load, for twenty-five dollars. That's for fifteen bags, and they sell it at three dollars a bag, so they get back forty-five bucks. Or they'll sell part of it and the rest they'll use to shoot up themselves. A vicious circle. And they have enough money to buy more and start all over again.

"Look at this junkie. That sonofabitch is flying. See that guy with the wheelchair? He's been locked up for selling junk. And right there, every one of 'em is a junkie. You can tell just by looking at 'em. They're either sick or high. And there's an overdose junkie. Too much heroin. He's probably just out of jail. Many of 'em die in jail.

"The junkies hafta steal. They need thirty, forty dollars a day at least. I say eliminate the junkies and you eliminate 90 percent of the crime in this city. Get rid of every junkie and crime will drop 90 percent. One guy says there's 30,000 junkies here, another guy'll say they're 50,000—*I* say there are 100,000 junkies. In this precinct alone, we must have 20,000. Just in this little area here!"

Joe paused, then said, "They stand in the weirdest positions, and their complexion is bad. The way they stand, their hands will touch the ground even, but they'll never fall down!"—Minelli laughed—"The way you tell the difference between a junkie and a drunk is that a drunk will fall down and a junkie won't. They never fall down. They just bend forward 90 degrees and hang there. You holler at 'em and they'll jump up and start marching around, and then they'll sink right back."

I asked him why there were so many addicts around. He told me, "A Negro boy here, he don't stand a chance—unless he's got good parents. Because if they let him go out on the streets wherever he wants, and not supervise him, he'll probably turn out a junkie, or a burglar—a purse snatcher, a mugger—anything. Not because he's Negro, but because of the environment. White kids, same thing. We got white junkies here, too. Plenty of 'em. Just 'cause he's Negro don't mean anything. It's environment. Right, Raphael?"

The small Puerto Rican boy was kneeling on the back seat, aiming his ray gun out the window, apparently not paying any attention to what the policeman was saying.

Minelli continued, "It's just that, in general, the Negroes care less for their children. But before anything's gonna get back to normal around here, you gotta eliminate *this* generation of junkies. Ah, the punishment isn't there, though. If they stayed in jail a minimum of five years, maybe—but once a junkie, always a junkie. It's a problem. A good junkie'll tell you he'll never get back. They never beat heroin once they're hooked good. And the longer you can put him away, that's the less trouble you're gonna have from that particular junkie.

"If you let him out, you gotta make him live under controls, so he has to report every night to a medical examiner or something. And you gotta put 'em into constructive places, give 'em lives. I guess they want not to be junkies, but they can't help themselves. They get themselves committed to places, just so they can cut down on their habit so they can *support* it. They have no intention of ever quitting.

"It's an impossible thing, because there's no such thing

as a junkie that's not on junk any more. Not if he's actually been hooked. They say it takes about two weeks to get hooked, and once you're hooked, you're hooked for life."

Joe obviously was caught up with the subject of drugs, and perhaps my presence afforded him a forum for his views that he otherwise would not have had. His words flowed without my prompting him. I also sensed that he felt it his duty to teach the new man.

"You need continuous pressure," he said. "All the bleeding-heart liberals, they can't see this, right? Well, just because he's had a marijuana cigarette, they say, you can't put him away for four years. What they don't understand is that a junkie is destroyed, he's a useless human being. He no longer exists. The crime one junkie commits, before he gets caught—or in his lifetime, a twenty-year span, say—*forget it*. The money! The aggravation! An IBM computer couldn't keep track of it. The machine would blow a fuse if you combined 'em all."

I asked Minelli about marijuana and he replied, "The college kids on marijuana; well, let 'em go ahead. If they wanna be junkies, what can I tell ya? They're liberals, right? You can't tell *them* they can't smoke marijuana. They wanna *legalize* it. Ha! It may not be habit-forming, but you certainly do become *dependent* on it. It certainly becomes a *start*. It may not be like heroin is, but you take 90 percent of your marijuana smokers, and if they've done enough of it, they'll end up taking heroin. As they say, you can't beat the horse."

Joe continued to move the car slowly. We crawled through a side street already darkened by shadows of tenement buildings, although evening had not yet come. Little Raphael crawled over the rookie's lap and then over mine to the opposite window. Neither he nor Minelli seemed too concerned over how long it was taking to return him to his home.

Kettle and Paul appeared to be listening to Minelli, as I was, but they occupied themselves while he talked. The large cop hung one arm out the window, periodically gesturing to children in the street or on the sidewalk. The police car seemed to be an extremely familiar sight in the ghetto, yet it still attracted a great deal of attention. The rookie flipped through his memo book as Joe spoke.

"Imagine the poor lower-class, the hard-working lower-middle-class guy," Minelli counseled us. "He skimps and scrapes to send his kids to college, only to find out the kid is using junk! What a kick in the ass! If he came back home for Easter I'd kill him. All them years of saving your heart out— if he don't wanna go to college, say so! *Become* a junkie, right? Going to college so he can be with the *in*crowd. What's the *in*crowd? All it takes is one idiot, right? All them years, of two jobs, skimping, saving, everything—you think he'll come out to be a good doctor, dentist, lawyer, Indian chief— he comes out a fucking junkie and robs you blind! Some kick in the ass. And it's not just the guys. The broads in college are no better."

Minelli paused, angry, and then became reflective.

"As I said, in my personal opinion, there isn't one cured addict in this country. Not one that's been hooked on heroin. Not one! Not one in the whole world, I don't think. Cured junkie? Not a chance, no such thing, no such animal. The only time they're cured is when they put 'em in that little plot of land six feet under."

Neither Kettle nor Paul disagreed with Minelli, and I asked him what he thought of government programs aimed at rehabilitating addicts.

"Ah, they're trying to appeal to the public. They're not accomplishing anything. If you eliminated all the junk, the Commies would send in junk by the truckload—*trailer*-truckloads. They *want* it over here. Just imagine what they'd do to a junkie in Russia. Probably shoot him on the spot. But here, this is a free country. You can do anything here. You can be a junkie if you want.

"Down here, everybody knows everybody, but they don't tell nobody. It's the 'code.' We kick junkies and the people yell at you—but then they get mugged by the same junkies!

You see that guy there in the green shirt? That's BooBoo. He got arrested for selling narcotics. Hey, BooBoo! Come here!"

The Negro boy, about seventeen, recognized Minelli and walked to the side of the car.

"How's things?" Minelli said.

"Eh."

"You on probation?"

"Yeah."

"How much time?"

"I dunno. You know, that regular youthful-offender thing, it's three years . . ."

"Well, as long as you keep your nose clean, right?"

"I'm going away, man. I'm gonna cut loose where I can do something. California, maybe. Someplace out west. Ride horses, maybe."

"Sounds good," said Minelli, but as he drove away, he turned to the rookie and said, "Now there's a real liar. He says he gonna go to school, then he's gonna get a job and go out west—and meanwhile he's still here on this block. It's only a matter of time before he gets grabbed again."

He pointed to a group of young men leaning against a gray brick wall. "These guys on the corner," Minelli said as they stared vacantly at us, "I've locked most of them up before, for one thing or another. All junkies."

Across the street, a middle-aged woman rounded the corner, her hands jammed into the pockets of her brown-leather jacket. "Hey, Alice," Minelli yelled. "How are ya?"

The woman looked up a moment, said, "Hi, Joe," and stuck her tongue out. Minelli laughed as she disappeared into a tenement building. "Ah, that Alice. Every time you see her she sticks her tongue out at you." The car stopped in front of a small laundry, where a group of Puerto Rican winos and junkies was standing. Kettle and Minelli began yelling: "Hi, guys! Behave! Good evening!" The sarcastic greeting by the cops was answered only by hate-filled stares from the group of listless, unkempt men.

"That guy reading the comic book," Joe said to me, "I

locked him up right here about two years ago. He was on the corner with a loaded gun, so we threw him in the car. We took him down the block and I saw two guys mugging a guy. About three in the morning. I grabbed them, too, and locked 'em all up.

"But you get a guy for assault and robbery, with a gun, and he gets only six months. And in four months he's back out on the street. You hit your head up against a brick wall. The guy maybe mugged fifty guys before he got caught, and when he gets out he's gonna mug fifty more, maybe a hundred more people, before he ever gets caught again.

"The politicians—everybody—they know what the cause of the problem is, but they don't do nothing to remedy it. Arrests? That ain't showing them nothing. And the junkie doctors around here, they're trying; they're fighting one of them losing battles, you know? They *feel* they're doing their bit, and that's what counts for them.

"In my opinion, you gotta lock up junkies for fifty years. Until they die in prison. We gotta start building some big buildings, or one, big junkie jail, escape-proof and everything. Don't even put *doors* on it.

"And the unlawful search and seizure, that's the whole deal. These people got rights! You *know* he's a junkie, *everybody* knows he's a junkie—but you can't search him. He's got rights! Rights, rights, rights, rights! Everybody's worried about the rights of the *criminal*. Nobody worries about the rights of the honest citizens who's bearing the brunt of all this. The honest citizen suffers. The *junkie* don't suffer. He don't care about nothing. You lock him up and he's happy, in a way. He gets a chance to clean up and rest awhile. He knows he ain't gonna get any more than six months . . ."

Outside Raphael's apartment building there were at least fifty people gathered almost as soon as Minelli parked the car. Joe honked the horn and yelled to the crowd: "Is this him?"

"Yes, yes, that's him!"

"Give his mother a holler, will ya?"

Minelli chattered away with the Puerto Rican youngsters who crowded around his window. One little boy was hitting Minelli on the arm. Faking the pain, Joe drew great laughter from the crowd. The mother appeared on the other side of the car, looking through the back-seat window at her son. "Raphael!" she screamed. "Get out! Get out of the car!"

The little boy hurled himself over Paul's lap and threw his arms about Minelli's neck from behind.

"Raphael, come here!"

"No!" Raphael aimed the ray gun at his mother. "No!"

Finally the boy was taken from the car and Minelli, laughing at the comical scene, said, "Ya see that? The kid wants to be a cop!" They watched as Raphael's mother picked him up and carried him into the building.

To the rest of the youthful crowd still around the car, Minelli shouted, "What's doin', men?"

"Hey Joe, give us a ride!"

"Ah, no, I can't now, I tell ya."

"Why not?"

"We got important things to do, man."

"So long, Joe!"

Minelli moved the car down the block to the corner and Kettle said, "Stop here, Joe, and I'll get us something to eat." Joe halted the car outside a small grocery store and Kettle bounced out, taking orders for ham wedges and soda as he went.

Alone with the rookie and me, Joe turned around to face the back seat. "These Puerto Ricans," he said, "at night they move from one apartment to another, from one *building* to another—in the middle of the night! At three o'clock in the morning, you see 'em with these u-haul-its. Loading up, moving. If a guy rents an apartment, I'll bet that six months later, ten families have lived there."

"Why do they do that?" asked Paul.

"I don't know why. To beat the landlord for the rent or something. But all night long, that's all you'll see: u-haul-its."

"I guess these people here are pretty poor," Paul said.

"Poor? It depends on how you look at it. This here is a *rich* ghetto. There's so much welfare and poverty money coming in and new schools . . . Look at me—I was a poor whitey! These people have the best. But the kids are all promoted or they'd never get out. The teachers are afraid to keep 'em back. Yet they never get any response from the parents. You know, if the Negroes keep getting so much money the whites'll start rioting some day."

"The Puerto Ricans don't do much rioting, do they?" the rookie asked Minelli.

"Nah, just once in a while. There's nobody here to instigate 'em and work 'em up like Negroes got. Anyhow, the *Negroes* even don't riot so much any more, because they got the city government so subverted. They probably figure, why should they ruin a good thing? But they got paid agitators here. I mean, they're not just agitating for nothing, or because they want better things outa life. 'Cause they got the best as it is now! How much better can you get? They *got* all that now —poverty programs, welfare . . . And they're all gettin' fat from it, and I mean *fat*. Because they're not *working* real hard for it. They just keep the pressure on the public officials. And who pays? The poor working person, white *and* Negro. I think this is the only city in the world where you get instant welfare. Just throw in your name and tell 'em you ain't working—and boom!—instant welfare. No wonder the city's becoming a garbage dump. And we're sitting right now at the bottom of the pile."

Paul had been sitting quietly through all of this conversation. He seemed to be uncomfortable with Joe's angry emotions, though he did not quarrel. His face was thin, very pale, and I think he was upset that I was jotting down notes while Minelli talked. At one point, Joe snapped, "Go on—write it down! All they can do is fire me!" I asked him if he thought the Negroes and Puerto Ricans got along well together.

"I don't know. Not so well, really. That's what makes you laugh, though. You hear the Negroes fighting for this and that in behalf of Negroes and Puerto Ricans. But the Puerto

Ricans don't get nothing outa that. The Negroes get it all. Federal money, state money, city money. The Negroes get it all.

"You see, the Puerto Ricans are *white,* you know? They're white people. I mean, they don't wanna be considered with the Negroes at all. Not nohow. Somebody that's Spanish, you know, from Spain—he arrives here, and his ancestors may go back to Spain and yet they're called Puerto Rican! What? Even the *Cubans* don't want to be associated with the Puerto Ricans. Or Venezuelans! Or any of those Latin American countries. And the Puerto Ricans, they resent the Cubans. It's all mixed up.

"But in Puerto Rico itself, a man there is usually a re-fined, respected, hard-working Puerto Rican. We get all the bums. It's just like taking a bunch of Bowery bums that are white—and we're white, you know?—and they go to Africa, and they establish a community there; and the Africans com-pare them to you. Well, maybe he's white, but that's as far as it goes. I'm no bum. A Puerto Rican with money doesn't want to associate with a Puerto Rican on welfare—or with a bunch of illegitimate kids, right? It's the same with the Ne-groes themselves. The middle-class Negroes, they don't wanna know the *lower* class."

"Well," said Paul, beginning to assert himself. "You seem to be making *all* the people out to be rotten."

"Between you and me," Minelli continued, "they could put all the Vietnam money in here and it would still be a shithouse in ten years. The people rip up brand-new apart-ments. You can't sit down. They don't even offer you a glass of water. I wouldn't take it, anyway. Probably get sick. There's usually piss all over the elevators. Every place is a toilet for these people."

"Don't you want to get transferred out of here?" asked the rookie, this time challenging Minelli.

"Me?" Joe looked astonished. "Nah, I *like* working here."

"Why is that?"

"I dunno. I've *been* here for twelve years."

There was an embarrassed silence. Finally, Joe said, "It's not *that* bad. The public housing is better than these rat traps. At least there's heat and hot water. All these buildings, someday they're coming down to make way for more co-ops or something. Insurance companies are gonna build 'em in six square blocks."

In midstream, Minelli's anger returned. "They're gonna charge $150- or $200-a-month rents, and yet you'll have home-reliefers in there. Unmarried, with a bunch of kids, deserve nothing, but they're gettin' home relief—now it ain't bad enough that they're here, but they gotta put 'em with hard-working, honest people who are paying $200 a month. They'll wreck the building, but the government's going to subsidize their rent. And that's what really burns you up. You work and you bust your ass, you *better* yourself in life, and these sons of bitches, for being nothing, for *doing the wrong thing,* are living as *well as you are,* on welfare! They get all kinds of money. It depends on how many kids they got and all. They don't care where they live—they don't care if the rent is *$400* a month, because welfare pays it!

"They'll keep it a secret. You don't know if the family next door to you is getting subsidized. But you can figure it out when you take a look at the pack of people they are. They got a half-dozen kids running up and down the halls, painting the walls . . . And no husband. And those are the ones who are really making it rotten for the working people. They got generations of people, family after family, of home-reliefers, who never worked a day in their lives—twenty-five, thirty years old—standing on the corner, on welfare!

"Now the welfare people want guaranteed incomes. We pay out a billion dollars a year in this city. A billion! And you wonder why people get disgusted and move out of the city. And if *that* ain't bad enough, with the junkies robbing you every day of the week, and purse-snatching, burglaries, stick-ups, pickpocketings . . ."

Addressing the rookie, Joe asked, "If you came up here

and said that if you were mayor of New York you were gonna stop all this, that you were gonna have it come right to a head, that you were gonna knock off the welfare from people who don't deserve it—how many votes do you think you'd get?"

"Not much, I guess," Paul answered.

"That's right," Minelli snapped. "Not even the *white* people would vote for you. And the politicians don't care, it's not their money. It's the taxpayers' money. But it'll get to the point where you'll have *no* taxpayers. Everybody's moving out of the city. So now they're trying to unload the welfare thing on the state, so they can tax the suburbanites. Over a million people have left the city, just to get *away* from the taxes. Look at the cops! Most every cop on the job lives out of the city. There are cops like Kettle, living sixty and seventy miles out on Long Island—so they can buy a cheap house they can afford. And they commute, just to get the hell outa the city.

"The welfare, it don't help nobody. The people need initiative. The whole system of welfare sets integration back fifty years, simply because it takes away incentive from people who need it. If you're living with your husband, they won't hardly give you anything. But if you go separate from him, they give you 400 bucks a month. So it pays to shack up! They break down the whole family life in this country. Those fags up in the welfare department, *they* need a little psychiatric help. They're all hippies. They even give welfare to *junkies*. Imagine that? Junkies on welfare!"

It was dark when Joe drove into a small parking lot behind some housing projects so we could eat our hero sandwiches and drink the cans of cold soda without being bothered. Minelli sank his teeth into the hard crust of the roll. His mouth was full when he looked up and saw a middle-aged Negro woman's face peering into the car.

"Hunh?"

"I'd like to talk to you," the woman said in a soft tone of voice. "My son, with those boys, they were just here—the kids were all here . . ."

"Looks like they're gone, now," Minelli replied, trying to pick up the thread of the woman's mind.

"No, just a few minutes, a minute ago—"

"I know, ma'am, but kids never stay in one spot too long."

"I wanted him to come in. He's running around—"

"Your boy?"

"Yes. He's fourteen. All over here, they're using marijuana. I don't know where they're getting it from, but they've got it. When he came upstairs my son beat him; my big boy beat him."

"Your other son is here, too?"

"I have another son, twenty-one, who's upstairs—this building right here."

"And—?"

"And he got him upstairs and he gave him a good beating. My husband is not here—"

"And the kid ran out again?"

"Yes. Now, he was just here about five minutes ago. I don't know where they went. Somewhere they're getting this marijuana . . ."

"Look, ma'am, why don't you get the housing police to work on this. You know, they have plainclothes men, too—"

"Every night, they get marijuana down here somewhere, from some men around here, but I don't know—"

"Your son could be any place."

"But I mean, I want him picked up, officer."

"Why don't you go to children's court or something?"

"I *did* go there. But they have so many other problems. They got so many problems that they don't consider playing hookey or things like that, they don't consider them bad . . ."

"Or smoking pot, either."

"I don't know. But I have this marriage license here that my son filled out. He said he was going to run away today."

"You're not gonna know anything until he gets caught."

"My son—what can I do?"

Minelli got out of the car while Kettle and the rookie continued to eat. He grabbed the marriage license and exclaimed, "Jeez, I just got one of these things on Friday. What's a fourteen-year-old kid doing with it? Your son's probably looking for this. You might call the doctor, the one who signed this thing. See, with us, there's not too much we can do about it, because we work in the radio car, we're on the outside. Go back to the housing police and make another complaint. Tell 'em you want to make a complaint about a *condition*. Because we have the outside. The only time we come here is when somebody calls us. But for us to get out of the radio car and just walk through the projects here, that's a job in itself. Because it's not only here, but it's the other projects, too . . ."

"Well, thank you . . ."

"Right. Well, you gotta keep on. If you don't keep on now, in a couple more years you won't be able to handle him. You know?"

"Thank you."

"All right. Good night."

Minelli stood by the car as the woman disappeared inside a tall housing project. Shaking his head, he swung himself back into the driver's seat and resumed eating his sandwich.

"There's one woman out of 10,000," Minelli reflected, "who wants to *do* something about her kid before he gets beyond help. But she doesn't have a chance. She's lookin' to straighten out her kid. But what can she do? Not when he's got fifty other kids around him that are *no* good. Kids whose old ladies don't give a damn about 'em. She can *try,* but I tell you if they send him to reform school, he'll come out three times worse than when he went in. He's smoking pot now, but it won't be long and he'll be shootin' up, with junk, with heroin."

Radio: "David . . . burglary in progress . . ."

Without a word, the cops hurtled out of the parking lot and raced three blocks, bucking furiously at red lights in order to avoid being struck by cars coming through the cross streets. They sped around a corner and into a side street, crossed another main avenue, and then screeched a short way through the block. Minelli and Kettle—and the rookie not far behind —jumped to the sidewalk and ran into the doorway of a tenement. There, they confronted a group of Negro men carrying furniture. Someone had phoned the station house thinking that a burglary was in progress on the ground floor, but these were only friends of a tenant who was moving. The cops were partially embarrassed; there was anxiety, fear, and combativeness on their faces. The Negro men smiled as if to say, "Don't get all worked up, men."

Outside, youngsters swarmed out of the doorways of their slum block and converged on the scene. The police car's radiator was smoking heavily. "It always does that when I race the engine," Joe said. A fire siren drowned out all the noise for a moment and then, as the cops returned to the sidewalk, a white dog attacked Kettle. Though he did not actually bite, he barked loudly and snapped at the huge cop's legs. The scene was chaotic, with the children on the car like ants crawling over a hill. Kettle, excited by the dog and the shouting, took out his flashlight and yelled, "Hey! Hey!" He beat the animal on the head, yelling, "Hey, Whitey! Hey, Whitey!" The dog growled and charged, and Kettle hit him away, shouting and laughing as if the previous series of events had generated a great deal of emotion inside him. The dog attacked him again and Kettle shouted, "Come on, Whitey, come on!"

Four little boys, each under seven years old, jumped into the back seat of the car. As the cops tried to grab them, two jumped out, but the remaining two youngsters refused to be moved.

Minelli and Kettle returned to the front seat. The dog had given up his fight with Kettle and now barked from a distance. The two Negro boys sat between me and the rookie in the back seat and as the car moved slowly through the hot, dark, crowded street, they began crying as loudly as they could, pretending they were being taken to jail. Residents of the block looked out of windows and those on the sidewalks glared at our car.

I was worried that the fake crying by our two passengers would provoke an incident of some kind. If Kettle also had that idea, he concealed it by joining in the act with the small boys.

"Hey!" Kettle yelled out his window, his voice echoing through the block. "You, Momma! We're taking your kids to jail!"

"Riot!" Minelli joined in, as if to unlease all of his frustrations. "Riot! Riot!"

At the corner, a Negro man rushed up to the car and begged to be let in. Minelli ordered the small boys out and they obeyed. "Go home, now," Joe commanded. The man, well dressed but smelling of alcohol, jumped into the back seat with the rookie and me. He pointed to a group of teenagers on the corner.

"They been trying to rob me!" he exclaimed.

"Where you going?" Minelli demanded.

"Brooklyn."

"We'll take you to the subway."

"You know them guys?" Kettle inquired.

"No, I don't know 'em," the man answered, out of breath shaking with fear.

"They were lookin' to rob you," Minelli observed, "because they think you got money. They was lookin' to beat your black ass."

"I ain't done nothing to nobody."

"I know it," Minelli replied. "But look at the shape you're in. That's why they're lookin' to rob you. You got a load on."

"You see 'em crowdin' me?"

"I saw them. Good thing we were there. They would have gone through your pockets . . ."

"They couldn't of got nothing."

"Maybe not," Minelli argued, "but *they* don't know that, not until they go through you, right? Meanwhile, you're sittin' there with a busted head."

"Yeah, maybe you're right."

"You *look* like you got money. That's all they need to know—and you got a load on."

"These black motherfuckers," the black man said. "I wish they'd all drop dead."

"That's your people, man," Minelli shouted. "What can I tell ya, hunh?"

"*My* people?"

"That's what *they* say. My people, my people!"

"What do you mean, *my* people? I'm glad you drove up just at the right time . . ." His words came out in a drunken, lazy flow. Suddenly a taxicab pulled alongside the police car. The Negro driver began yelling at Minelli and pointing to his white passenger.

"Looks like another one got robbed," Minelli said, laughing.

"I'm sick and tired of his mouth!" the cabbie shouted to Minelli, pointing to the white-haired gentleman in his cab. "So do me a favor—take him outa my cab!"

"Whattaya want me to take him out, for?" Joe screamed.

"Because he tells me he's a cop! I'm on my way downtown—what the hell does he expect outa me? He's drunk—he can't walk a straight line—and he's telling me to drive around and around in circles!"

"So what do you want with me?" Minelli shouted at the cab driver. "*You* picked him up! You're not supposed to pick up drunks."

"I'll take this guy to the subway," Kettle said, referring to the Negro man. Minelli jumped out to see if he could help the cab driver. The rookie and I were left alone in the back seat as the car idled, blocking traffic.

"All right," Minelli said to the white-haired gentleman, "get out of the cab." The man obeyed though he was drunker than Kettle's charge. He informed Minelli that he was an employee of the U.S. Department of Justice. As Minelli flagged down another cab, he asked the Justice Department employee, "Where you going? Come on, where?"

"To Grand Central Station—I live in Connecticut."

"Take this guy to Grand Central," Minelli ordered the new cab driver. Then Joe hopped back in the prowl car with us to wait for Kettle.

"Have you ever seen such a mess!" Joe exclaimed. "And look—I haven't even eaten half my sandwich!"

"I thought we were gonna start a riot back there," I said, referring to the kids who had been in the car.

"Well, all of 'em are great for rumors. Those kids could have said we took 'em to Central Park and beat the shit out of 'em. Then everyone twists it until everyone believes it—and there's a riot." Minelli became thoughtful for a moment, then added, "The *people* don't mind seeing a cop, at least the good people don't mind. They know us and we know them. It's the junkies—they don't like to see you. You try not to set a pattern on this job, to catch them off guard. They don't think nothing of mugging somebody right in the street. They usually don't bother young guys that are sober. They pick on old men and old ladies, and guys that look like they got a load on."

Radio: "Disorderly youths . . ."

"That's not our sector. Those cab drivers, if they're not getting beat up on for a fare they're getting mugged. See that woman there, the way she's walking? I hope she's not carrying money in her purse. Because somebody'll come along and snatch her purse right out of her hand. Look, she's dangling it on two fingers. If the guy knocks her down while he's taking her purse, then it's *robbery*. And then they'll call us and we'll yell for the mugger to stop running. Of course, he knows we're not allowed to shoot him, so he'll keep right on going. It's a matter of who can run the fastest, the cop or the mugger. The muggers, they stand around those check-cashing places, and when someone comes out—whoop—they whip the purses right out of their hands."

The car radio broke in: "Charlie . . . two armed men on loose . . . they ran into housing project . . ."

"Try and find 'em!" Minelli shouted to the radio, knowing he could not be heard. He went on more quietly, "We have a criminal element here that exists by stealing off of others, mostly narcotics addicts. In broad daylight, if you walk with a suitcase, say—I'll start you at 120th Street, and I'd almost be willing to bet that you don't make it to 125th Street—in certain blocks. Lately, these delivery trucks, you know, they're gettin' hit bad. I met a truck driver last night—he drives a laundry truck—who's ready to shoot every nigger in sight. People either blame *all* Negroes or *all* cops, which of course is stupid. But still, more than 300 drivers have been attacked and robbed in the last few months, while making deliveries to grocery stores. Hey—remind me, I've gotta call my fiancée later."

"I want to get married myself," the rookie said. "My girlfriend is afraid of cops, though."

"Yeah? She's afraid of *you*?"

"Not of me, but of cops in general. But I told her, this job has some security. You know you're going to get a paycheck, at least."

"Yeah," said Minelli. "That's what I told my wife when I became a cop. So she divorced me." Minelli laughed hard at his own statement.

"She divorced you because you became a cop?" the rookie asked in an incredulous voice.

"Well, not exactly. She got afraid, for one thing. But that wasn't it, either. It wasn't the *fact* that I became a cop, it was what happened to me *after* I was a cop four or five years."

"What do you mean? What happened?" Paul asked.

"I'm not sure. All of a sudden, the years go by . . . You don't believe nothing, you don't trust nobody . . . All you gotta do is ask any cop's wife. Ask her about the time between the day he came on the job, and now. Has the guy changed? Well, you've hardened, I guess. Nothing bothers you. If someone gets run over by a train, you go over and look at it, and you might say, 'Well, one guy less.' Nothing's gonna faze you . . . not any more . . . All the shit keeps going on, right? Oh, you feel *sorry,* you know. But you become a different person. I hope my fiancée can stand me after we're married."

We all were silent for a minute. Then Joe said, "I'm watching everything, it seems. On and off the job, really. I've been around this precinct a million times. I go round and round, I'm going into myself, you know? Especially when there's nothing happening. The longer you're here, the less you see the danger. You *see* it, but you have to deal with the people, you have to get down to their level. You can't say please or anything. You gotta play the part. So sure, I'm a different guy when I get home . . ."

Kettle returned after having placed the drunken man on the subway. "Hey," he asked, "where did that guy want to go, anyway?"

"Brooklyn."

"Oh, man, I put him on the *up*town subway—the one that goes to the Bronx!"

"He's got a load on—probably won't know the difference," Minelli said, laughing. "Ya know, Kettle, you got a great mind. Really."

"Joe, baby—"

"Listen, I'm gonna go eat the rest of this sandwich."

For a few blocks, Minelli drove under the railroad tracks and over the cobblestone street, through the shadows of Harlem. The car crept down a side street and we heard whistle signals; Minelli and Kettle laughed to each other and whistled back, joining the strange sounds of human communication outside the car. We cruised past a watermelon stand and paused briefly in front of a bar. Kettle jokingly wondered if we should stop in to look at the "go-go" girls. But Minelli moved on, pointing out a bar and grill that used to be "strictly Irish" that was filled with "nothing but junkies now, all junkies—look at 'em."

A bus passed the patrol car, with a small Negro boy hanging on the back.

"Hey! Get off there!"

Kettle's command was obeyed. The radio dispatcher said, "A man with a gun." "Not our sector," Joe answered aloud. The night air and the way the people stood, staring emptily at the prowl car, combined to make this new period of waiting very tense for all of us. Overtly, the cops were trying to find a place to eat, but actually they were waiting for something to happen, for something that would light a fuse. In the process they built up their nerve by becoming haughty: "Hey, nigger cats, hey man, hey boy, hey mother-fucker!" Kettle's voice did not reach the outside of the car.

"Other cops from other parts of the city," Kettle said suddenly, "they don't realize how tough this precinct is. If a guy is standing there on the corner and calling me a motherfucker all the time, and I throw my fist after half an hour, the television will show just that, and everyone'll say, 'Police brutality.' Well, the law of the land is respect. They can't think they can shit on you. You gotta bust 'em down. Sure, you *talk* to them. You talk to them the way they talk to you! But then they charge 'verbal' brutality. Well, most of the time we're baited and baited, but we don't fall for it."

"There was this one guy," Minelli added, "who said he thought this country was full of crap. I asked him why don't he go to Cuba, then. He said no. I said how about Russia? And he said that that ain't so bad. So I said you wanna go? I'll pay your way!"

"Hey, Fatty," said Kettle to a large woman who waved back in recognition. The cops paused at a corner to watch a black man and woman fighting. When she hit him with her purse, Kettle yelled, "Kick him in the balls, honey!"

"Look, there's a junkie brigade," said Minelli. "There's Weepy." He pointed to a stooped-over Negro man. "He's always being chased—he *thinks* he's always being chased by the narko guys; and he's always crying and saying, 'I ain't done nothing.'"

On the sidewalk, a Negro addict was dancing in circles. "He's high on some good stuff," Kettle said with a trace of admiration.

Minelli moved down the block and stopped next to another band of young boys. They stared at the police car and the cops stared back.

"What are you lookin' at?" Minelli asked at last. One boy had a radio pressed against his ear. Another walked around in a circle, reading a magazine.

Radio: "All cars, be on lookout for lost child, male, Negro, six years of age . . ."

"A good dictatorship would straighten this country out," Kettle said to us as the car moved again. "There's too much fancy living, by all the people. There are no family ties left. That's what this country needs for a while—a good dictatorship."

"Like the drunks and winos in the park," Minelli injected. "We used to bring a wagon down here every day and haul 'em all off. They don't do it now because it would be violating their civil rights. Now muggers can do anything they want. If they wanna mug somebody, they mug somebody. How liberal can you get? It's not even liberal—it's extreme!"

"You gonna stop and eat your sandwich, Joe?" asked Kettle.

"Yeah, if I can find a place to eat without people running up to the car. They got the longest noses in the world, these people. No matter what happens, within five minutes you'll have a hundred people there. If there was a guy with his head chopped off and lying dead, everybody in this area would be there to look at him and stare at him, and not even make a face—just stare as if to say, 'Well, one guy less.'

"You begin to eat in the radio car and everyone comes up and looks at you like an idiot. How about if I came up and watched *you* eat? You could be parked in the street, eating a sandwich, and people'll walk a block out of their way, just to walk past the radio car to see what you're doing. They look to see if you're drinking beer, maybe, or something. They try to get you on any little thing."

"Stop here a second, Joe." The car stopped across the street from a tavern. "Hey, Vicky! Thelma!" Kettle summoned the two Puerto Rican women, both prostitutes and good friends of the cops. "Come here, girls, and watch Joe eat his sandwich."

One of them was Vicky the Rug, whose hairpieces had provided the inspiration for her name. She leaned her drawn face through the window and teased Minelli's hair. Thelma, at Kettle's window, shouted, "Hi, Joe!" Her dirty-blond hair was cropped like a boy's.

"Look at Thelma," Joe said to me. "She's got gangrene on her arm from dirty needles. How many times you been locked up, Thelma?"

"Twenty-seven times," she said. "That I *remember,* anyway."

Vicky the Rug said, "My cat had kittens."

"Yeah?" replied Minelli, visibly excited by the announcement. "How many?"

"Five."

"We got busted and just got out," said Thelma.

"Hey, Thelma," Kettle said, "we're gonna have a bachelor party later on. Wanna come?"

"Who's gettin' married?"

"Joe!"

"*Really,* Joe?" said Thelma, flashing her yellow teeth.

"Yeah. She's a telephone operator," Joe replied.

"Thelma," Kettle soothed, "if I leave my wife I'll go with you."

For twenty minutes the cops exchanged jokes and gossip with the two addicted prostitutes. "Vicky," said Joe, "when are you gonna take that policewoman exam?"

"Who's your undertaker, Thelma?" Kettle joked. "You settled on one yet? Look at Thelma, Paul. She's as screwed up as anyone I know. She looks like death warmed over—ankles swollen, scabs and scars . . ."

"How many wigs you got now?" Joe asked Vicky the Rug.

"Oh, ten, maybe."

"Ten!" Minelli turned to me and said, "Vicky the Rug has ten wigs—but she swipes 'em. Right, Vicky?"

"Oh, Joe! You think I'd do that?" she whined.

"She got a red wig, a blond one, this black one you got on—hey, there goes one of your friends."

Minelli was referring to a younger girl, Dottie, who was disliked by these older prostitutes. To the rookie, Minelli said, "That's Dottie, crossing the street there. A junkie whore, eighteen years old. She had to withdraw her baby from heroin. She was on junk when she had the baby. Been a junkie for three years, since she was fifteen. There's a million kids in her family. She was eleven years old when I first met her. Since then she's been married, divorced, and God knows what."

As soon as Minelli had stopped joking, the prostitutes took their leave of the patrol car. Joe turned onto Park Avenue near 127th Street, mumbling, "That Thelma, if you'd seen that broad twelve years ago you wouldn't know her. Now, she walks the streets, night and day."

Parking next to an abandoned building, away from any lights, Joe went back to his sandwich. In between bites, he said, "A lot of times, some of your best information comes from prostitutes. It works if you have a favorite girl out here, one that knows you and you know her. A rookie like you, Paul, you wouldn't know her, see? But a cop who's been here, he's watched her. You may have seen her go to school. In fact, maybe you crossed her at the school crossing. And now, ten years later, she's a big whore and a junkie. She knows you, right? And she's not your enemy. And she *could* be your friend. So once in a while, you may ask her about something like a shooting, and she may give you some information. Bee-yootiful! This is how crimes are solved." After a pause, Joe said to Kettle, "That Puerto Rican girl, Hilda . . . Have you seen her around lately?"

"I don't know."

"You know what? When she was nine years old, I went to her birthday party! No kidding. She's twenty-one now, I guess. I remember Hilda when she was little, when she used to come home from school . . . I crossed her at the school crossing and she used to wave at me, you know? Jeez, I hope she's not a junkie. I watched her grow right up. She graduated high school, one of the *few* that graduated. I don't think she grew up in the *exact* poverty that everybody else grew up in. As the years went by, she became quite a gal. When I worked the late tour, I used to see her going to the subway in the early morning—well dressed—and I might say hello and talk to her, you know? She graduated at seventeen and I know she worked downtown for about two years. She was making about seventy-something a week, looked real proud. But I haven't seen her for weeks now. I hope to hell that she hasn't given it all up for junk . . ."

Another police car pulled up next to Minelli and, from the rear window, the captain's face appeared.

"Hello, captain," said Joe. The captain gave a slight nod as his car moved away. "The captain," Joe complained, "he's the only captain around here like that, you know? He's gotta go around and *show* he's a captain. He probably never sees his wife. She probably divorced him two years ago and he hasn't found out yet. He's gotta let everybody know he's out here and all that, you know?"

The captain of a precinct is subject to caricaturization much like the principal of a high school. The men of this precinct had variously named their leaders "Captain Nice," "Captain Top," and "Captain I-Love-Me"—the first because he was a gentle soul, constantly urging the men to be "nice" to the community; the second because he always read aloud the Temporary Operating Procedures (TOP); and the third and present captain (I-Love-Me), not because he loved himself, but because he had an excessive passion for his work.

Minelli seemed loyal to each of these men but he had his gripes as well. He described one of them to me. "He gave us our usual briefing today: 'Know when and how to use your gun.' I been here twelve years and I still hear the same lecture. Rules and procedures! Of course, the captain himself never walked the street *here*. When *he* walked the streets, there was more respect for the uniform. There was a time, you know, when it *meant* something to be a cop. But this job, you get it from all ends, from the people and from the bosses. You never know where the hell you're gonna get it from. And then, all you really are is a number, right?"

"The captain *talks* a good fight," said Kettle. "But maybe the job has passed him by. Nowadays there's no respect, nobody's afraid of you. Damn the theories. The captain told me, 'If you're right, I'm right behind you; but if you're wrong, shame on you.' Hell, if I'm *right* I don't *need* him. But I want to be backed up when I make an honest mistake."

"If you make a good arrest," Minelli interjected, "the captain might give you a day off. That's his discretion. Like if you catch a guy with a gun—in another part of the city, they'd give you a *citation*. But us, it's so common here, they just give us a day off."

"Has either of you ever used your gun?" I asked.

"Nope."

"Me neither," Kettle said.

"I shot at cab tires once," Minelli offered. "A psycho woman stole it. She was a Bible reader and a prostitute, with a bottle of gin in her bag. She stole this cab and we had to chase her all through Harlem. She was blind as a bat, no glasses. I put five bullets in the back tires, but the goddamn tubeless tires took fifteen minutes to go flat. She finally smashed into the Willis Avenue Bridge."

"I just want to be backed up, Joe!" Kettle shouted,

breaking in. "I can't go home at night and tell my kids I got bricks thrown at me! The captain, I want him to *back me up.* The people here spit at you, but there's no teeth in this job. They want the people to shoot at *you* first. What do we *have* the gun for?"

"Look," Minelli counseled, "people nowadays don't want any restrictions in their lives. They want freedom. And a cop is a symbol of restriction, right? So people don't like cops. It's that simple."

"If my son was looting a store," Kettle said, "and if I had to kill him—my son!—I'd kill him."

"In a way," Minelli said to me after a pause, "we're kind of lucky up here. Our balls get broken, so the bosses are good to us. The job has changed, though. It's the pressure. It's making us a tighter-knit unit. The bosses at least treat you like a human being, now. Captain I-Love-Me is a rare breed. He wants to work forever."

"At the Police Academy—" the rookie started to say.

"Horseshit!" Kettle interrupted.

"Well," Minelli said, "what Kettle means is that down at the Academy, where you went, they want you to be a super Boy Scout. Don't do this, don't do that—don't use your gun —and some of these guys, like yourself, they come on this job with a bunch of theory that don't work. The city's so short of manpower that they dump young kids on the street right away. You can't *analyze* everything, see. That's great for book people, or *ex*-cops, or guys who wanna be teachers. You go to the Academy and get all the bullshit, and you come out on the street and you're in a whole different world. And the bosses—none of 'em have any idea! Not really. They play games, they make up memos, they look up books—but it's the cop in the street who's gotta put up with all this shit. Psychos, hospital cases, burglaries—the *bosses* don't respond to them. They might go to a stickup or something big like that, maybe. But they don't get stone-throwers and hydrants. Something happens around here and you simmer it down— and the bosses don't even know it's happened! It's over with!

"How about the guys who were charging us the other night on 105th Street, right? Fifty, sixty kids coming right *at* us. Full steam ahead! Sticks, bats, everything! Three of us are standing there, looking at 'em. 'Where you going, fellas?' They could have run us over, right? But the bosses'll never know about it. All these Monday-morning quarterbacks, they'll never know about it, because the incident was killed right then and there! But if the fifty kids had jumped on us and kicked the shit out of us, then we'd have to find out *why* this thing happened. Oh, we were in their *way*. Who were *we* to be *standing there*? It's their street! You're only a public servant, blah, blah, blah. They come up with a million excuses. And all the bosses know is when we put in for a day off, or what you put on paper—when you make an arrest or when something happens to you."

"People don't like the law," Kettle joined in, "and so they just don't pay any attention to it. If you don't like a law like going through a red light, go ahead through it! Oh, you don't *approve* of that law. So you shouldn't be found guilty?"

"The rich liberals," Minelli said, gesturing to the rookie with his finger, "they only remember when *they* were kids. They might remember the old cop kicking them in the ass. But today, things are the complete opposite. They don't know what's going on now. And those were good neighborhoods, where the wealthy stiffs lived. They aren't afraid, see. But suppose all of a sudden all these people in Harlem got on a train and started wrecking the houses up in the suburbs? They'd be the first to start buying guns. Just like the guy who asked the mayor, 'How come *your* kid don't go to public school?' Tell the liberals, take *your* kids and put 'em down here to school. Go ahead! If you're so liberal. But see, *their* kids aren't getting raped and mugged . . ."

Radio: "David . . . psycho . . ."

"That's us. It's in the projects." Minelli put his hat on and crumpled his sandwich wrapper. "It makes you sick, these jobs. All the housing police have two-way radios now, and everyone in the housing projects has the number of the housing cops, right? So who do they call? Us! Why? Because they don't want the housing police up there on their disputes. They're afraid that they're liable to get thrown outa the projects. Sometimes even the housing cops *themselves* call the station, pretending to be a neighbor, and we have to respond. Because they don't wanna handle the jobs. Too messy."

Joe cruised slowly past an abandoned car, one of hundreds in the area which had been stripped completely and turned into a shell, a skeleton of what once was a car. "Look at those guys," Minelli said, pointing to a group of Negro youngsters moving like shadows in the hot night. "Nothing like using a fire escape for a basketball net, you know. Then the people complain, because the fire escape keeps vibrating. I'll take any five of those guys, though, and I'll bet they'd give a professional team a good game."

As a firework exploded in the darkness, Kettle said, "We had a cop shot dead right here, in a small riot."

"I worked every riot in Harlem," Joe added. "Most of the time, in the riots, you get calls to assist patrolmen. In 1964, when all the rioting started, every two minutes you had another assist-patrolman. In all the riots, you just go from one place to another. We were going back and forth, up and down Lenox Avenue . . . you chase 'em all off the corner, you grab a few guys, and they take off. Next thing you're back in the car and they start heaving bottles at you—which now is normal—and you've driving down the block and *more* bottles will be flying at you. You'd see a cop who was by himself who needed help, so you jump out and help him, fire a few shots in the air to scare 'em away—and they'd all run. Then they'd regroup down the block and start all over again. I was rapping them in the legs, mostly, you know? With my nightstick. Rappin' 'em in the ass. Because most of 'em'll run, you know? We'd get four or five guys and we'd charge the bunch, and while you're chasing them away, somebody's trying to burn your radio car. So you get back in the car, listen to the radio, and there's another assist-patrolman two blocks away . . .

"All well-planned, the riots. Organized. Where could

you get all those bottles all of a sudden? It got to the point where I was picking up the bottles that didn't break and throwing them back at the rioters!"

"It's the way everybody's coddling the people who break the law," Kettle added. "I don't have to *beat up* people, it's not that. But a criminal is a criminal! And I treat him exactly how he treats me. If he swings at me I'm gonna whack him right in the puss. Fair is fair, don't hit me! I'm doing my *job* out here. *They* are the criminal, not me! Don't raise your hands, who the hell are you to raise your hands to me?"

Minelli was checking his memo book to make sure he was heading for the right address. Kettle went on, speaking to me and the rookie. "I usually have an understanding with the people I'm arresting right away. I tell 'em, 'Now, friend, you're gettin' locked up. Don't be a smart guy, and you and I'll get along fine. I just got you for what I got you for, and that's it. I'm not gonna pile it on you or frame you or anything. I'm not looking for any more from you. You're wrong. You're in. It's the game, friend. You play it, sometimes you lose. And tonight, you lost. You got caught. That's all.'

"I talked to a priest from Argentina the other day. He has a parish here in Harlem. He called me because some kids were throwing rocks at the nuns' convent in back. He said to me, 'You know, in Argentina we may have a dictator, but I assure you of some things—they don't smash windows and they don't steal in Argentina.' I'll bet that country has one of the lowest crime rates in the world. Do you know why? Well, this priest said the very same thing that I've always said. He spoke about fear and respect. For policemen, for the law. He says that in Argentina if a man breaks a window and steals something, a policeman has the right to shoot him on the spot. Because it's a *crime*—against the *people*."

"Well," Joe said, "the trend swings around. It goes all the way around. From hard to easy and back to hard again. People are getting sick of the bullshit. The white people wanna see these people get a good shake here, but they're gettin' sick and tired of getting threatened, 'If you don't give me this or that, we're gonna blow the world up.' Well, all you're doing is blowing up your *own* world, or neighborhood. You ain't blowing up *my* neighborhood. Hard to soft, and it's *gotta* get hard again. Either that or we might as well all pack it in."

Paul said quietly, "I believe that discrimination is wrong."

"So do I," Minelli snapped. "Who the hell cares about color? But what sells papers, a cop locking up a white man or a cop locking up a black man? You'll sell more of one than the other, right? But there *is no racism* here—that's baloney. Very seldom do you hear any of the good people around here say that you're doing something because they're black and you're white. *Very* seldom. The people are sick of hearing that garbage. The colored people themselves! In some blocks or areas you get it more, and that's because they instigate it. They pull 'racism' on a cop and they think he'll let 'em go.

"They make the cop give them his shield number and then they think he's gonna get scared off from making an arrest. I had a woman do that to me. She wrote a letter on me. A long, nasty letter. Of course she admitted the fact that she was drunk, stone drunk. But that don't count. I went down for a hearing, then down for a brainwashing, then down for *another* brainwashing—and that was the end of it. I gave 'em such a hard time they threw me out of the office. They're not gonna brainwash *me*. I've been working here twelve years! They're gonna tell me how to work with these people? I mean, how lenient can you get? How lenient? Well, maybe they don't need me. I might as well stay home!"

As Minelli pulled up outside the projects where the "psycho case" had been reported, we saw dark shapes moving quickly through the night. They were youngsters, first one and then, twenty yards behind, a gang chasing him. The mob bore down on the fleeing boy, chasing him over the grass lawns of the housing projects. "Well," said Minelli, "I hope that psycho case can wait a moment." With that, the police car shook with motion, tearing back, then forward and around a corner in order to cut off the mob of young boys. Minelli deftly maneuvered the car—siren wailing—to where the terrified boy rushed into the street. Kettle hopped out and confronted the mob, which immediately backed off and dispersed.

"What happened to you?" Minelli asked the boy, who was shaking and vomiting at the side of the patrol car. "Man, they were coming at ya with chair legs, sticks, bats—you're lucky you're not dead!"

Breathing heavily, the boy said, "Puerto Ricans. My friends."

"Your *friends*?"

The boy, a nineteen-year-old Negro, explained that he had made friends with several Puerto Rican youngsters. When a Puerto Rican boy he did not know approached him with a knife, he ran, only to find that all his "friends" were chasing him, too.

"You know you ain't gonna get no fair fight around here," Minelli told him. "Even if you *win,* you lose."

"That's right," the boy said in a whisper.

"They'll never back you up. You find that out."

"Yeah," Kettle said, "you'd just about had it when we got here."

"Come on, get in the car," Minelli ordered. "We'll take you home." The boy got in the front seat, between Joe and Kettle.

Joe drove back to the front of the housing project where they had first seen the mob of youngsters. "Paul and I'll take care of the psycho case," he told Kettle. "You bring this guy home and we'll see you back here." I got out with Joe and Paul.

As we walked up the sidewalk to the housing project, Minelli said to the rookie, "Well, maybe we made half a friend."

Kettle told me later about his conversation with the boy. He asked, "You go to school?"

"Nah, I graduated already. I work in the Stock Exchange."

"Really!"

"Yep. And I'm gonna make a million bucks one day, too."

"Well," Kettle said to himself, "how do you like that? I just helped save the life of a millionaire—from Harlem!"

In the lobby of the housing project, Minelli yelled to someone entering the elevator, "Hey, hold that door!"

In the elevator was a man in his thirties, dressed in a light-blue shirt, dark-blue pants, light-blue socks, and dark-blue shoes. He had some change in his pocket and he wiggled his body as the elevator climbed to the tenth floor. He shook his head, jiggled his body—and mumbled something in clear defiance of the patrolmen. Minelli, his face red and his dark-brown eyes glued to the young man, tapped his hand against his leg. It became a staring contest between Minelli and the man, who, as he walked from the elevator, said, "Man, I just rode with whitey."

Kicking the door open again, Minelli jumped into the corridor. "You got something to say?" he yelled.

"Me? No, man. Don't get nervous on 'count of me, man."

Minelli stood with one foot in the elevator door for a moment, reddening with anger. Then he came back into the elevator car with Paul and me. "If looks could kill, I woulda been dead, right? Dead! On the spot!"

We got off on the twelfth floor. Minelli knocked on an apartment door and it was opened by a short Negro man, drenched with blood—on his face, on his white T-shirt, on his hands. "Come in," he told the cops, shaking all over. The officers moved into the room and I followed. There was blood on the bare floor and furniture had been overturned. Two long-playing record albums were on the floor: *How the West Was Won* and *Soul and Inspiration*. A Negro woman sauntered in from the back room, wearing a red dress stretched tight across her bulging stomach. Her ankles were swollen and her face was painted, Indian-style, with red streaks and blue dots.

"I think," she told Minelli, "that I shall never see a poem, as lovely as your cock!"

"She threw the television out the window," the man said.

"He brought a woman into my bedroom!" his wife countered.

She walked to the record player and turned on some exotic music. She wept, danced, kicked the coffee table, which was already on its side, across the room.

"You know what?" Minelli whispered jokingly to the rookie, "I don't know which one of 'em is the psycho case."

Trembling, the man said, "There is poison in this room. Look—where she scratched me. You have to take her away. She's been beating up our kid."

"A kid? Where's the kid?"

The man pointed to the back room but his wife jumped in front of Minelli. "You got a dick?" she screamed, jumping around him and grabbing at the rookie's crotch. Minelli put his arms around her, but she was almost too big for him. Finally he wrestled her to the couch and put handcuffs on her. "Help this guy clean himself up," he told Paul, who grabbed a washcloth from the small kitchen. Minelli backed away from the woman to turn off the record player. She slumped down on the couch, with the handcuffs on, yelling incoherently.

"Give me a gun!" she screamed. "I'll kill myself! I ain't going to no hospital!"

"Psychopath," Joe informed me, matter-of-factly. "Just crazy. Most of 'em are outpatients from a nuthouse. They go off the deep end again, after they get out. They'll take her to the hospital—we'll have to go over there and stay with her a while—and then send her home. Give her some pills. Or maybe if they got any room, they'll put her back in the nuthouse."

"I still got my pussy!" the woman screamed. "I still have my pussy—and God!"

"People are always flipping their lids around here,"

Minelli observed, almost as if he were conducting a guided tour. Then he walked into the back room and picked up a six-month-old girl from her crib. The baby's face was rigid, her eyes looking off in abstract horror.

"Oh," the rookie moaned at the sight of the child.

"We just gotta wait for the ambulance," Minelli said, holding the child, obviously struggling to keep his own face from showing any expression . . .

I went downstairs and outside the housing project, where Kettle was waiting in the squad car. I told him that the ambulance had not yet arrived and he said, "That's par for the course." I climbed into the front seat and Kettle decided to go for some cigarettes. He drove slowly, humming to himself, as I watched the various colors of the night splash onto the windshield and reflect off the hood—red, green (WALK), white, pink, orange, blue, red-orange (DON'T WALK). Kettle pulled alongside a *Daily News* truck and the man handed him a late edition. Then we turned down a side street.

A black man, in a stunning white suit, was standing on the curb halfway down the block, waving. Kettle pulled up next to him. The man leaned his face into the opposite window and, in an articulate, sophisticated tone, said, "Officer, I was just coming home from work—I work late—and I heard something fire, I don't know if it was a .22 or what. I think it was some kids on the roof."

"Which roof?"

"Just down this block."

"Get in the back seat."

Kettle drove to the end of the block. "Last night," the man said, "at about this same time, I almost was hit by a brick. If these kids are beginning to get away with this now— well, I'm not telling you your business, but if they *are* stopped now it'll save a lot of trouble in the future."

"They've *been* getting away with it," Kettle said. "Let's put it that way. Okay?"

"Last August, I was stabbed with a sword," the man said. "Something has to be done. You can't let them run you. Of course, I can understand that these kids have too much time on their hands, nothing to do . . ."

"Of course," Kettle said, "we'll never catch them now, because they hide in all these buildings, all through the hallways."

"Where else can they spend their time? That's part of the trouble."

Kettle asked the man where he worked. When he replied, "Over at the Welfare Department," Kettle muttered something in which I detected a note of derision.

After a few minutes, Kettle let the man out and turned uptown again, driving the wrong way on a one-way street. Then he drove through another narrow block and stopped near the corner. He walked into a small grocery store to get his cigarettes. I waited in the squad car.

As Kettle emerged from the grocery store a woman yelled to him: "Officer, I think someone is in my apartment."

"Where?"

As they turned toward her building, a Negro man in his mid-thirties was walking calmly down the steps with a bundle of packages in his arms. The woman said, "He don't live in my building."

Kettle rushed over and confronted the man: "You live in this building?"

"No, I don' live here."

"Come with me." Taking him by the arm, Kettle led him back up the steps and into the hallway of the building, the woman following. I left the car and joined them.

"He's got my uncle's property," she said.

"Put 'em on the floor, buddy."

"Yes, all these are from my apartment," the woman continued. "I had this one gift-wrapped and my Aunt Dolly's name is on the card—see?"

The man leaned his back against the wall, looking calm

and resigned. "It's okay, pal," Kettle said easily. "You're under arrest. You lost the game today."

As Kettle reached for his handcuffs, the man suddenly jumped over the packages and dashed for the door. Kettle raced after him, hit him against the wall, and struggled to bring him down and put the handcuffs on him. But the man fought like an animal, as if he had made up his mind that he would never be caught. The struggle continued until both men tumbled down the steps to the sidewalk. The man rolled free and took out a knife. Kettle grabbed him, but the man's sweater ripped completely free, revealing a bare torso. When he reached for him a second time, the knife sliced the palm of Kettle's hand, making a deep cut that immediately drew a rush of blood.

Now the burglar was running away and Kettle followed. He fired two shots in the air and yelled, "Halt! Halt!" But the burglar continued to run, so Kettle leaned against a lamp-post—hugged it, actually—and aimed his gun at the man's back. He fired two shots and it was over. It was over almost before beginning, with no meaning.

Kettle reached inside the squad car and called for assistance. As we waited, the only thing that was on his mind was whether the law, the bosses, would uphold his right to shoot the man. He had apparently decided for himself that he was definitely in the right. He seemed completely calm. Now, for the first time, he had killed a man. He had survived.

Breathing heavily, Kettle said there would be a thousand more nights like this for him, before he could retire. We heard a siren and Kettle laughed: "The boys are coming." There would be some good laughs, he said. Minelli would put it in his gossip column.

"Maybe the *Daily News*'ll print something," he said, smiling. "The man was a burglar. He was nothing. It was self-defense. He committed a felonious assault on a cop! I had to use any means necessary to apprehend him!" Kettle seemed to be looking over his shoulder, as if he were being attacked or reprimanded. "A cop is a human being before he's a cop, right? What else is there to say? He played the game, he lost. It's all a game ..."

"I've locked up that guy before," Joe Minelli said, pointing to the dead burglar soon after he and the rookie arrived at the scene as passengers in another patrol car. "He's been locked up twenty-five times before. It's the judges who let the guy back on the street that are guilty! It's no incentive for *me* to go and do a job. Here's a guy with at least twenty-five previous arrests, and yet he was still out on the street, burglarizing a place! Imagine what he would have done to a *civilian* if he thought nothing of knifing a *cop*! Can you imagine?"

Kettle was taken to a private hospital to get his hand cleaned up and bandaged. "He'll be out for a week or ten days," Minelli informed me as if he were commenting on a baseball pitcher's arm injury. "Then they'll assign him to the detectives for about a week, just to keep him off the streets and away from the community. And he'll have to go before the grand jury to tell his story. They'll have to return a justifiable homicide, when they get all the facts. It takes maybe a month. They don't rush it. Everything is by the book, no fooling around, no covering up or anything."

I asked Minelli whether he thought there would be trouble in Harlem because of the shooting. He said, "As for the community, they'll just make up their own story. Some guy just told me—you hear him?—that some so-called representative from the community called the station house. And you know what he asked? 'Is the cop suspended or fired?' Imagine that? The people here, they'll say anything. They'll swear they saw Kettle put the guy against the wall and pump three bullets in his back. They'll swear on the Bible that that's what he did. These instigators and agitators around here, they know their job. They'll start something over anything, any little thing.

"Of course, the guy shouldn't have even been on the street. The courts, they're the biggest contributors to crime. Out of every hundred arrests, I'll bet you that eighty-five had previous convictions—second, third, fourth, fifth, sixth, thirtieth offenders. Leniency in the courts! Of course, our liberal judges don't have to live here. We lock 'em up and the criminals beat me back here!

"You make a law, make an arrest, so the Civil Liberties Union brings it all the way up to the Supreme Court, and they say it's unconstitutional. They're all leftists. But nobody's got the guts to say it. And yet everybody *knows* that that is so. The communists are lookin' to beat this whole country without firing a shot. And they're doing a damn good job. What's a liberal? Another name for a communist. If the communists ever took over this country, well, you think Hitler was bad? First of all, they'd kill every nigger in this country. Second of all, they'd kill every Jew. And Earl Warren, they'd make a *statue* to him, for his service on the Supreme Court. And they'd thank him greatly for permitting this country to go down under.

"I locked up a woman who in concert with another woman took a thousand dollars out of a liquor store. I charged her with burglary. I wasn't even in that court more than *five* minutes when I went before the judge and he knocked it down from burglary to a goddamn *unlawful trespass*. Hey—this is a burglary! But you can't talk back. They wouldn't listen to you. They're the boss in that court, the judges. They wanna expedite the calendar, not get tied up. Or maybe they ain't got enough jails? Well, *build* 'em!

"It's always when you're not looking to go to court when something happens, you know? You got something to do— like I'm supposed to be gettin' married Saturday. I'll probably lock somebody up and have to go to court or something. I seen a guy with *two felony convictions,* a week ago, get *four* months in jail. On a *robbery*. It was reduced to a misdemeanor, but even then, for that misdemeanor, he should have gotten a *year*! Minimum! And the judge gave him four months. If that don't make you sick, nothing will. Especially if you've had to go back to court four or five times, and the complainant loses four or five days' pay. You and the complainant keep coming to court and the case keeps getting adjourned, right? And you finally convict the guy or he pleads guilty to a misdemeanor and the judge accepts it. And he gets four months in jail. But he's out in three months for good behavior. So the complainant loses a week's pay, there's no justice, and besides, he got robbed in the first place.

"I got one of the guys who threw a brick at a fireman and nearly killed him. There was three of 'em. We came in that morning, Kettle and I, and we found out about it. After about three hours, we got one of the guys. Sixteen years old. We go on trial in Supreme Court and they convicted him. He got five years. And you wanna know? The other two were fourteen and fifteen years old, so they went to children's court. The judge chewed the ass out of the *cops!* The judge! He wanted to know where did they get off arresting these kids with no corroboration to the testimony. Somebody to corroborate the fact that these kids did throw those bricks at the fireman. So he turned them loose! But where you gonna get a witness around here? That's the *real* joke, trying to dig up a witness. But if you want a laugh, go to children's court. You'll squeak your sides laughing. You'll wonder why, when *you* were under sixteen you didn't go out and steal and rob and mug and everything else. Because there's nothing gonna happen to you. Absolutely nothing! You should see the cops after they walk out of that hearing room. Bitter? More than bitter. About 90 percent of the time the judge ends up yelling at the cops. So why do your job?

"There are too many cops on this job who are afraid of getting involved. It isn't that they're afraid of work, but that's the big thing today—'don't get involved.' The average cop walks around today and he's afraid of what's gonna happen to him, what with civilian-complaint review boards and liberal bosses. But personally, I don't feel that way. I mean, at least I go up to people and I talk right out to them. Because I feel I'm never gonna say anything that can be used against me. If I say something to them, this is my conviction. I *feel* this way. Is that a crime? And I'm not gonna do anything to knock 'em down—the truth is truth and fair is fair. If they want to go to my commander and tell him I said something that displeased them, well, I'll go and *repeat* it to him!

"That's just like, when I go on a job and they start this black-and-white bit. Whoa! Hold on! I didn't come here to look at you because you're black! I don't wanna *hear* anything about that. You called me. I'm here to do a job. If you're a black man, that's what you are! But I'm not looking at you because you're black. And believe me, after twelve years, you do a job and you *never* think of them as being black people."

He turned to Paul, "Maybe to a kid like you, a rookie, you come here and maybe you see black—because it's new and you're not calloused.

"If you have two separate groups, the only way you can please both groups is to do what's fair. The man who looks over his shoulder when he says, 'Negro'—to see if he's said the right or wrong thing—he's prejudiced. I just say what I feel."

I learned that the "psycho" woman had been taken in an ambulance to the public hospital. Now Minelli was driving his own patrol car again, with the rookie in front and me in back, heading for the hospital to follow up the job. "I gotta see what happens to the psycho," he explained, "so I can call in a disposition of the job."

"What's going on in there?" I asked, pointing to a crowded storefront we were driving past.

"That used to be a gin mill, but it lost its license and now it's a church. Every time a place closes down it becomes a church. There's almost as many storefront churches here as bars."

We sat in the idling car a moment and listened to the black people chanting inside. "They like their singing," Joe commented as he crept up the block, trying to avoid the broken glass in the street. "This is like driving an obstacle course."

A car was illegally double-parked, but Minelli stopped behind it rather than immediately serve a summons. After a few moments, the owner rushed out of a delicatessen.

"Wanna move it?" was Minelli's stony-faced request. "Giving summonses out," he asserted, "is one thing that annoys me in my job. I give 'em out, but I don't like anybody telling me that I *have* to give a summons out. Or that I have to give out so many per week. Not that the captain *says* this, but it's like a boss saying to you, 'You've been out there twenty days this month, and you mean you couldn't give five summonses out?' Even this annoys me. Because I feel I know my job, that I'll do my job—and if I see a real flagrant violation, there's no two ways about it, I'll give it out. But I'm my own man, my own boss out here when it comes to that! The law's gotta be tempered with a certain amount of justice, right? A little discretion! I tell ya—I'm not a liberal. I'm not even half a liberal. Not many cops are. I just believe in fair play. It's also that summonses are bad public relations."

Radio: "10-13 . . ."

"That's an assist-patrolman in the other precinct," Joe explained casually. "It means that some cop is getting the shit kicked out of him. The 10-28 is an assist-on-carry case. I think I hate to hear that more than anything. That means you gotta carry somebody down a building—a sick case, a dead body, anything. A 10-32 is any condition there's no other number for. You go there and you're liable to see *anything*. But the 10-13, there's no mistaking it. It's not 10-14 or 10-15 —it's 10-13, you know? I mean, it don't *sound* like a 10-14, you know?" The rookie was beginning to laugh at Joe's analysis of the police signals. "The 10-13 is easily discernible," Minelli added.

Now openly laughing, Paul said, "I think 10-14 sounds pretty discernible."

Suddenly catching the humor in his own logic, Joe shouted, "Ten-Tur-teen! Ten-Tur-teen!"

Minelli laughed with us, then went back to his point. "It's not only summonses. We need our image promoted, like the FBI. And we need distinctive uniforms! These guys who wear uniforms like cops but who *ain't* cops—they give us a poor image. You see a guy walking up the street with his pants up to his knees, he's wearing a big stick, and he *looks* like a policeman, but he's a guard or something—it's disgraceful. When I see one of those guys I run and hide in the radio car. And they walk into stores and get free stuff, on the house. We need to become a group that's distinguished from all the other groups. The sanitation patrolmen—they walk around with *shields* on, but they're *garbage* men! And they give out sanitation summonses, in their blue uniforms. Why does *he* have to be dressed like *me*? I mean, it's a way to survive, when you wear this uniform."

We got out of the car and walked into the emergency ward of the public hospital, where a huge Negro man was lying on his back, tied to a table, bleeding from the head and howling as if he had been tortured beyond toleration. The nurses and interns were smiling, apparently because they had seen so much of this. A woman was strapped to a wheelchair; and, writhing, she screamed, "I'm cracking up! Oh, Lawd, have mercy on me! I can't go home! They'll kill me! Oh, *no*!" No one appeared distressed at her savage outbursts.

A few other cops were inside, waiting to be dismissed. Like Minelli, they had assisted on cases where an ambulance had been required. Joe's "psycho" was in one of the small rooms off the main floor and he peeked inside. He told the rookie, "She'll be put away again." They chatted for a moment with the other cops, and then Joe, his young partner and I walked out of the hospital to the car. "That's a real shithouse," Minelli commented. "If I got shot, I wouldn't want to go to the public hospital. 'Cause they don't give a shit if you're out there dying—you wait on line with the rest of 'em. They don't care how bad you are. Staffed mostly by Negro doctors and nurses. I wouldn't say they have an *attitude,* but I've known of cops who've gone there with injuries, real bad injuries, and they've sat down and waited. More than once. They tell you, 'Sit down and wait. We'll get to you, don't worry.' And you could be dying. Plus they got them half-ass interns up there. They don't know what the hell is happening."

The fire sirens were still raging in the night. Spotting an engine, fire-buff Minelli stepped on the gas. As he cut in front of a taxi, the cab almost hit the patrol car. "Those cabbies," Joe screamed as he weaved through the street, "a radio car up here don't mean nothing to 'em. They'd just as soon run me over as *look* at me." The rookie, in the front seat, was holding on to the car by keeping his hand out the window and pressing it against the door. "See any flames shootin' up in the air?" Minelli yelled. "Probably food on the stove. They're more fires of food on the stove than you can shake a stick at. Either that or a faulty oil burner or a stuck incinerator. But when we *do* get a good fire"—he whistled—"it's usually a five-alarmer. The whole building goes. These tenements, they burn real good. They have about thirty layers of old paint, and old dumbwaiter shafts loaded with garbage, never been cleaned. The flames go from the cellar right up to the roof."

Suddenly there was an urgency in Minelli's driving. He raced down a side street and now we could see a mass of people in the darkness, crowded about a conglomeration of smoke, fumes, firemen, hose, trucks, ladders, spray, and sound. Bright-orange flames were licking the night air from a fourth-floor window of an old tenement building. "Hope there's no people still in there," Minelli said as he leaped from the car. "C'mon, let's go play usher."

"Look," the rookie said. "There's a man in the window."

Paul pointed toward a man whose apartment was filled with smoke. The flames were leaping from a window next to his. "He's okay," Minelli replied. "Even though the whole building is going up, these firemen'll have it under control. They're so used to it that it doesn't bother them." The firemen were running up a ladder and pouring water into the building. Minelli gestured to the crowd to stay back. Suddenly the water stopped coming from the hose. A youngster had put a wrench to the hydrant and turned it shut. "Who did that!" Joe screamed, but the crowd said nothing. Then the water returned and the flames disappeared.

Walking back to the radio car, Minelli said to me, "You know, you can get nervous on this job. That's taken for granted. I mean, you're gonna be nervous. Everything is split-second. See, the firemen don't make a move unless the lieutenant says, 'Do this,' and, 'Do that.' They don't think for themselves. With us, you're out here all alone, and who's gonna tell us what to do? You can't assign a sergeant to every patrolman, so he can say, 'Oh, shoot that man,' or, 'Hey, don't shoot that man.' You know? But a fireman, he'll stand there and watch a building burn to the ground before he'll go in, unless the lieutenant tells him to go in there. And yet they get better benefits than we do."

Three young Puerto Rican men walked by the radio car and greeted Minelli. "How're you doing?" Joe asked.

"Okay. Pretty good."

As they moved on, Joe yelled to them, "Tell your boss you wanna get paid!" They laughed and Minelli added, "Take it easy, I'll see you later."

"Who are they?" I asked.

"Auxiliary police. They do it for nothing—because they like it. The Negro guys on the West Side, they're getting ninety bucks a week. That's hot stuff, hunh? Thousands of guys in East Harlem have been doing it for nothing, and all of a sudden those guys on the West Side are getting ninety dollars a week. And half of 'em got prison records. Ninety a week for nothing, just to walk around with brown jackets on. And these guys here, like we just talked to, they go out and buy their own uniforms and everything. And they get paid absolutely nothing." Minelli lit a cigarette and then, in his side-view mirror, he saw a pretty girl of about 20, dressed in a pants suit with black and white checks, walking arm in arm with a large Negro man. Minelli waited until the pair passed the radio car. Then he said, "Hilda?"

The Puerto Rican girl turned, recognized him, and said nothing.

"Hilda, come here."

"What do you want?"

Joe whispered to us, "Hear that? She was *never* indignant before. Now she's wise. She figures I caught on to her. Look at the big junkie she's with."

"Hilda, come here," Joe repeated. Leaving the junkie, she walked to the car. "Hilda, are you playing around with junk?"

"No!"

Although still youthful, Hilda's eyes were sunken and shadowed. Though she did not yet have the gaunt, aging face of the prostitute, it was apparent that her body was being burned and consumed by heroin.

"I don't see you going to work any more," Joe said. Hilda responded with a resigned shrug. "You don't come down to take that subway any more in the morning."

"So what?"

"So what are you doing with that junkie—and with them other junkies people've seen you with?"

"They're friends."

"Come on, Hilda. They're not your friends. You're using junk!"

"I'm *not* using junk."

"Hilda, you're using junk. If I catch you with a needle—with anything!—I'm gonna lock you up."

Hilda's weary eyes suddenly became red and she turned slightly. The tears began to roll down her cheek and Minelli said quietly, "Hilda, how the hell did you get hooked into this? Here you were, a girl, graduated from high school, you had a job . . . making seventy-something a week . . ."

"It was my cousin's fault," she replied in a tiny voice. "She called me to go to the Bronx with her, to a party . . . a bunch of girls, we got together in the bathroom, all sniffing . . . popping skin . . . I was a weekend user, for kicks, then Monday also . . . now six, seven, eight bags a day . . . what can I tell you?"

Joe was silent, then asked, "You whoring?"

"What do *you* think, you goddamn cop? I couldn't hold the job. The time interval didn't allow me . . ." She shook her head. "What can I tell you? It happened . . ."

"Didn't you ever want to try and stop?"

"I gotta go."

She ran away to catch up with the large Negro man, who had begun to walk around the corner. "I watched her grow up for eleven years," Minelli said. "You know what? I got a daughter that same age. I see her on weekends, or whenever I'm not *working* the weekends, which is almost never. I got divorced and my daughter doesn't hate me, but I'm a cop and Hilda and I got along, too. Now Hilda's a junkie whore and she probably can't stand the sight of me. But then, later on, like these other girls, she'll be good for information . . ."

Minelli was still angry and upset, so that when the radio dispatcher indicated that he should respond to a "dispute" he abruptly announced to us that we would first get some coffee. He stopped outside a shop and I went with him. The waitress handed him the containers in a white bag and stood waiting for the money. Joe fiddled in his pocket for the change and paid her, embarrassed at having figured that she would give the coffee free of charge.

"One time," he said as we climbed back into the car, "they had a raid on dope and all the junkies congregated on this block. The panic reached here when they ran out of junk. All of a sudden we had a lot of homicides then, too. Guys would be selling duds. They fill the glacine packets with quinine instead of heroin and sell it for three dollars a bag. And the junkie would come back after he found out he was robbed, with a gun, and shoot the guy who sold it to him. Or stab him or something. We had about half a dozen homicides."

Although we were supposed to be heading for a family dispute, the radio dispatcher interrupted with a fresh call to go to a "looting in progress." Once again, without a word, our car sped through lights and up a side street, turning onto a main avenue where a group of young men was marching down the block.

Minelli looked out at them and said with sarcasm, "So where's all the looting that's supposed to be in progress? They must have meant those Muslim basketball players that just passed."

Turning the car around in the street, Minelli said, "Look at that rat hole." He pointed to a dilapidated tenement we were passing. "Kids are always in there, inside that crumbling place, hiding in the halls, drinking wine, smoking glue and pot. The younger kids drink a lot of wine, for a cheap, fast drunk. When they get older their stomachs get shot, and then they *have* to drink wine. Listen to the bongos—they play all night long."

Joe drove past a row of housing projects and then stopped in front of one of them. "What's the address on that dispute?" The rookie had jotted it down in his memo book.

"This is it," Paul said.

As we went into the building, Minelli said, "Husbands are always beating up their old ladies here. If we locked 'em all up there'd be no cops left on the street—they'd all be in court. The other night, a guy fired four shots at his wife and *missed*. Another guy shot at his wife twice—and *he* missed too! But the women, they never miss."

On the fourteenth floor, we met two housing policemen who were standing in the hallway, apparently helpless. Minelli walked past them and opened the apartment door. A Negro woman in tears stood holding a baby. Her husband was sitting in a chair in the living room.

With deep emotion and wild fury, the woman screamed at Minelli, gesturing to the man inside: "He has to go back! You have to go back!"

"Why?" Minelli demanded.

"Because I'm tellin' you why now! You mean to tell me a woman has to be *beat on* and nobody can do anything—"

"You can! Go to court, lady! You can do it!"

"Well, *do* something for me!"

"*You* can do it, *I* can't" Minelli screamed.

"You get him outa here, tonight!"

"You can leave, if you want to," Joe answered.

"Where? Where can I go? With children?" She continued yelling at Minelli, who kept saying, "Thank you, ma'am, thank you." Taking the rookie by the arm, he walked straight to the elevator, his face blushing with anger.

"Same old shit, seven days a week," he said as we went down the elevator. "Let the housing cops handle it. She says she wants her husband to leave. So how do we tell a guy to leave his own apartment? On *her* say so? If she wants to leave, she can leave. But I'll bet she wouldn't go to court, anyway. They never go. It's a rat race. She thinks the only way she can get results is hollering and screaming. Good-bye, lady, you called me, I didn't call you."

Minelli, still shaking his head and grumbling inside the radio car, continued, "You know, you go up on these family fights, and you hear this broad mouthing off: 'He's beatin' on me, beatin' on me, and if you don't get that man outa here he's gonna be dead, blah, blah, blah,' but why bother to call us? Why didn't she kill him before we got there? Because that's why she *called* us: so she can get her licks in without the husband rapping her back. Because the broads, they're always lily-white, you know? Pure! *They* don't do nothing wrong. He's beating on her because he's got nothing else to do. Right? Don't everybody beat their wives every night because they got nothing else to do? That's the *impression* the broads give you. But if you listen to the husband's side of the story you feel like you want to kick her in the ass yourself! The broads, they leave their kids alone, you know, for eight hours—and they think nothing of it. How many times do you find dead kids in a fire, and where's the old lady? Down at the gin mill! Oh, but they're always right!

"It's never the husband that calls the cops, it's always the wife. You hear so much that you don't even pay attention

—just go to court, lady, go to court. And they try to tell you things—I don't want to hear it, lady!— but they tell you personal things that you wouldn't tell *nobody*. But they tell me! Who the hell wants it? Hell, I don't wanna hear your problems. I got my own! You try to con the husband into taking a walk for a couple of hours, or to go stay at his mother's house for the night. That way, at least, you know you got one word of peace. But you know, that deal where the woman kicks the old man out of the house—see, those days are gone.

"And you learn little things, like the little boy comes outa the bedroom, right? The mother and father are in the hallway, fighting, and you go in there, you half-listen and rub the kid's head a little bit. And you talk with him and you say, 'Whatcha watching? TV? Ah, you're a big boy' . . . And all of a sudden the two of 'em will stop fighting—and now they're looking at you playing around with their little boy there. Or little girl, right? They stop fighting! And now you've got your foot in the door. You're not a big bad boogeyman here, you're like the average human being, you come to work eight hours a day, you have a family, you go home, you eat, you fight with *your* wife, too. You beat your own kids, slap 'em once in a while if they're mean. You get into the room— and now you're a *part* of the situation here. You *don't* throw the husband down the stairs. You let the woman know where she stands. Usually, the guy'll say, 'Well, look what *she* did to *me*!' Maybe she hit *him* first. This whole business of taking advantage of a man because he's a gentleman—the woman slapping him and not getting slapped back—that don't work up here in Harlem. If the old lady slaps him up here, he's gonna slap her back, and they'd better understand it. That's their way of life."

Minelli parked beneath the railroad tracks to fill out numerous forms. "Duplications, overlapping," he grumbled, "that's all we get. The housing police make out forms and then we make out forms on the same case. It's such a senseless thing . . ."

"It's nice to relax once in a while," he said. "It goes in spurts. For a while you get a bunch of jobs, then for a while you get nothing. A foot man like yourself, Paul, you go buggy for eight hours. Of course, I say we're doing nothing now, but we got these forms . . . Everybody thinks you just sit in the car and do nothing, that you sit and drink beer or smoke cigarettes. Believe it or not, one night last week me and Kettle had only three jobs all night—but they took eight hours, filling out forms and all . . . It's actually pretty quiet tonight. The real good days are the first and fifteenth of the month, when the welfare checks come through. Then everybody's drunk. But it's a full moon tonight. I'm surprised at how quiet it is. Usually everybody's cuckoo around here."

A heavy-set black woman, walking on the other side of the cobblestone underpass, waved to Minelli.

"Hello, Florence," he yelled.

"Hi, honey!"

Florence had just gotten off the train at 125th Street, the Harlem station. Joe told me she had spent her day and most of the night as a maid in the suburbs.

"I'm glad to see you back," said Minelli as she walked over.

"I have something for you, Joe."

"Oh, forget about that."

"No, no."

"Come on—" Joe protested.

"I'll see you in the car and I'll give it to you."

"Okay, Florence. I'll see ya." Minelli shook his head. "Now," Joe explained, "I know her a long time, right? And she wants to show her gratitude, she wants to give me something. But I don't *want* anything. But you see how the people are?

"I locked her son up twelve years ago, when I first came here on foot patrol. And we became good friends. I know her family, her daughter, and whatnot. And last week we had a psycho case—and it was her! I was shocked. I didn't know she was like that. She was *gone*: stockings down, carrying on something awful . . . about the days down south on the farm.

She flipped her lid. She was in another world. So I took her to Harlem Hospital and I stayed with her through the whole thing there, and I gave her that little 'extra,' see? So now she's out and she says, the other day, 'Of all people to have my case, it had to be you!' She was ashamed or something. So now she's got some cigars for me or something—from where her husband works. She knows I like to chew cigars once in a while."

The cops were silent for several minutes. As they filled out the forms, they listened to the police radio. "Listen to Lieutenant Orange Cheeks," Minelli said. "He's always calling in with dispositions. Either that or he's checking the tire pressure of the patrol cars. He'll tell you that you need a shot of air of something. He's hot stuff. I just shake my head and walk away from him."

Radio: "David, an overdose—tranquilizer . . ."

"Ah, that's us. Hope it's not a DOA. I don't feel much like going to the morgue in the morning. You need a strong stomach. They got a dozen tables, bodies all over. They use a buzz saw to slice the tops of the heads off."

"Uh-hunh," the rookie replied, shifting his body in the front seat, apparently repulsed by Minelli's glib but vivid imagery.

"I do my job the same way every day," Joe said, taking his time in responding to the call. "Most of the horseshit is in the administrative end. They have things that are senseless, that serve no purpose whatsoever out here. Sometimes I wonder how people can sit down, these supposedly intelligent administrators and planners, and think these things up."

"Like what?" Paul asked, almost challenging him.

"Well, like taxi checks. They'll take a radio car and sit him on the corner all night. I can't see what he's *there* for! They say that every taxi driver, when he's in trouble, runs for the patrol car sitting there—but it just doesn't happen that way. The bosses, they just don't know things through experience. But you know what bothers me most? That I *know* it's a cover-up! It's to be able to say to the mayor and the governor and all the inquisitive people in the newspapers that,

'Yes, we're doing something about taxi holdups.' How? 'Well, we've got taxi checks all over the city.' But they're not doing a goddamn thing about it! They *still* stick up cabs. In two years of taxi checks, there hasn't been an arrest made. Oh, *I* made one. It was *on my way* to the taxi check that I caught a purse snatcher. On my way!

"And let's say that there's been a homicide in the park, but two years ago. So for the next *two years* they'll have three cops standing at the park. This is what I call a cover-up. Because they don't wanna be caught with their pants down if *another* homicide occurs there. Now they'll be able to say, 'We tried to prevent it, because we had policemen there.' See? But this is stupid. It's things like that that annoy you."

"Well, maybe taxi checks *prevent* holdups," the rookie offered.

"Prevent? Hell, they stick up the cabs two blocks over, that's all."

"Where is the overdose case?" the rookie asked, as if to remind Minelli.

"That's in the projects," Joe answered, lighting a cigarette and beginning to drive. "See this school? It's got an Olympic swimming pool! Something like a hundred yards long. In my home neighborhood in the Bronx, they've been trying to build a new school for the last fifty years. But you come to Harlem and every block's getting a brand-new school. Ultramodern, too; not just an ordinary school. How many schools can you build? They get so much money they don't know what to do with it. They put $100,000 murals in 'em, just to burn up the money. They're gonna have a school for every goddamn grade here, by the time they get finished. They'll have one school for each pupil. Just a little pressure and everybody shits in their pants and gives 'em what they want. If not, they threaten more riots. Well, go ahead and riot! Let's get this riot *over with.*

"Of course, you wouldn't know it, but a riot happens to be a crime. But everybody beats around the bush and caters to one group or another. I mean, if the objective of civil rights, and of the people of Harlem, is to gain those things which they think they're being deprived of, and they have a *way* to go about this—well, all well and good. But if in their objectives they turn around and step on the rights of *other* people, then this is wrong. The very thing that they started out to do, that they want corrected, they're now beginning to do themselves, to gain their end. And two wrongs don't make a right.

"And the only way you can control rioting is if they know they'll be shot. But, of course, how do you shoot a looter? If there's no sign of force against me, I wouldn't shoot anybody. I could have shot a thousand in that case. If I'm standing there and there's fifty people looting a store, am I gonna start shooting at fifty people? I'll probably end up dead myself, because all I'll get is six shots off and then they'll have a gun and shoot me. That's why murders here are so common —they all have guns.

"The Russians, they want riots to continue. Imagine if the Negroes took over this country. How long would they last? Russia would attack tomorrow. You break down law enforcement in a country and what's left? That's the main thing, that's what holds everybody in line, right? You break it down and there's no law and order, and it's all over, right? They're disarming the citizen with all these gun laws. And when you disarm the citizen it makes it just that more easy for the enemy. How many millions of guns are they getting out of the hands of the private citizen? Where's your private militia? A citizen army that could be formed if there was an invasion? You'd have at least a thousand people with a thousand guns. Now you got a thousand people with nothing. I'm not talking about unlawful possession of guns, pistols, and stuff—that's unnecessary. I'm talking about rifles and shotguns, whereby if it's necessary the people can arm and defend themselves.

"You see the swing of everything, right? Look at the looting. Everybody's looting, but all the politicians just look at 'em, to let 'em stay happy. That's the policy. They don't want the police to walk in, so you can't do a job. They think you might agitate 'em, you know? Well, it's got to the point where the people are gonna say, 'Let's just get this riot *over with* and whoever's the winner will take over! If you win, *you* run the country; if we win, *we'll* run the country!' For Christ's sake, if the Negroes ever got control of this country, forget it! They'd kill each other! And you'd have segregation like you've never seen before. All the white people would be living in the desert. Or up on the top of Mount Everest.

"They get everything they want—so why not keep rioting? Everything their heart desires. When they were looting a big supermarket here, a cop in uniform walked in and got behind the cash register. He started yelling to the looters, 'This is the express line! Eight items and under! Right over here, check-out!' And the people were filing right by him. The cop had been told to *do nothing,* right? So he made a big joke out of it. That's some way to run a country, hunh?

"It's gonna come to the day when it's gonna come to a head. The big shots, they wanna appease the people until they get promoted. Then the next guy comes in, and *he's* looking to get promoted, so he starts in with the cops, 'No incidents! No incidents!' And anything that happens, they say, 'Let it happen!' If the Negroes don't have any buses on one block, that means they should burn down the community, right?

"Of course, it's not exactly true, what the politicians read in the newspapers about the riots. I've seen all the riots here, but to read the newspapers you'd think that all Harlem was ablaze and that *all* the people in Harlem were all involved in everything—which isn't true! The people here get a raw deal just like the cops! I don't see *all* the people involved in riots, just like I don't see *all* cops as lousy bums. I tell you what I see: I see a half-million Negroes up here, and the Puerto Ricans; and at any given time in any riot, 498,000 of 'em are home sleeping in bed. Which leaves 2,000 trouble-makers running around the streets—but not *all* the people, by any means.

"But you watch television, and you're led to believe that the entire community is rioting *because it's a ghetto.* And then your politicians come along, and your civil-rights leaders—and they use common sense and they capitalize on the thing. They come along and they *don't* say that last night there were 2,000 *young youths* out there in the streets, raising hell. The politicians tell you that the riots happened because all the people are living in a ghetto. And so they start giving the impression that we have to erase all these poor and bad conditions *because of riots.* This is very misleading, because most of the people up here are not involved in riots, and they *deplore* the riots. The ones *I* speak to. I mean, they think it's ridiculous. They can't understand how the police force can't put the thing down, as soon as it starts. You read the newspapers and you read that the riots are because of lack of job opportunities, because it's a ghetto area, this, that, and the other thing—and sure, all these conditions exist!—but they're *not* the reason for riots! Like I said, most of the people want us, the cops, to put down riots."

As we stopped outside the housing project, Paul said, "But how can you stop them? I mean, you yourself said you couldn't shoot at looters."

"I just say there should be a *fear*—of the fact that the policeman is out here to enforce the law. And the fear on the part of the criminal who commits an evil crime that he may well be shot by the policeman. Or what's a policeman *here* for? He's guardian of *all* the people. He's not just for a few. And he has a job to do, and if the criminal thinks that he can commit these kind of crimes and if he can outrace the policeman he's home, scot-free, I don't think this is good. And *most* of these people out here—black, white, Puerto Rican, you name it—they think like *I* think! I mean aren't we all on the same side?"

Two housing patrolmen were already inside the apartment. A young man with a shaved head, wearing a green T-shirt, was telling them that his name was Willie and he was twenty-six years old. Minelli and the rookie walked into the living room, where the man's wife and small baby were watching a television commercial.

"He looks about fifteen," Joe commented.

Smirking at the line-up of cops, Willie took his hat off the door and covered his head. He was glassy-eyed but otherwise seemed all right. There was total silence in the apartment until the ambulance attendant arrived. Then everyone headed for the elevator—the cops, the ambulance attendant, and Willie—and we all went down to the lobby without speaking.

In the patrol car, following the ambulance to the hospital, Minelli said, "Willie is probably faking, to get pity from his old lady or something." As Joe went through a red light, another car nearly hit him. "Idiots here always drive with their windows closed and the car radio going full blast—they never hear you even if you got the siren on."

Minelli swerved into the rear parking lot of a huge white hospital. The cops got out and walked with Willie and the attendant into the emergency ward. "We just tag along," Joe explained to me, "in case Willie here gets violent. He just took a few too many pills, though, that's all."

Inside, they stood around and joked with a young doctor and his girlfriend. Nearby, an elderly Puerto Rican woman was crying. She sat down, leaning her heavy body wearily against the wall, to weep more intensely. Her young son stood next to her, helpless, holding her pocketbook. Meanwhile, the cops were laughing as they waited for Willie, who now had a tube in his nose.

"He just might pull through," Joe said sarcastically.

"Are you going to stay around for a while for this fellow?" the doctor asked.

"Do we have to?" Joe complained.

The doctor said they should stay. Eventually they learned that Willie had been injured recently and had wanted to be admitted to the hospital for plastic surgery. Someone had told him that the only way he would be admitted was to try to kill himself. Therefore, he had taken the tranquilizers.

When we got back in the car, the radio dispatcher was calling for a disposition of this case, because there had been a burglary in Joe's sector. "Well, that's nothing new," he said. "We got some of the most industrious burglars in the world, here. They sneak in, sneak out, hundreds of times a day. There probably isn't a store or apartment that hasn't been burglarized. The mailbox of that store there, they ripped it out and chopped the rest of the bricks out—and zoop, they're inside the store. The thieves go through brick walls, they're like rats. Sometimes you catch a burglar but the store owner, all he wants is his property back. He won't even bother to sign a complaint. The good people are being dragged down. The guy who owned that bar there, he was scared stiff. He came up to me once and said, 'You want a bar? I'll *give* you the bar now and you can pay me as you make the money. Take it, before I get killed in here.' Two weeks later, he got killed. It's like whenever I see a guy running down the street, I always look where he came from—I look to see if anybody's chasing him, or if he's killed somebody.

"I'm tired of all this, just like the people here. Off the job, I avoid everything and anything. Like if I see a couple of people arguing, I just go the other way. You're still a cop, you carry the gun, but you don't go sticking your nose in. Because you end up in court, on your own time, and who needs it? If it's something serious, that's a different story."

Minelli turned to the rookie, challenging him: "Like you, just out of the Academy, you were told that you're a cop 'twenty-four hours a day.' Right? Well, after a few years you'll learn the hard way. Like at home, when the neighbors find out I'm a cop, they'll call me instead of calling the police. I don't know if they think they're doing me a favor, or what. When I go drinking, I don't tell anybody in the bar that I'm a cop. Not even when I drive a cab, which I've only done three times. I got a hack license, you know. It's hard work, aggravating. But when I need the money, I do it. Sometimes I find myself thinking I'm driving a *police* car. I find myself driving three miles an hour, watching the junkies, looking for burglars . . . And everybody starts blowing their horn at me. Hey—I still gotta call my fiancée, don't I?"

Although it was nearing the end of Joe's tour of duty this night, he was walking up five flights of filth-ridden stairs again, just as he had done at the beginning of the tour. This time the victim was a Puerto Rican woman whose husband had told her never to leave the apartment because it had been robbed twice before. Now there was almost nothing left in the two small rooms.

"What'd they take this time?" Joe asked.

The woman, pacing the floor and breathing frantically, tried to control herself; but her life seemed to be closing around her while the cops stood and watched. "They took the television—and records," she said, the tears coming. "What can I do? I just went to a friend's house. Now he'll kill me! But I can't stay inside all day and night!"

"My partner blew away one of them burglars today," Joe said. "But that leaves the other 999,000 of 'em."

"Why don't they go down to Park Avenue and rob someone with a lot of money?" the woman cried. "Instead of robbing poor people?"

"Yeah," Minelli joined in, "*then* they'll give the orders to shoot to kill, right? But if it happens here, they don't care."

The cops jotted down the items stolen and suddenly Minelli said to the woman, "I think I met you before. Don't you have a little girl, about twelve years old? That got pregnant?"

"Yes, I do . . ."

"I thought I recognized you," Joe said. The conversation stopped there.

We walked down to the street again. Fire sirens still wailed in the darkness and the people still filled the sidewalks and the streets. "Life never stops here," Joe said.

We sat in the radio car while the men filled out more forms. "Let's get back to the station house," Joe suggested as he rolled the car down the block.

Radio: "All cars respond. Someone is popping shots off a roof of housing project . . . Which cars are responding?"

"David here, David responding."

The sudden blast from the radio, and the quick response of the car to Joe's pressure on the gas pedal, shocked us into an anxious silence. The siren was frantic and the radio operator was insisting that more cars respond. Our car joined another, both speeding against the traffic. When we arrived at the address, a large crowd already had gathered. Joe leaped from the car and the rookie followed behind. A patrolman pointed to the roof of a housing project and yelled, "Someone with a rifle—shooting down in the street!" Joe ran across the street and then into the lobby of the building. I noticed, as we got on the elevator, that the rookie was not with us, but Minelli did not stop. When the elevator came to the top floor, he looked cautiously into the hallway. He found the stairs to the roof, climbed them and walked through the door into the night air. I followed behind as he took out his flashlight and moved its beam around in the dark. No one. He walked to the middle of the gravel-covered roof. Then, there was a noise. Minelli turned, ready to pull out his gun. It was the rookie.

"I'm sorry," said Paul. "I tripped and fell on the curb when we got out of the car."

"It's okay," Minelli said. "We lost the guy anyhow."

"Some people started laughing when I tripped," the rookie said, out of breath. He seemed frightened and angry.

"Don't worry about that," Joe replied. "Look, you can see all over the goddamn city from here."

"Horseshit," Paul responded.

"What do you mean, horseshit? Christ, you've only been on the job one day!"

"*You* don't like this job," the rookie said. "*You* don't get along with the Negroes, or—"

"What do you mean?"

"I mean," the rookie shouted, "that I never wanted to be a cop—and I still don't!" Joe began to laugh but the rookie continued, "And *you* don't even like this job, you don't even like the *people*. Not the Negroes, not the—"

"Don't start in on that, not *you*," Minelli said, looking hurt. "Look, I'm gonna *boast* a little bit now. All right?"

"I don't care..."

"I'll boast a little bit. And I'd be willing to confront these people any time, any one of these so-called police experts. I'm here over twelve years! I've been riding in that car down there steady for ten years—in this same area, with these same people—and I've handled maybe 10,000 assignments. I've handled Negro babies when they're born. I've handled them when they've been born and they've died, at their birth. I've delivered Negro babies. I've had Negro women with miscarriages. I've had little Negro babies fall out the fifty-story windows! I've had *suicides* among the Negroes. I've lived with all their family disputes here. *You name it, and I've been there,* with the Negroes here. Triple homicides! Lost children! Birth, marriage, death, divorce, psycho cases, heroin cases, burglaries, murders! I've seen it. I've heard it. I've been a very part of their lives! They wouldn't even accept you into their home, maybe. An outsider, not even a Negro next-door *neighbor* they wouldn't let in to know their business. But they called *me*. I didn't *guess* to go there. *Why* did they call me? Because they *hate* me? Because they think that I have no authority? Or because they think that I'm such a bad man? They didn't call me for that reason. They called me because they *recognized* me. They recognized what the policeman stands for, even if they won't admit it. The policeman is the solution to their immediate problem if they can't get it anywhere else, and that's the most *ignorant* Negro who knows that, with no education at all! Who does he call—every time? Who does he call when his little old toilet runs over? He calls the policeman! And *I,* in all of my experience, can only name you very few times when I've ever been greeted with any sort of arrogance when I've walked in—under normal circumstances. People say to me, 'Hello, officer.' They do!

"Now, I'm speaking *in general.* I'm not saying, I don't want it said, that there aren't arrogant Negroes out here. There *are.* There are *plenty of* arrogant Negroes out here. There are Negroes who hate a cop just because he's a cop— and for what reason, nothing more than maybe a cop told 'em to get off the corner at one time or another. Or a cop broke up their dice game. Or maybe a cop locked 'em up for committing a crime, or for fighting in the street! If this makes a cop a bad man, well, what can you say about it? And in general, I don't think you'd find, if the Negro people voted on it, that the majority of them think that cops are sadists or something. Or that they hate cops. I have used my nightstick in twelve years here, and in 10,000 assignments, I have used my nightstick, in times other than riots, on *two* occasions. Two! And I've made better than a 150 arrests, or close to 200. And I have used my nightstick on two occasions—and both times were for my own self-protection. One time was when a guy threatened me, that he had a gun in his pocket, on Fifth Avenue, and he grabbed me by the throat. And the second time I used my nightstick was at 110th Street and Madison Avenue, when a real big guy was throwing cans through the windows. When I approached him he reached out and grabbed my summer blouse, and I gave *him* a whack, too. On two occasions—both to protect myself. I have never had to shoot anybody, though I won't say that I haven't had the occasion to. But I *haven't* done it, on second thought. Most arrests I've made were without a struggle. But a man who has been a policeman, I don't see how anyone can say he doesn't have any compassion, after what he's seen . . ."

After a pause, Minelli added, "I don't mean to say that everything is wonderful. I'm disillusioned with the job now. I *like* my job. I *like* what I do. But I get sick when I have politicians over me who say I can't *do* my job, and people can riot and people can steal . . . I mean, what *is* a cop, hunh?"

Patrolman Joe Minelli switched off his flashlight. The rookie waited in respectful silence while Minelli, almost invisible in the darkness, urinated on the roof of the housing project.

Detective Ernie Cox
South Side, Chicago

The seventeen-year-old boy was wanted for five shootings. His apartment was four steps down from the sidewalk, on the ground floor of a dilapidated Victorian building. I stood behind Detective Ernie Cox as he knocked on the door and stepped to one side, his hand rubbing the edge of the gun beneath his sports jacket. An elderly Negro woman answered. Behind her, in the dark, damp living room, the television was on. Dressed in a faded pink bathrobe and with a large towel wrapped about her head, the woman stared at the black detective without expression.

"Police officer, ma'am. Is Donald Baggot here?"

"No. He's not here."

"Well, I'd like to speak with you, ma'am. I'm Officer Cox."

"I'd like to know what it's about," she said, letting Ernie and me into the drab room.

"I'd like to talk to your son."

"Mmmm."

"May we sit down?"

"Mmmm."

"Where is Donald now, ma'am?"

"Donnie went over to his father's place. He stayed there last night. He never gave me no trouble. He's been picked up one or two times for questioning, that's all."

"Is he with his father now?"

"I said, he went over to his father's last night."

"Where does his father live?"

"I don't really know . . ."

"Well—"

"Look, mister man, my son never be out after eight o'clock at night, he's always at home or inside, causing no trouble."

"Well, ma'am, can you call him at his father's? Do you have a phone number there?"

"No. His father got no phone. But I can call Donnie's brother and tell him to relay a message to his father that y'all are lookin' for Donnie."

"Maybe you can give me the brother's address and phone number."

"No, I'll make a phone call."

"Never mind that, ma'am."

"No trouble." The woman went to the telephone and dialed, while Ernie squirmed in his chair. "Hello, Georgie? It's me. The po-leece are lookin' for Donnie . . . No, they won't tell me what the trouble is. Now, you see if he's at his father's house, all right? 'Cause the po-leece are here, right with me, you hear?"

When she returned, Ernie stood up and said, "Now, who were you just talking to, ma'am?"

"I was talking to Donnie's brother Georgie. His oldest brother."

"Is he your son?"

"No, he's my *husband's* son. Donnie is *my* son. Donnie's my baby. And he never got in with no trouble."

"Now, ma'am—"

"See, I can give an *account* of him. I really can do that! And then I have proof!"

"Yes, ma'am. Now, can you call Georgie back and have him give you your husband's address?"

"Yeah, I can do that."

"Thank you."

The woman picked herself up again, suddenly looking weary and alone, and went to the telephone. "Hello, Georgie? Now, the po-leece are *still* here, and they want you to give me your father's address . . . Mmmm . . . Mmmm . . . Okay, Georgie, thank you. Now, you *call* your father, hear? And tell him that the *po-leece* are lookin' for Donnie . . . Thank you, Georgie."

She set down the receiver slowly and shuffled back into the room. She handed a slip of paper to Ernie. He copied down the address in his note book and then politely said, "I thought your husband had no phone, ma'am."

"He *don't* have no phone."

"Well, ma'am, you just told Georgie to *call* him."

"No, I did not. I told him to *get in touch* with his father."

"But—"

"Don't you tell me what I did with my mouth, boy!"

"Yes, ma'am. If you see Donald, give me a call at police headquarters. I just want to talk with him and straighten a few things out, that's all. Here's my card, and thank you."

"You're thanked as well."

"Good day."

Waiting for us outside were several young black men. One of them, apparently the leader, cocked his elbow, making a clenched fist in the air. Then he said, "Who runs it?"

Ernie raised his own black fist and asked, "How're you doing, brother?"

"Who runs it?" Ernie smiled but made no reply. The entire group chanted, "Stones run it!" The statement meant that the Blackstone Rangers, the leading street gang in Chicago, had control of this neighborhood in the South Side. Ernie maintained his stoical smile as the leader stepped forward. His hair was cut short on the sides and an orange cloth was tied around his head, knotted in front, making a headband.

"You know," the young man said, grinning, "you is in the middle of a revolution."

"Yeah, I know that."

"Well, uh, you're an Uncle Tom. You know that, too?"

"What you mean I'm an Uncle Tom, man?"

"You're a dick, ain't you? You're working for the honkies."

"Well . . . Would you rather it be *all* white policeman? I mean, wouldn't you like to see somebody on your side?"

"Sure." Smiling again, with a glance at me, the young man added softly, "But you ain't *on* my side, man."

"But why you say I'm an Uncle Tom? I mean, you don't even know how I feel 'bout that particular subject. You just throwing all the apples in the same barrel."

"That's right, same barrel!"

"Don't you think I have *any* of your interests at all?"

"You're a dick, right?"

"That's right. You want to have all white cops instead?"

"Well, for the good you colored ones do, they might as well all be white."

"But just honestly, would you rather there be *no* black policemen? I mean, then you'd be crying that we had a segregated police department."

"Well . . . Maybe some colored. But we don't have no black cops come to our meetings or nothing, except when they're spying on us. We don't see you around, except like now, when you're trying to bust one of your own black brothers. You in another world, man."

"How do you know what world I'm in?"

"Look, man . . ." Turning to his friends, the leader began to laugh. As the group started to move away, he pointed his finger at Ernie and shouted, "I'll tell you one thing, man! We got the names and addresses of all the black policemen in Chicago, and when the Big Thing comes, y'all are gonna be some of the first to go!"

"*Who runs it?*"

"*Stones run it!*"

Later in the afternoon, I went with Ernie to his brownstone apartment. For half an hour he worked out with barbells, stretching and pulling the muscles of his solid, black body, which was soon drenched in sweat. I watched, drinking coffee. Before ducking into the shower Ernie turned on his favorite Tchaikovsky record for me.

We sat talking, flipping through magazines. I asked him about the encounter with the young militant, wondering how he felt when he was called an Uncle Tom.

"That boy was right," Ernie said, smiling. "I *have* spied during riots. I put on clothes to infiltrate the arsonists and the snipers, to find out who and where they were. A black cop can get closer to the action, so to speak, before being detected."

For a moment I was distracted by the sounds of children outside Ernie's window, but he continued, "I can't speak for all Negro policemen—and maybe I'm too police-oriented—but I personally feel that arson and sniping and looting are no good. I *sympathize* with what supposedly they're doing this *for*. I mean, they're protesting the injustices and so forth. I sympathize with that 100 percent! But I don't believe that you can accomplish anything by burning your own neighborhood down."

Ernie poured me some more coffee. He spoke freely and sincerely, yet he seemed to be the sort of person who enjoys solitude. At thirty-nine, Detective Ernie Cox is one of thirty-three homicide men who cover a twelve-square-mile area bordering Lake Michigan. The unit, one of six in the Chicago Police Department, handles cases in parts of the Loop, the Near South Side, and the South Side. Ernie had asked to work in the latter section.

"That's where I was born and raised," he told me. "Hell, I was a gang leader myself. I wanted to work as a detective among my own people, because I just know it better. I know my way about over there better, because it's where I come up at."

Ernie thought a moment and said, "Some of these extremely militant cats believe that the black man's world should be owned, operated, and controlled by the black people and that there should be no white people around, period. They should leave. To me, this is the extreme. And these cats wear sandals and robes and all those things, they let their hair grow out a foot long, and they say, 'We're seeking our identification.' Well, to me, I don't *want* to be identified in that way. I want to be identified as American, rather than as African."

Ernie stood up and paced about the room. "I mean," he continued thoughtfully, "I'm *proud* of my African heritage, but where I am *now* and where I've been all my life, here in Chicago, it isn't a good thing. I want to merge into Wall Street or Madison Avenue, in a manner of speaking."

As he paced the room, I could see that he had dressed for duty in black, newly shined shoes with tassles; long, black

socks; neatly pressed gray pants; gold-rimmed green cuff-
links on a pale-blue shirt; and dark-green tie. He also wore
a navy-blue jacket with silver buttons. Two guns were concealed on his belt.

"I want to walk around without people saying I'm an
oddity or an oddball," he said. "In other words, I want to
merge into the mainstream of the American scene. I don't
want people looking at me and saying, 'Look at him, he
comes from Africa.' To me, this is not my bag. So some guys
can call me an Uncle Tom, but I don't *feel* like no Uncle Tom.
I'm as militant as anybody else, as any other Negro, when
it comes to getting what I'm rightfully due. I want everything
I have coming to me and I don't want to be obstructed from
it—but *not* because I'm colored. I'll be militant, but I don't
want to wear travel garb. I don't want to be an oddity one
way or another, unless it comes to my profession. There, I
like to stand out—you know, in my work, being a real good
detective."

I asked if there were many Negro policemen who would
be considered militant. "Sure," said Ernie. "You're looking
at one. But I don't know of any black cops who preach race
hatred. If a guy who's a police officer is very extreme *that*
way, he's in trouble. There are many who want more identity
with their African heritage, but if a cop hates whites he'd
better not broadcast it so people can hear it. We're supposed
to be impartial and so forth. They'll fire a white racist in short
order, and they'd do the same thing if they found a black
racist on the force."

Ernie interrupted himself here, laughing. "One thing,
after every riot there's a rash of resignations from white cops.
At least a dozen or so resign each time. And that's not too
logical, because the perpetrators of a riot don't particularly
care what color the policeman is. When they see that uniform,
it's just like raising a red flag in front of a bull. Color don't
mean too much in a riot. They'll shoot me just as quickly as
they'll shoot a white cop—if we're in uniform. The badge and
the uniform represent what they're rioting about. We're the

enemy, and even if I *am* black, I'm the enemy along with the white cop. Of course, I don't wear a uniform, so that helps . . ."

Sitting down again, the detective folded his hands and spoke thoughtfully. "On the other hand, without a doubt, being colored is an advantage on this job. Yes, sir. And now, at this particular time, with this turmoil and social change, we have situations where it's almost impossible for a white policeman to effectively function—because all the doors are closed when he comes in. Before all this change started taking place, a white policeman, just by the advantage of *fear,* could go in and do something or get information, because the people were *afraid* of him. Now, he's afraid of *them.* Also, we colored cops know the people's habits and everything better. We understand 'em better. We know how they think, and the Negro people figure that we're harder to fool than a white detective, say. That's why so many of the ultramilitants hate us so much.

"To me, though, I figure that the sooner the riot is over with, the less likelihood that more of my people will be killed. So I do it with dispatch, if possible. One time in a riot a colored man with a whole lot of loot said to me, 'Hey, man, you're black like we are—so what are you doing? You're grabbing people and all this, but you ought to be laying back. You're out here making a big deal, but we're all the same color!' And I looked at him and thought to myself, 'My mother worked for seven years like a slave and I'm gonna let him burn her building down?'

"I feel like a riot in a ghetto neighborhood would be a difficult thing without colored policemen, because I *know* that they're hurting my own people, in my own neighborhood. Without colored policemen, there'd be no one to put in there who could move with any amount of safety. If there were just all white policeman, the man downtown would be in a hell of a fix.

"Personally, I advocate the NAACP-type movement. I like that, because they're not extreme one way or the other.

They just give a steady push for an equal-rights bag. And the Urban League, too. This is the practical way of going about the thing.

"One of my suggestions to the Police Department once was that courses in urban sociology be taught to the police recruits. Because many times, white and black alike are unfamiliar with the reasons for the problems that we have here. They need an insight into the possible reasons and a crash course in psychology. Then they would know better how to deal with the people they come in contact with, and to understand how criminals got that way, as well as helping them to understand themselves. Older policemen say they've been getting along without it, but have they really been getting along? I don't know what happened to the suggestion. I never heard anything about it."

At three o'clock Ernie was ready to leave his apartment again. We walked to his three-year-old Cadillac and in a minute we were swerving past the University of Chicago and heading for his office.

"To me," Ernie remarked, "the man's got to have a little old-fashioned mother wit, a little street savvy or common sense, mixed in with some education. You learn alleywise, and on the street you sometimes have to improvise as you go along. I know some cops with lots of college, but they can't put a patch on a good policeman's behind. That's because they haven't come from the ghetto. But if the man with street savvy has an education as well, he's operating with the best of both worlds."

I learned later that for the past three years Ernie had been attending criminology courses every Monday evening. As the leader of a three-man detective squad, he is known to perform very well. Ernie and his partners act as a follow-up team, working on homicides, serious stabbings, shootings, beatings, rapes, sex crimes, crimes against children, incest, and anything else that falls within the category of "Homicide —Sex and Aggravated Assault."

The detectives operate from an office in an ivy-covered

building surrounded by grass, trees, and shrubs. The park serves as a temporary shelter from the 300,000 people among whom the detectives work, and the office is laden with files and records that further depersonalize the population. The most important file cabinet includes all homicide cases, ninety percent of which have been solved. Some of these files have red tags attached to them, signifying that the offender is "known but flown." The unsolved cases have become part of each detective's total routine workload. A few nights before, Ernie had worked from four in the afternoon until nine the following morning, on a murder case several months old. He had worked on it piecemeal, when he was not involved in something else, and "moved in on it" when enough information had been obtained to make an arrest.

This afternoon he had tried to pick up the seventeen-year-old boy, Donald, who was wanted for five shootings, hoping to "make the grab" on his own time. "The boy hadn't *killed* anybody yet," Ernie said, "but he did an awful good job of *wounding* five people."

"What happened, Ernie?" asked another detective.

"Ah, the usual thing. Parents protecting their children. His mother probably thought I was going to frame him or something. Next time, I'll probably be looking for him on a murder charge." To me he added, "I'm sure she knew where he was. By the time we could have gotten to his father's house, he would have been over the hill and gone. Cat-and-mouse bullshit! He'll convince his mother that he's innocent. He's been accused of five shootings—at least five that I know of. But it'll never occur to his mother that maybe she should let the law take its course. She'll probably send him away, believing she's doing the right thing. Man, I don't think I've ever met a parent who thinks the kid is guilty."

The backlog of cases in this office continues to grow faster than the unit can dispose of them. By July 4 there had been seventy-five murders in the unit's area this year, whereas it had taken until September the previous year for that many homicides to occur. The detectives constantly check with the hospitals to see if patients on the "critical board" have died, in which case they become victims of homicide. Some of the men work only from the "sex board," a thick catalog of the most perverted activities imaginable. "It makes good reading," one detective informed me. Also, there is a huge backlog of minor assault and sex crimes to be solved, and these are apportioned to members of the unit as "spare-time" work.

However, as the boss put it to Ernie, "Dead people take precedence in this office," so that only a select portion of the new reports—which are stacked high from each preceding day —is acted upon with immediacy. Added to the rise of violent crimes is the current unrest in the ghetto, which has depleted manpower. "Some of the dicks are back in uniform," Ernie said. "They're still detectives, but they're back in the hole for civil disorders. We're the survivors, so to speak. We have two teams going out tonight, but there should be four. The boss wants us to keep below seventy-five hours of overtime, but it's hard. I've got 200 hours stockpiled, so if I spend only two or three hours extra, I don't even bother to put in a slip."

The two men who work on Ernie's team, Roy Jackson and John Brice, are also Negroes. Jackson is tall and lean, wears a thin mustache, and occasionally quotes from Freud and Descartes. Originally from Birmingham, Alabama, Roy appeared sensitive about life in general and his work in particular. He had accumulated ninety semester hours in education, the fruits of three years spent at Illinois Teachers College, and his wife was studying for her master's degree in psychology at Roosevelt University.

Brice is a powerfully built man, overweight, in fact, who seems constantly on the verge of laughter. "He has no guile, no trickery in him," Ernie said of his smiling partner. "I keep him in the background sometimes, because he's such a bad liar. He's so damned straightforward! He loves to eat, read, and laugh. Can you imagine a cop with an *account* at a bookstore? He's always reading. And he looks less like a cop than anyone I know. He and I went to school together, but John was a good little boy."

When I later met him, John explained to me, "I never figured that I was tough enough or smart enough to be a cop. Then I saw some of the idiots that were *on* there and I said, 'Well, damn, I *know* I can do *that* well.' I walked into the police school and saw Ernie sitting there and I said, 'What is this? I thought this guy was in the penitentiary! This guy's gonna be a *cop*? Damn, they're letting *everybody* in here!' It turned out Ernie was suited for the job real well."

"John was one of the little boys I used to pounce on," Ernie said.

"That's right," John agreed, laughing again. "I remember one time when me and this guy Frank—we were strictly schoolboys, he was on the order of me—saw Ernie and got scared. Frank and me avoided all trouble. So one day during high school we were walking down the street and we start to go into a housing-project playground and he says, 'Hey, wait a minute! That's some of the 13 Cats over there! Man, those guys'll rob you in a minute!' I looked and I said, 'Hey, I *know* that shorter fella there!' He says, 'You *know* him?' and I says, 'Yeah, that's Ernie Cox.' And so we walked past them, and Ernie and his friends were glaring at us, and I waved and shouted, 'Hi, there, Ernie! How're you doing, Ernie! Hi there, it's *me,* John Brice! Hi, Ernie!' You might say that Ernie sort of protected me."

I learned that John had worked a great deal in order to buy his mother and father a home outside the ghetto. However, almost as soon as they moved in, his father and then his mother died. John, who had been divorced, remarried and brought his new wife, with her four children, into the house.

"John always wanted a family," Ernie told me privately. "He used to teach Sunday school. He's no popsicle, though. He's fearless, actually; more so than me. He would go after a guy without calling for help—that is, even if he *could* call for help. I'm responsible for his and Roy's conduct, and the boss don't want us to take chances. But John would work the average man to death. He'll konk off after twenty-four hours, but he won't complain. While other guys are ducking work, he'll volunteer. He's got a memory like an elephant, too. The only trouble with him is he can't act, can't play a part. He starts laughing or something. He's useful for squares—old folks, children, or church women. Straights. I use certain guys for certain situations. Myself, I handle hoodlums, thugs, slickers. A detective needs a cast of characters available to play different roles, to get certain people to open up and talk. Roy is good for the young ladies."

Roy wears colorful sports jackets, occasionally with a pink shirt and black tie. Unlike Ernie and John, he wears only one gun; and a small one at that, in order to diminish the bulge in his clothing. Ernie is fond of kidding him by saying, "Hey, brother, when are you gonna get a *man*-sized gun?" From behind dark glasses, Roy's eyes usually smile in response, although his lips remain unchanged. Alluding to a certain craftiness about himself, he said, "I used to run a gambling concession in high school, over on the West Side. It was my 'thing.' You know—dice, poker, and so on."

Ernie, Roy, and John maintain a schedule whereby two of them are always working together. This particular Wednesday was John's holiday, but he had come in to do some paper work. Roy was also there, typing some reports.

"I've got about five things for us to do," Ernie told him.

"Don't count on it," Roy replied. "We've got to get over to the hospital. I got a call from a guy named Wilton James who says his brother was murdered. The body might still be at the hospital. Also, there's been a drowning that we'd better check on. And if we have time, I want to stop in and see the young boy who lost his kidney in that shooting."

Outside one ground-floor window of the office, a family softball game was under way. Out another window, I could see an unusual scene. A Negro man in a bathing suit hung by his feet from the limb of a tree. A white detective had been sitting on the window sill, watching him periodically and shaking his head. "Hey," the detective shouted, "can't we go out and arrest that guy?"

"What for?" the commander asked.

"For hanging upside down!"

"What's wrong with that? There's no law against it."

"That's the possum," Ernie explained. "If you walk up to him he'll get embarrassed and hang blankets around himself so you can't see him."

"He makes me nervous," the first man said.

"I've talked with him," Ernie briefed me. "He hangs there for eight hours at a time—says it's healthy."

"Here's what I have on this James murder, so far," Roy interrupted, handing Ernie a brief report.

The information was, indeed, scanty. On Tuesday morning two radio-car patrolmen had been called to the Acco Hotel in the heart of the South Side ghetto. There they found Rudolph James on the floor of his tiny, third-floor room: "Officers found victim unconscious and unable to talk. Victim had multiple contusions on face, arms, and legs, abrasions on right elbow and a possible skull fracture. Victim was brought to hospital, remained in deep coma until death in hospital Wednesday. Location of murder: unknown. Offender(s): unknown. Motive and manner: unknown."

In the unmarked car on our way to the hospital, Ernie and Roy expressed their thoughts to me about an unsavory aspect of the detectives' job: the handling of dead bodies.

"You know something that has happened to me?" Roy said. "I can't remember the guy's face. Can't ever remember the faces of the bodies. I really can't. That may be a psychological factor on my part, but I block out the face. Anything about the *body* I remember, but already I begin to forget the face. It might be healthy, psychologically, because I sleep better at night."

Ernie added, "When I first started on homicide, I got a kind of quickening feeling—a lump, you know? Smelling the bodies and all that kind of thing. I was kind of apprehensive about handling them. I mean, if I didn't have to handle them I wouldn't do it. If I could get around it somehow, I did.

But now, I don't feel nothing, or at least it doesn't bother me as much. Now they're just a problem, a professional problem. Now I'm anxious to get to handling it, to get the clothes off and see where the wounds are, to get to positioning where the missile went in the body, to find out how many times he was cut and so on—because many times, there are a lot of wounds under the clothes that you don't see . . .

"So now, I don't even get bothered. When I'm handling a dead person—after they're dead and then it's just a large piece of flesh—I try to see *how* it happened, rather than think about *what* actually occurred. I mean, I just don't say that I'm dealing with something valuable. I don't feel that this is a dead man or a dead woman or a dead child. I feel like I can help him if I find out why he *got* this way. A lot of times you find out why he got this way and when you *do* find out, you feel like, well, he asked for it. Personally, you feel that. To me, though, I'm going to try and, at this point, and when we first get on any homicide, try to get the most expeditious answer. I mean, the truest, quickest, most accurate account as to how the dead man got this way. You just, I mean you just . . . Once they're dead, as I say, you just don't feel like it's . . . You don't have any compassion any more. It's just a cold thing, a job, and I want to get through with it, without missing anything."

At the hospital a nurse said that the body of Rudolph James had already been taken to the morgue. A doctor added, "The guy was just beaten up all over. No bullets, no knife cuts, or anything like that—just a terrible beating."

"Did he say anything?" Ernie asked.

"No. He never regained consciousness."

The emergency section of the hospital was crowded as usual, and I stood with Ernie and Roy a few moments while they looked in various rooms for the body of the drowning victim. At least 200 people lined the hallway, packed together in grief. Nearly all of them were black. Some were uncon-

scious or bleeding profusely, and others were weeping softly
—for themselves or their friends or loved ones—and still
others were yelling and banging on the walls. It was almost
impossible for the interns to wheel a dying patient through
the crowd. The nurses and doctors appeared so far behind
that several times they seemed out of control.

"It's like all the horror of the city bunched in one place,"
Ernie commented. "And each one of 'em has a story. There's
some background music behind each of them wounded people."

"There's never a slack," Roy added. "It sometimes takes
from one to twelve hours to get to someone, because so many
of them are really bad off."

Two young, white patrolmen were sitting in the corner
of a crowded room where a nurse was trying to bring about
a semblance of order. The officers were waiting for detectives
to arrive so that they could complete their "dead-on-arrival"
report. Trying to make themselves heard above the sounds
of wailing and moaning, Ernie and Roy exchanged information with the patrolmen. The nurse, one of the few white
people, looked up and frowned, muttering, "You guys are
always taking up room." Then in a loud voice she said to
Ernie, "Will you please get out of the way?"

We stepped aside as a sheet-covered body was wheeled
slowly through the confusion. "That's ours," Roy said. We
followed the body down the hall and into a small room,
where it was wheeled behind a pair of white curtains. To the
intern, Ernie asked, "Is this the boy who drowned?" The
young man nodded and hurried away.

The detectives rolled back the sheet, revealing the body of
a sixteen-year-old boy. Ernie lifted one arm, Roy the other,
and like two rubbery eels the arms fell dangling lifeless over
the floor. The boy's body was large for its age, making it difficult to inspect. The boy was wearing only a small pair of
black, elastic swimming trunks.

"He's in here!'
"Oh, no! No!"

"Bobby! Bobby!"

The detectives stepped aside as members of the boy's family rushed into the small room. Ernie quickly covered the body again, but the boy's brother ripped the sheet back. Seeing the familiar face, he screamed, "Bobby!" Others surged inside—a sister, a friend, a girlfriend, another sister, the father. The brother began kicking the wall. The sister dropped to the floor, unconscious. For at least five minutes the room swirled with the moans and screams of the boy's family and friends. The two detectives stood by, waiting to get back to the body. Several times the girlfriend dropped to the floor and Ernie had to pick her up. "Please," he said, "you can't do anything now . . ." Meanwhile, Roy tried to hold the brother back from damaging the wall. A nurse came in with a long needle and told Ernie to hold the sister who had collapsed. Now she was flaying her arms about. The nurse approached with the needle, the girl struggled but Ernie held on. She screamed, louder and louder, another nurse came in and helped to hold her down, she pleaded with her last surge of strength and the needle went in . . .

At last, the room was cleared and the detectives went back to their examination of the body, rolling it over and back, looking for any sign of suspicious injury. Satisfied that it had been an accident, the detectives walked outside, through the crowd, to another room in order to wash their hands. Then Ernie interviewed members of the family about the drowning. Had they been drinking? No, they said, although Ernie had smelled alcohol on the dead boy's body. Finally, we boarded the hospital elevator.

"That was a nice clean body," Ernie told me.

"I don't think there was any foul play," Roy said. "Just routine—although to the family, I don't imagine it was routine."

"I thought that wailing would go on all night," Ernie commented.

On the third floor of the hospital, there was none of the frantic activity we had just left. We walked through the dimly lit, quiet corridor, checking the room numbers. In one of the rooms lay a Negro boy, his body curled up and shaking.

"This is him," Roy said. "He was shot twice. Had his kidney removed. Now he's getting telephone threats—right here in the hospital—that if he brings charges they'll finish him off."

"How're you doing, man?" Ernie asked him.

Realizing that the boy was still frightened and worried, the detectives merely assured him that he would be taken care of. The boy, although constantly shaking, managed to smile.

"And don't worry 'bout them phone calls," Ernie advised as we left the room.

The detectives returned to the Rudolph James murder case. The dead man's brother, Wilton James, lived on the fourteenth floor of a high-rise complex on the Near South Side. Middle-income Negroes and whites lived together in this tall, glass-encased, ultramodern structure that stood in sharp contrast to the row of dilapidated, wood-frame slums across the street.

Wilton, a Negro high-school teacher, was still in his tie and jacket ("I teach mathematics in the summer," he explained). His wife, a heavy-set white woman with red hair, greeted the detectives and showed us into a brightly lit living room, furnished with a pale-green rug and bright-orange sofa. "It takes a few moments for the air conditioning to work," Mrs. James noted. The detectives sat facing the couple across the coffee table. I watched from a chair in the corner.

Ernie began: "Now, when was the last time you saw your brother?"

"Tuesday. Last evening. I went to the hospital and he was unconscious. And he died this afternoon. Never recovered."

"Before that, when did you see him?"

"The Saturday before last."

"Now, do you know anything at all about what might have happened to him?"

"Well, after I went to the hospital last evening, and I had seen how badly Rudolph had been beaten up, I took a ride down to the hotel. I went up to the third floor and knocked on the door next to my brother's room—where he was found on the floor—and talked with a fellow named Robert Dagger. I asked Dagger if he knew what had happened to Rudolph, and he said my brother told him he was going to meet somebody under the el. Dagger said my brother left the hotel—this was Monday evening—and came back about fifteen minutes later, all banged up."

"Did this guy Dagger say he talked to your brother then?"

"Yes, he did. He said he asked him what happened and that Rudolph said somebody jumped him under the el. So Dagger says he wanted to call the police and have him taken to the hospital, but that Rudolph told him not to, that he would be all right. So Dagger says he helped him into his room and put him to bed."

"And that's the last time that Dagger said he saw your brother?"

"Yes. Well, until the next day, when somebody must have called the police and they came and found Rudolph in his room, unconscious."

Ernie made some notes in his book and asked, "Anything else?"

"Yes. Definitely yes. You see, I know that Dagger was lying."

"What do you mean?"

"He was lying about my brother coming back all beat up. He got beat up right there, right in the hotel!"

"Why do you say that?"

"Because I went back to the hospital—all this was last night—and I asked the nurse on duty, 'Could my brother have walked anywhere in his condition?' I asked her specifically, 'Could he have walked five blocks?' which is the dis-

tance from the el to the Acco Hotel. And the nurse said that
no, he couldn't have walked *one* block, not in his condition.
Yet this Dagger guy claims that Rudolph just walked all the
way from the el, back to the hotel and up to his room! And
when he was telling me this, I knew he was lying."

"How could you tell?"

"Because his eyes were jumping all around, while he
was talking to me. He was holding back something. I just
know it happened in the hotel."

There was a silence. Roy asked him to repeat Robert
Dagger's name and room number. Wilton did so, adding,
"He's your number-one suspect."

Ernie asked, "How well do you think Dagger knew your
brother?"

"He said he didn't know my brother too well, and here
again is a funny thing. Dagger says that before Rudolph left
the hotel, before he *supposedly* left the hotel, he had been
gambling in another room. Dagger says he too was gambling,
and that my brother had won a good deal of money."

"And Rudolph left in the middle of the game, while he
was ahead?"

"Yes. And Dagger also admitted that he himself had
lost a lot of money. So you have a motive there, also. And
further, I want to tell you that my brother never, never gambled. So something's fishy."

"Now," Roy interrupted, "is there anything else about
your brother that you should be telling us?"

"No, not of any importance."

"Well," Roy continued, "I have his record here, and it
seems that he had been arrested for drugs . . ."

"That's true."

"Well, he wasn't popping no more, was he?"

"No."

"You sure?"

"I'm pretty damn sure. Listen, he was *murdered*—you
can't *arrest* him or something! I tried to keep track of him as
best I could. He was in the process of changing his life, which

is a hard thing at age thirty-seven. He was a loner, a drifter, he had nothing, no friends. He was just starting to do *nice things,* like he bought my mother a Martin Luther King necklace. He was becoming more outgoing, generous . . ."

"Was he upset about anything, do you know?"

"He was very even-tempered, sir. And he liked to read a great deal."

"He wasn't upset?"

"Well, he had this girlfriend, but she ran out on him. She went back to Memphis two months ago, and I think this was on his mind a lot. As I say, I tried to keep a check on him. Every Saturday I'd go to see him. But . . . Last Saturday, I didn't go . . ."

"Tell them," said Mrs. James, seeing that her husband was becoming emotional, "about the man borrowing the car." Brushing aside her hair and placing a hand on Wilton's shoulder, she added, "Tell them, honey."

"Well, this guy Dagger, when he was talking to me in the hotel, he seemed very upset, nervous. He said that after the gambling, after the dice game and after he put my brother to bed, that he went out and borrowed a car, to take out his girl. Now, to me, that sounded completely phony. It sounded like a plot."

"A plot?" Ernie repeated.

"Look, *I* don't know! My brother was *nothing,* just nothing! He was a nothing in this life, but you dicks better think different! He was the only brother I had!"

Wilton held his hands over his face and Ernie stood up. "Listen," he said, "we don't care who the hell your brother was. We treat each case like it was the President."

Also rising, Wilton shouted, "I don't want bullshit! I want satisfaction!" His wife clutched his hand.

As we rode southward on Prairie Avenue, Ernie said to me, "You know, one thing I've learned from being a policeman is not to make up your mind too quickly before you get all the facts. Because a lot of times you're in for a big surprise. When you start taking things for granted, that's when you're in trouble, because it precludes you from doing things that you should do, from finding out more about it."

"Old Wilton wasn't too ready to tell me about his brother's involvement with drugs, was he?" said Roy, laughing.

"Well," Ernie explained for my benefit, "he don't want to believe that maybe his brother was in trouble or something. Rudolph could have been mixed up with all kinds of people that Wilton didn't know about. Anyway, now we head for the Acco Hotel. If our solution looks forthcoming, like *now,* then maybe we can call up the boss and tell him we can't take no more jobs today. Of course, we'd better not do that until we're almost getting ready to put our hands on a guy. Otherwise he'll want us available. It's like I feel we'd better get to that hotel or we'll be sidetracked, though. Ask 'em if we got any new assignments and hope for the best."

Roy grabbed the microphone under the dashboard and said, "Give us a back-up for 7144." The radio dispatcher said there were no new assignments.

"Good," Ernie said. To me he went on, "That's what bothers me—that we get sidetracked so damn often. Right in the middle of something we're doing, we're liable to get another job. Try to get through it as fast as possible and then get back. If it's a big murder mystery they might not give us any other assignments for about three or four hours. But this Rudolph James beating actually took place on Monday, so unless it was a hell of an extraordinary case, we're not going to be able to work on it exclusively. It would have to be someone of great prominence who got killed. I told Wilton that we treat every case like it was the President, but you and I know that that's only partially true. Every case is the same as far as *I'm* concerned. I don't care who the guy was. But murders are so frequent among poor people that I can't even find most of our cases in the newspaper. Not even news any more. Now, I guess a person of consequence is different. Instead of us working on all these different investiga-

tions we got in the briefcase, they'd probably have us working
on *that* and nothing else. They'd want that solved right away,
because public indignation is a factor. Or if there was some
lewd rape-murder around the University of Chicago, well,
the university can generate a lot of heat. And like the Speck
case where the eight nurses were killed, there wasn't no piecemeal work on that case, no sir."

"I suppose," Roy said, "that Rudolph James wasn't too
important in the world, except to his brother, Wilton."

"Just a dead man in a room, found in a junky hotel in
the ghetto. Just one nigger less. But it's important to *me*, see.
He may be nothing to the white people who pay the taxes,
and who pay my salary, but if I'm assigned to clear it up and
find out who killed him, it's very important to me. He was
one of my people, also. And if I *can't* find out who did it,
then that's a reflection on me, professionally; and I wouldn't
want somebody to come behind me and do it. If we turned
the case loose, just let it stand and let the leads all peter out,
that would be a terrible blow, as far as I'm concerned. Especially if another dick came right behind me and got the answer. I take that personally. I feel that if I get off a case and
it's not solved, well, I like to think that nobody else can solve
it either. If they do, I'm *glad* that they solved it, but on the
other hand, I'm sorry that *I* didn't."

The Acco Hotel was indistinguishable from the old Victorian buildings on each side of it. Purple-tinted streetlights
cast an eerie glow into the evening air and a large tree smoth-
ered the face of the hotel with its shadow.

"I remember when all the slicks used to come in here,"
Ernie remarked to me. "Everyone from judges to musicians
to dope peddlers. There was even a time when *I* spent a little
bread in here, bringing girls upstairs for a few hours. Now I
don't think I could stand to be inside this place for one night."

"Why not?" I asked.

"The smell, man, the smell."

The desk clerk, a plump Negro woman, sat behind a dusty window to the right as we entered the dank hallway. Ernie held his badge to the window. After a moment, a buzzer rang and we went through the door. The woman remained seated, her face without expression.

"Police officers, ma'am. I'm Cox, this is Jackson. (I was 'Inspector Whittemore.') We're here in regard to, uh, Mr. Rudolph James."

"Oh. Yeah."

"I understand that you were working down here and heard a big fight going on upstairs," Ernie lied.

"No, no. I ain't heard no fight."

"Did you see Rudolph James on Monday night?"

"No, no. Whatever happened, I don't know it."

Before Ernie could ask another question, a tall black man dressed in dark-green work clothes came down the stairs. Pausing, he asked, "What's happening here?" The man leaned his head forward. His breath smelled of liquor and his eyes danced about in the semidarkness. "What in the world's going on here? It looks like something *mighty* serious."

Turning, Ernie said, "We're police officers."

"Ooh, well *that* explains *everything*. How interesting. My, my . . ."

"What's your name?" Ernie said, visibly annoyed.

"Me? My little old name?"

"That's right."

"Well, I'm just an interested passer-by, just a spectator of human goings-on."

"What's your *name,* man?"

"Well, it ain't Rudolph James, I'll tell you that. Because he's dead. He died and that's why you fellas are here, right?"

"You hit it on the head, brother."

"How *interesting.* My, my. And now you're investigating! That was quite a shame, I'd say. Do you have any clues?"

"Look," Ernie snapped, "are you gonna give us your name?"

"I don't think I'd *prefer* it, to be honestly truthful with y'all."

"Well, listen, step down here in the hall," Ernie said, grabbing the man by the arm and swiftly pulling him aside. "I want to talk to you," Ernie added, putting his face close to the man's and softening his tone. "Now, you don't *have* to give your name to me. I'm not trying to front you off. Everything's gonna be mellow, brother, don't worry about it. Just give me a little hint about this fellow, Rudolph James. I'm with you, man. Now, what's your name?"

"Robert Dagger, in person."

"Okay, Mr. Dagger. Now, we'd like to talk to you about this whole thing—"

"I ain't talking."

"Why not?"

"Because talking is trouble. Silence is cool."

"Well, get your jacket on, we'll go down to the station. Come on, put your jacket on and—"

"Wait a minute, now! What if we talk here? I mean, what do we have to go down to the station for? What do you mean, go to the station? What for?"

"Just get your jacket, there. You gonna argue with me, or what?"

"Look, we can talk right here, man."

"Okay, let's go to your room."

"Sure, sure. Be my guest. Come with me, gentlemen!"

We followed Robert Dagger up two flights of stairs. Dagger skipped two and three steps at a time, turned repeatedly, and gestured to us to follow. His lean body was in constant motion, large hands gesturing, eyes darting about, a smile lighting up his face. As we walked through the narrow hall on the third floor, Dagger pointed to the room Rudolph James had occupied.

"And this one is mine. Come in, gentlemen." Dagger's small room had dirty-yellow, undecorated walls. Its one window faced the solid rear wall of another building only ten feet away. "It's not a very good view, I admit," Dagger explained. "Sometimes I can look down and hear *all kinds* of things going on in the alley below my window. Very crude goings-on. I have to keep the window open for some air. I also have to keep it closed because of the soot that comes in, and because the smell from the garbage comes in."

"What do you do?" Ernie asked. "Keep it open or closed?"

"I try to do a little of both," said Dagger, his smile broadening. He sat on the window sill and offered Roy the one chair in the room. I remained standing. Ernie lifted up one of three science-fiction magazines lying on the bureau. Dagger's eyes widened and he said, "You hip to that stuff, man?"

"Yeah, sure, I dig this jazz."

"I'll lend you that copy."

"No . . ."

"You *should* read it, man! Before you say, 'No,' read it and see for yourself. It's nice, really nice."

Ernie threw the magazine back and sat down on Dagger's rumpled bed. "Now," he began, taking out his notebook, "I want you to run down what you know about what happened to Rudolph James."

"Well," Dagger replied, rubbing his hands together and enjoying the attention directed at him, "I want to ask you a personal question, first-off."

"Sure."

"If I was doing something to violate the law, this would not be held against me—is that right?"

"That's right."

"Okay, that sets my brain at ease. You see, we was up there in another room, shootin' dice."

"Don't worry 'bout that, man."

"I won't. I offer you my full trust. Now, me and Rudolph James and some other guys was up there, shootin' dice. No big stakes, you know, but we was gambling."

"Did Rudolph do a lot of that? I mean, did he gamble often?"

"Yeah. Oh, yeah. Very often."

"Go on."

"Well, he was winning pretty good. I mean, he was ahead about twelve dollars. And suddenly he says he has to leave, to meet somebody under the el."

"What was the argument about?"

"No argument, man."

"Okay, go ahead."

"I was losing about four dollars at that point, myself. So Rudolph leaves the hotel, and he comes back, oh, about twenty minutes later, and he's all messed up. He looked like he had done some pretty mean tussling. So I tried to help him, call the police or something, but he said he'd be all right. I helped him into his room and he got in bed. And I walked out, closed the door."

"Now, you see any boxing, man?"

"Nah."

"Look, nobody knows what anybody says to me. Where information comes from, I don't care. Understand? Now, you know what I want."

"Yeah, but you don't want it from me, because there's one little man who may be able to supply you . . ."

"Who's that?"

"The fellow who had Rudolph James' room before James came in. Name is Williams, Leroy Williams."

"What about him?"

"Well, now, I knew Leroy Williams because he lived here right next door, before James came in. And just a few hours ago I seen him on the street and I said, 'Hey, Brother Williams, you know the dude that got your old room?' And he said, 'No, I don't know the dude.' I told him, 'Well, he was killed.' And Leroy seemed real interested, because he said, 'Yeah? When?' And I said, 'Well, he got in some kind of fight on Monday and he died today.' See, I saw his brother come into the hotel today—I had talked to him last night, by the way—and he took his brother's clothes and things. Anyway, Leroy thought a minute and then he said, 'Well, I saw a dude and a cat fightin' over under the el on Monday evening.' And we two concluded that this fight Leroy seen was the one where Rudolph James got messed up."

"Now, this Leroy fellow, how old is he?"

"Oh, 'bout forty give or take a little. A good five years older than me. He's a good little dude."

"You know where he's living at now?"

"No, can't say."

"Now, listen, Brother Dagger. Tell me about that car you borrowed right after you put Rudolph in his room that night."

"I didn't borrow no car, man."

"Well, we got information to the contrary, Brother Dagger."

"I didn't *borrow* no car. I *rented* a car. Here, I'll show you the receipt." Dagger fished inside his pocket and pulled out a crumpled, pink piece of paper. As he unfolded it, a white envelope dropped to the floor.

"What's that?" Ernie asked. Dagger picked it up, smiling and shaking his head. "Come on, what's that?" Ernie held out his hand and Dagger reluctantly gave him the envelope, which contained some leaves of marijuana. "Seaweed," Ernie said, adding, "You do a little smoking, hunh?"

"A little. You caught me! You guys are keen, all right! You're not gonna hang that on me, is you?"

"Of course not, man. Not as long as you're on our side."

Roy asked, "Do you pop, man? You don't shoot any shit, do you?"

"Me? Hell, no. I don't mess with that stuff. I ain't nothing near to a junkie, man."

"Okay," Ernie said. "Now, what about the car?"

"Here's the receipt that I was going to show, before we was so rudely interrupted by that little bit of grass. I rented a car and took my girl to a motel. I do that all the time, when I get me a paycheck."

"You in the habit of keeping receipts like that—to prove where you been?"

"No, man, the receipt is what I show some cats who don't believe I got me a woman. Or they say I don't treat her right, you know? Well, I got me some proof, that's all."

"Why don't you take care of your business in here?"

"Here? Be serious, man! I can't take no broad in here. I got to make an impression!" Laughing, Dagger added, "I take me a rented car, bring her to a motel, do my business in style."

"Well," Ernie said, also laughing, "I seen this bed in here, and that's all I figured you'd need."

"What do you take me for, man? I got a little dignity, you know."

"Listen, Brother Dagger, one more thing. Who called for the police to come get Rudolph James?"

"Now, I don't know for sure. See, it was yesterday, Tuesday, that they came and got him. I was off at work, then. But you might try the gal who lives down the hall, in 321. I could pin a little guess on her."

"Okay. Thanks. Now, there's some doeskin in this kind of thing, so I want you to keep your ears open, okay? I mean, we'll put a little something in your pocket. Here's my card, and if you see Leroy Williams, tell him we want to see him. Tell him to call us at that number. Or if you hear anything about this thing, give us a call yourself. There's no exposure involved, no court. Just a phone call, and they'll be half a note for you. You hear?"

Dagger sat on the window sill, his eyes gleaming at the prospect of earning money from the police. He nodded his head slowly, enjoying the moment. Suddenly, looking at Ernie, he winked. With that, we left the room.

In room 321, which was even smaller than Dagger's, a woman and two men seemed enveloped by cigarette smoke. The woman was in bed with the older of the men, a sheet covering them to the waist. The man chain-smoked while the woman flipped through a movie-star magazine. The other man sat on the window sill, also smoking. When we appeared, the woman got out of bed—dressed only in bra and pants. For a moment Ernie hesitated, apparently repulsed by the dirt, smoke, and heat in the room. After a brief exchange with the woman, however, the detectives walked inside, remaining on their feet as the woman returned to the bed. Suddenly Ernie said to her, "You were in my class—in high school. Is that right?"

"Me? Oh . . . Yeah . . . I remember you . . ."

"And I think you were in the projects, too."

"That's right," she said.

"Man, seems like a long time."

"You're a cop, now."

"Mmmm."

"Some of the football team became cops."

"Yeah that's right." After a pause, Ernie said, "Listen, we're here about that guy who died, uh, Rudolph James."

"Well, he's out of it, now," she mumbled.

"Out of it?"

"Yeah. Like you. You got out. You look like you're doin' okay for yourself. And he's dead, so he's out of it, too."

After another pause, Ernie said, "You know anything about what happened to him?"

"No . . ."

"Okay. I know y'all wouldn't put us on.'

"Only thing I know," the woman replied, "is that all night the guy was in his room, moaning. All Monday night. He must have kept falling off his bed. Wham! He'd crash onto the floor. Then you could hear him moaning, you know? And then again a bit later: wham! I went downstairs, tried to get the woman at the desk to come up and take a look at the man. But she said, 'Just as long as it didn't happen in this hotel, it ain't none of my business.' So he was in that room, all night, dying . . . It was horrible. Finally the next day I called the police."

"From a phone booth?"

"No. A friend's house."

"You know anything about the guy?"

"No. Not anything for sure. It looked like he was hustling. He was in and out of the hotel all the time."

"Well, baby, here's my card. Give us a call if you hear any ol' thing."

"You remember Pigeon?" she asked.

"Why?"

"Pigeon. From school . . ."

"Oh, yeah," said Ernie. "I remember. He must be in the big place, the penitentiary, by now."

"No, he ain't. He's a security guard at one of the schools."

"No kidding? Man, that's a shock."

"Sure is," she said. "Just like seeing you. Let's see"—reading his card—" 'Ernie Cox—Detective Division; Homicide—Sex, and Aggravated Assault Section.' Very impressive, young man."

"Thanks, baby. We'll see y'all."

The woman's smile left her face.

Back in the car, Ernie told me, "That gal, I couldn't hardly recognize her at first. I knew her in high school. She looks about twenty years older than me, don't she? It don't *look* like we went to school together, does it? She looks like she's at least fifty or so. She's an alcoholic, could you tell? She's probably a junkie as well. She did a little whoring on the side, too. I *know* she did some whoring, because I seen her walking the corners . . ."

"Looks like she was a pretty girl at one time," I said.

"Man, man! I see a lot of school friends on this job. Some don't even remember me, especially when, you know, they're fouled up, using narcotics, or when they're alcoholics. They lose their wits, memories, intelligence, and everything else. A little step above a vegetable, walking around the streets. But that helps them loosen up a bit, 'cause she knows me. Of course, she didn't seem to have too much to tell us."

"What'd you think of Dagger's story?" I asked.

"Well, he's a character, that's all. You know, he rents

cars and probably keeps a fancy suit that he puts on for his
girl. I don't think he's lying, like Rudolph's brother thought.
He's just a hep cat, you know? He's sort of in a twilight zone.
He likes to drink, smokes a few reefers, has a good time when
he can. Meanwhile, he just exists. He has a job he holds
down."

"Think it happened in the hotel?" I pressed him.

"I'm inclined *not* to think it happened in there, but I'm
still harboring the thought. It's possible. I wouldn't give it a
hundred percent no, but the possibility is in favor of it *not*
happening in the hotel."

"I enjoyed watching Dagger's face," I said, "when you
found those marijuana leaves."

"Yeah, he looked kind of apprehensive about it," said
Ernie, laughing. "Now, I'd rather let Dagger keep those couple of leaves and keep him as a friend, or a source of information. If I had taken them leaves away from him, he wouldn't
be so cooperative."

"He wasn't *planning* to be so helpful in the beginning,"
Roy noted.

"No, man. When he said he wasn't going to give his
name," Ernie explained to me, "I took the *stern* attitude with
him. In other words, I didn't give him no choice. I made him
think he had to talk to me, either at the station or in the hotel.
If I had just kept saying, 'Well, you better give me your name,'
we would probably still be standing there with the whole thing
still up in the air. But as soon as he softened up, I said, 'Let's
go to your room.' Then he was submitting. He might not have
realized it, but I was getting control. Like, I was telling him
to do something and he was doing it, obeying me.

"When I'm talking with people over on the *North* Side,
or like over in Wilton's high-rise, I use a different tack alto-
gether. I'm very reserved and proper, and all that kind of
stuff. But over here, you gotta come on with a different bag.
One thing I noticed about Dagger right away—he seemed
to be taking a defiant attitude because that hotel clerk was
there and he didn't want to get in trouble, get kicked out, or

anything. So I took him away from there. You take a guy away from his audience and make it just you and him, face to face. And it can't be you up there looking down on them: you gotta be looking each other in the eye. Dagger felt more comfortable that way. Like I was up there laughing with him, but I was dead serious, I had a purpose. I didn't see nothing funny, but I was laughing. I feel if I do that, he'll talk more. You form a kind of kindredship when you talk the same language as they are, joking about this and that, and sometimes they'll loosen up a little more.

"Everybody's doing an acting job. Dagger, for example, he knows the 'code' about not talking to the police and not giving no information. So I'm in there to get him to talk, and we got to sell *ourselves,* first; and *then* go for the information. Find some common ground, like those books up there on the bureau? I don't read that shit, but I tried to make him *think* that I do. To break the ice, so to speak. Gotta relate to people on their own ground. Take a friendly role, like two buddies talking to each other. Even a *murderer*—I'm for him, too, until I get what I want. With Dagger, I had to get it out of his mind that I was a police officer who was going to do something *bad* to somebody because of what Dagger tells me."

Laughing, Roy said, "I don't think you ever completely erased that thought from Brother Dagger's mind."

"A lot of times," Ernie continued, "I'll give the impression that I know something, from the way I phrase a question. Like I asked Dagger, 'What was the argument about?' Well, I didn't know there was any argument. But I just threw it out there, to see what his reaction would be. And before he answered, I was watching his face *very* carefully. To see if there was any hint of strain, or deception; but he answered right off. His expression never changed. He said, 'No argument, man.' I like to go fishing like that. That gets kind of risky, though, because if he gets the idea that I don't know what I'm talking about, then he's got the advantage. He'll think, 'Well,

I can tell this guy *anything*.' So I don't try that *too* many times. It's a little game and you just don't ever want to let a guy catch you bluffing. He'll lose respect. And of course I gave Dagger a little financial incentive, there. Make him a little more eager to talk. I don't know how much I'd give him. It depends on how good the information is. If it's good information, it could be a lot of money, but I'll probably give him something out of my pocket—five or ten dollars."

"Your former schoolmate, she seems to think that Rudolph James was a fruit hustler (a male prostitute)," Roy noted.

"Maybe. And according to Dagger, he gambled all the time. Remember how Wilton emphatically said his brother never gambled?"

"That's the thing," Roy told me, "when any two people live apart, one thinks he knows a lot about the other, but often he knows only a small part of the story. Rudolph was probably wearing at least two hats, playing little games out here like us."

"Well," Ernie said, "now we gotta find us a witness who saw some blows being perpetrated"—we laughed at the pompous language—"on the victim by the offender."

Under the rusty el there were neon lights, dark shadows, and constantly moving groups of people, some coming down the stairs from the train, others mingling on the busy commercial street, still others appearing and disappearing through the cracks of what Ernie called "a crossroads for crime in the ghetto." There were grocery stores, pawn shops, bars, pool halls, cleaners, tailors, laundries, record shops blaring soul music into the night, signs advertising "whopper burgers" and Polish sausages, blinking lights promising "checks cashed" and "loans," posters calling attention to an array of assorted causes and grievances. Teen-age boys yelled, ducking behind park cars; adults stood aimlessly or wandered from one corner to another; a young couple walked slowly along the sidewalk, past three young men outside a tavern, staring at our unmarked police car.

"That fight probably took place right around here," Ernie said, parking the car several stores away from the stairs of the el. For a while the detectives merely watched the people—it was like having a front seat for an unrehearsed show of prostitutes, con men, dope peddlers, hustlers, informants . . . "Maybe we can find somebody who seen the fight," Ernie continued, "assuming that it did occur over here. I mean, you can't take anything for granted. Maybe we can find this Leroy Williams, or someone else who might have seen it. I figure that the best way to find out is to give the impression that one of the participants did *not* die. I mean, we ain't gonna tell anyone we're working on a homicide. Possibly the *offender* don't even know that it's a murder case—not yet, maybe. And possibly none of these people on the street know it yet, because a beating on the street here is a common occurrence, something that happens every day, so nobody really pays any attention to it, or follows it to the degree that they find out what happened."

Turning occasionally to address me in the back seat, Ernie continued, "On the other hand, the 'word' might be out, right out all around here and we wouldn't even know it. It could be just floating around, with us the only ones in the dark, like two outsiders. Already there's a hundred people who've seen us since we parked here five minutes ago, and they know we're police. And with you in the car, a white man, they figure you're either a cop or a prisoner. Most likely a cop. See those three cats outside the tavern, staring at us? I'll bet they're wanted by the police for something—not by us, but another division. The people here don't get *too* alarmed when they see a police car, because there's cops around here all the time. I'm in the habit of looking at every damn movement, every face, every suspicious thing, every deviation—and there are so many deviations in the ghetto, and oddities. It's one large pot of deviations. I watch it all because of the 'known but flown' people from three, four, five years back. There's always a chance we'll see that one guy that we've been trying to find for over three years—a face suddenly the same as the one on a photograph..."

"Well," Roy said, squirming in his seat impatiently, "I'd like to find Leroy Williams. At least he's a definite witness."

"Well, we'll check his name out when we get time. See if he's got a record. And we'll get a photo along with it. Sometimes," Ernie confided to me, "when I'm looking for a guy but I don't know what he looks like, I go near a group of cats and yell, 'Say, Leroy!' And then he'll look up, you know?" Ernie laughed at his own thought and added, "And I *got* him."

"Or," Roy offered, "these little, tiny kids who haven't been indoctrinated yet, who don't know the 'code' yet, *they'll* talk to us. We walk up to 'em and say, 'Hey little boy, where Leroy live?' And right in front of all the grown people who are keeping their mouths shut, he'll say, 'Oh, Leroy live right over there!' "

Laughing, Ernie and Roy left the car to mingle with the people. I followed Roy into the tavern, which was filled with Negro customers. We stood at the end of the bar and lit cigarettes. The bartender finally noticed us and smiled.

"Listen, brother," Roy said, "you see them two dudes boxing over there the other day?"

"Two dudes?"

"At least two. You see any scuffling under the el?"

"I don't pay attention..."

Meanwhile, Ernie walked beneath the el, across the street and down the opposite sidewalk, where I met him. A woman had said to him, "Are you the junk man?"

"No, ma'am," Ernie had replied. He explained to me, "They think I'm either a cop or a dope peddler." He moved on, smiling to himself, and we went inside an ice-cream parlor. The woman behind the counter looked up and Ernie said, casually, "Hi, I'm just checking on a little fight that was going on outside here. Would you know anything about that?"

"You the man?"

"Mmmm."

"Well, now, *I* didn't see no fight, but I got a lady friend who might know what you want."

"Did she see a fight out here?"

"Well, she mentioned to me that she seen a woman and a man beating up on one man. That's all she said. 'Course somebody's always fighting out here, so I don't know if it's the incident you're talking about or not. Somebody's always gettin' their ass kicked up and down here."

"Do you know where I can find this woman who saw the fight?"

"No, but she comes in the store all the time. For ice cream."

"When she comes in next time, will you have her call me?"

"I'll try, but I doubt if she will. She wouldn't wanna get mixed up with no po-leece."

"I understand," Ernie said.

"I'm sho' you do."

"Well, when she comes in, you get her to describe to *you* what the people looked like that were jumping on the man, and then you can tell me. This way I still won't know who she is, if she don't want to talk to the police. Otherwise, here's my card. Give her that number."

Ernie thanked the woman and we stepped outside again. We walked slowly past the record shop, watching the young boys and girls who clapped their hands to the music. As Ernie walked toward his car, a man greeted him by lifting his hat briefly.

"How's business?" Ernie asked.

"Not too good. The buses are on strike, so I can't work 'em."

"Well," Ernie replied, "the el trains are running."

"Yeah, but them dudes up there are being asleep! That's for them jack-rollers, you know. They'd have to be *awake* before *I* bother 'em. I don't bother nobody that's asleep."

"Why not? Money's money, ain't it?"

"Hell, that's *common thieves* up there pulling that shit. I ain't no criminal. You can search me, man. No gun, no knife—no violence. I'm a *confidence* man, brother. I don't go in for that violence bag."

"You pick their pockets, though . . ."

"Well, I got to make a living. But I ain't no jack-roller, 'cause that don't take no skill or nothing. Like that man you see over there? He's just a crude, underhanded, elementary *thief.*"

"Okay, brother. Stay out of trouble, now."

Ernie walked into the street and climbed behind the wheel of his car again. "Who was that?" I asked.

"That's the Mouse, a professional pickpocket. He used to go to school with me. I always see him around the el stations. He's a pro, and a good one, brother. Every time I talk with him I always feel myself. I know he wouldn't pick *my* pockets, but it's in my mind, you know? The police have picked him up a lot of times. He's good, though. He's got a real pride in his profession."

The detectives remained parked for another ten minutes, saying little to each other while they continued to watch the movements of the people. "See this guy standing here talking to himself?" Ernie asked me, pointing to an aimless-looking black man. "I locked him up one time in regard to a murder. It turned out his friend did it. But he was seen sleeping in the car with the victim, shortly before the victim's death. Now he's got to the point where he carries on two- or three-way conversations with himself. He's gotten worse in the last few years."

Over the car radio came a report that more than 100 teen-agers were marching on a district police station.

"Sounds like a little action tonight," Roy mused. "That's just outside our area, ain't it?"

"Yeah," said Ernie, explaining to me that detectives don't answer such calls. "See that woman? She's up here on the corner all the time. She always thinks she dropped something. You watch her and she's looking at the ground all the time, thinking she lost her money or something."

Then we watched a young Negro girl, perhaps ten years old, cross the street. She wore shorts and thick, red socks up to her knees. "Man," Ernie said, "she must be hot in those socks."

"They're stylish," Roy replied. "Hey—look at that broad. She really poured herself into those slacks . . . You see that down there, Ernie?"

"What, that scuffling?"

"Yeah."

"It's nothing, just a couple of guys getting something out of their systems." Ernie pulled out of his parking space and drove slowly through the street, taking a last look at the activity under the el. He turned the car back into the residential section of the ghetto. "Used to be all swells living down here in the 1920s," Ernie said, driving slowly for my benefit. "All aristocrats. These old Victorian buildings with the common walls, they were like castles in those days, I guess. Now they look like old, haunted houses, full of too many people. When I was ten or eleven—that was around 1941 or so—I used to work on a watermelon wagon all through these streets. I'd help the guy load up the wagon and ride around, up and down these streets, yelling, 'Red, ripe watermelon!' Got paid fifty, seventy-five cents a day and all the watermelon I could eat. I used to sell vegetables, too. Walked the streets with a basket, with different kinds of vetegables in it, selling them to people on the street or up in the houses—whoever would buy—and they paid us ten cents on a dollar . . . By that time it was all colored folk, of course, like it is now. I never got out of the ghetto—literally never set foot out of it—until after I was fourteen or so. That big ugly school back there on the left is the high school where I went."

Roy broke in here explaining that he had not lived in the area as a child.

"I went to high school on the West Side," he commented. "Didn't leave Alabama till I was twelve. Even then, I was aware of the problems down there. When I came up here to Chicago, I got off the train and yelled, 'I'm up north!' I felt a real release up here. No 'yessirs' and 'yes ma'ams' any more. At least the Negroes in the north have that release, even if it *is* crowded and so on.

"I don't know, I mean sometimes I don't know what I'm supposed to feel when somebody's telling me to help stop a riot, for example. I mean, I know that rioting is no good, but when I get off work sometimes, I like to go listen to the black-power people. I was in Washington Park for one of their rallies the other day. They didn't know I'm a cop or I would have been in trouble, because I guess I shouldn't have been there. But I wanted to hear what they were talking about, you know?"

"About how we're working for the honkies," Ernie said, looking at me and grinning.

"Well, who else can we work for in this job? My grandmother's home was bombed by whites down in Birmingham, six years ago, so I don't have to be told about honkies. But you have to make a living. You have to live.

"Take my son, for instance. He's fourteen just this week and I never said a word to him about racial trouble. It was kind of an experiment, to see how long he could go through life without bothering about black and white. Then he came to me, at age eleven, and we had to sit down and discuss the whole thing. He said he felt that the white man hates him, and he was learning to hate back. I tried to tell him, 'What good is hate going to do you?' It's a hard thing."

We rode in silence a while until Ernie said, "This is the pool room I went to as a teen-ager . . . I once lived in a floppy house that used to be where that housing project is now. The one in back of this row of slums. We lived there quite a long time, till they tore it down. I remember my grandfather. He was a slave on an Indian reservation and he had real white hair. He used to sit on the sun porch all day long, never saying a word to nobody. The only thing I remember about him was once when my father got real mean to my mother. The old man got out of his chair on the porch, went inside and laid out my father with one blow! Then he went back out on the porch like nothing had happened. I was real small then . . .

"There's this one colored reporter who's always calling me up. He works for a militant newspaper. I went to high school with him. At that time, he was timid as hell! Somewhere along the line, with the whole black-power thing, he got up some brass in him. Now he never shuts up . . . You know, the girl who gave our valedictory speech became the biggest whore on 47th Street. I met her once on a raid . . . See that little tavern over there? I used to go with the barmaid in there, go out with her. We was tight. That was some years back . . ."

Ernie parked the car outside a "colored" restaurant. Children were playing on the streets and sidewalks wherever you looked. One little boy, perhaps five years old, walked up to Ernie's window and stared at him. Ernie smiled; the boy hesitated and then waved.

"Hi," said Ernie, and the boy walked away. Turning to me he said, "Now, that little boy never had seen my face before. We got no uniforms and this car is just like any other car, but somehow he knows right away that we're cops. We're the man, and as far as that little boy is concerned, we might as well have a siren on. We might be able to go up on the North Side and they wouldn't know we're cops, but here they got a sixth sense. Because they're exposed to cops all the time . . . Stopping, going into their buildings, or their brother was locked up by a policeman, or their mother or father or *somebody,* you know. So the kids in the ghetto, they're always on the lookout for the police. They want to know where we are and what we're doing, all the time. It's like police watching is a daily pastime in the ghetto.

"One day I put on an old pair of overalls, an old hat, and some old, floppy-looking shoes. Dark glasses, too. I was working on a case and I wanted to be inconspicuous at this particular time. I'm standing there in a doorway and some itty-bitty boys came by and one of 'em looked up at me and said, 'Hi, Mister Policeman!' " Ernie laughed at himself. "Man, my feathers really fell. Out of the mouths of babes.

"Now, I'm sitting here using the word 'ghetto' for this place because that's the only word for it I know. Whatever the right word is, this place is it. See, most people, when they hear 'ghetto' they think about crime and drinking and prostitution and promiscuity, and all this kind of thing—ADC, charity, welfare recipients, unwed mothers, bastards, all this. This is what they relate to the ghetto. But most of the time, they don't know the true meaning of the word 'ghetto.' They don't think about what *promotes* this thing, you know? And about what's *keeping* it this way. They're just too far away; they're not close. They're outside, trying to look in here.

"The people on the outside, the white people who say they're concerned, they're not really looking in, they're looking *on*. Of course you can't have but a few people that look in. Otherwise, the streets of the ghetto would be full of folks riding around and just looking in. Now, if you could get all the congressmen and all the senators and ride *them* around, take 'em into these houses to talk with the people and all that —taking a straight look at everything—that would help."

"The trouble with that," said Roy, "is that the politician has to relate to his constituency. And they don't know what the hell's going on. He can stand up and say to them, 'Listen, we should do this and that and the other, because I know that this is the case.' But if he said that *too* many times, he'd no longer be a representative of his constituency. They wouldn't vote for him no more. Because they don't know what the hell he's talking about. He's *been* there and they haven't."

"Like Robert Kennedy," Ernie offered. "He got down with it, but when he started telling people about this injustice bag, a lot of folks turned against him. They didn't want to hear that, because they hadn't been where *he'd* been. So they couldn't understand his viewpoint."

"In the back of their mind," Roy said, "they may have felt he was right, but not strong enough to have gone and supported him. They probably said, 'Well, that might be true, but we ain't ready for that. Them colored people, they'll straighten themselves out. We don't have to get involved yet.' "

"The people on the outside," Ernie went on, "they see a guy who committed a lot of robbery, or he killed somebody, and they see another guy who committed a lot of rapes and so on, and they say, 'Well, that guy, he's no good. He should be in the penitentiary. He should be executed.' Well, by this time he's probably beyond any help because he's committed these dastardly deeds, but they never think about what started him off on that road: dropping out of school, the broken home, the cockroaches all over everywhere, he don't want to stay in the house, he has nothing to come home to at night, so he stays in the damn street—he stays out all night, he drinks wine, smokes reefers. He don't have nothing at home; he ain't got a decent bed to lay in. He's got to sleep on the floor, or sleep in there with the vermin crawling all around, or either his mother is a drunkard or she's got a different guy in the house every time he comes in. Here's a kid, ten or twelve years old, growing up. Well, you know, this is going to have some impression on him.

"So the kid just don't seem to be getting any place, so what the hell? He gets in there with the other crowd, the wrongdoers and this and that, and he wants to be identified as being somebody. So here's the gang-banger, the potential stickup man. He wants to be recognized, but he can't get recognized by any *good* deeds because he can't fit in, he don't have any education, he dropped out of school, and all this kind of stuff. So the only way he can get recognition now is to do something *bad*. Like the Blackstone Rangers and all them other hoodlums out here—they're getting recognition because they're causing trouble."

"Well," Roy said, "that's why we have so many homicides involving teen-agers. The gang activities are a whole big factor in the ghetto. Because there's so many, many teen-agers and everybody belongs."

"I've seen a few isolated cases," Ernie said, "where a kid lives right in the middle of the ghetto and has absolutely no gang attachments. But I agree—that's an exception rather than a rule."

"Someday I'd like to count up all the murders," Roy went on, "where a rival gang member comes into a neighborhood where he has no business and gets killed. A lot of people don't believe that this is the reason for so many murders in the ghetto. They think it's an exaggeration."

"They ain't been living with it, that's all," Ernie said, glancing at me. "For a kid in the ghetto, violence and death are so damn commonplace. Fighting and death, robbery and theft, sex crimes, narcotics—damn, that's an everyday occurrence. For these little kids to see somebody fighting on the street or a man getting stabbed or shot, well, this is no big thing for them. They see it all the time."

"Another thing," Roy said, "is how we get almost as much activity in the alleys as on the sidewalks. Outside folk would come through here and see all these people in front of the houses, but they wouldn't believe that there's an equal number in *back* of 'em, on those old crumbly porches where the wood looks like it's about to fall into a pile."

"And the *kids* use the alleys all the time," Ernie added. "Like that bunch of hoods that just went down the block. Any time I see a bunch of kids walking around late at night, I'm watching to see what's gonna happen. They're just like a pack of little wolves, or foxes, just going around looking for whatever they can get into. See—they ducked into an alley. Before I'd chase them, especially at night, I had better know the place. That's what I feel, because they can duck inside any of these big raggedy buildings and I'd *never* see them again."

"And a lot of these buildings have five or six ways to

get out," Roy said. "The kids know them like the back of their hand, and a good cop does, too. Somewhere down the line, it could save his life."

"I'd say," Ernie observed, "that this is the worst and most dangerous part of our area. From here on down. Where anything can happen. See that group on the corner? Only young kids, brother, but they'd kill us in a minute; and they have the means to do it with."

"This whole area is a militant black-power stronghold," Roy said to me. "I don't think you as a white man could get more than a block here before you got robbed. If you got through unmolested, it would be a small miracle."

Laughing, Ernie said, "A white *policeman* has to be extremely careful walking through here. In fact, they *don't* walk in here. A lot of 'em won't even *drive* through."

"You can't hardly blame 'em, Ernie," said Roy.

"Heh, heh. I may have been born and raised here, but I *still* think it's a dangerous neighborhood. I don't think there's nowhere any worse in the whole country. No foot patrolmen at all! Black or white. I'd walk in here as a detective, but not with a uniform on my back. Walk down one of these dark streets at night, man, and they never *would* hear of you no more."

"Even the people who *live* here are afraid," said Roy. "They don't want to venture out at night. At least, the older people don't. Some of the guys in their thirties or forties, they've been living down here so long that they're just as tough as the toughs. They'll go out at night with a knife or gun in their pocket. But most of the decent people are afraid to come out after dark."

"I don't blame 'em. How 'bout that old man last week— in broad daylight." Ernie added for my sake, "He comes out of church and two kids ask him for a quarter. So he just waves 'em away like old people do, and they take a shotgun and blow the top of his head off."

"He was a colored man, too," said Roy. "So how do you

figure these kids? They shout black power and then kill a colored man."

"They kill each other, too," Ernie said. "What gets me is the white salesmen who hire Negro boys to go around with them as some kind of protection. Remember the white insurance salesman who had the Negro kids as a 'security squad'?"

"Yeah. Two other kids tried to rob the salesman," Roy told me. "So one of the bodyguards took out his gun and shot one of the kids in the head. Killed him. I think the kid who died was fifteen. We caught the kid that did it. He was seventeen."

The detectives got out of the car and I accompanied them to a restaurant. On a wall next to the sidewalk there were huge scribblings in various colors of paint: "Suicide . . . Thunder . . . Watusi . . . Maniac Counts . . . Nova Stone . . . Satan Lovers . . . Jokers . . . Pimple Stones . . . Stones Run it . . ."

"Cries for recognition," Ernie said.

Over a dinner of "ribs, greens, slaw, and biscuits," I learned more about Ernie's background. His parents had come to Chicago from Meridian, Mississippi. They separated when Ernie was twelve years old.

"Before they split up," he said, "I had been indoctrinated so strong as to family prayer and that kind of thing. They taught me that it was terrible for a child to disgrace his parents and so forth. I just had that *beat* into me. Even so, I still went out and ran around with the bad kids. I was a leader, had my own little gang. I just loved to fight, period. I was a terror outside the house. Got this scar on my forehead in a fight when I was a kid. Occasionally we'd mess up somebody bad, but we never would *shoot* nobody or nothing like that. We robbed other little kids from rival gangs. If we caught another kid in the neighborhood who didn't live there, his money was automatically taken, or his coat; or if he had a nice pair of shoes or whatever, we'd take it from him. This was just SOP, standard operational procedure.

"But in school I never gave any trouble. Just minor stuff, you know. And I never even thought about quitting school. That was out of the question, as far as I was concerned, because from the time I was a little, small child, my mother and father both were very, very strong on this going to school. And for me to miss a day going to school? I'd have to be dead!

"But I would go out, when I got out of school, and raise *particular* hell! Of course, from a child I always wanted to be a policeman. I don't know why, really. Even when I first started working at jobs, I always figured that it was just a stopping-off place and eventually I would be a policeman. I think that this is one reason why I didn't get into more trouble than I would have, when I was a teen-ager, because somewhere along the line I found out about the consequences of having a record. It was my mother and father, I guess. They always told me, 'Once you get a record, you'll never be able to be a policeman.' Now, they knew I always wanted to be the man, so I guess they used this as a kind of stick over my head. So I would always have that fear of getting into any kind of difficulty that would cause me to come in contact with the police.

"I thank my parents very much, for helping me to get out, so to speak. They were both very deportment-conscious, education-minded. My mother had to come up to the grammar school one time. I had a fight with a boy. I knocked him through a window, a ground-level window. Actually, it was more of a push than a knock. Anyway, my mother had to come to the school. So she came and the teacher told her what I had done and so forth, but she didn't say anything. When I got back home, she told me I couldn't go out and to go to bed. I usually took a bath every night before I went to bed, so I guess I must have been about eleven then, and I was just getting ready to get out of the tub, to dry off, and she came into the bathroom with a strap, a razor strap. And she beat my ass to the bone! While I was still in the bathtub, wet, and, brother, I never will forget that. That was the worst whipping I ever got in my life.

"My father only spanked me once in his lifetime. I never crossed no words with him, though, until I got grown, until I got married. If he told me something, that was it. I mean, there wasn't no question as to whether I was going to comply or not. And my mother, no backtalk, never! If she told me something and I made a face, she'd slap me in the mouth, immediately, without preamble, just—wham!

"I don't know if my parents were extreme when it came to discipline or not, but they were very effective; because I never, never entertained no thoughts of being insolent or anything like that. They'd always preach about respecting grown people and all this kind of thing. I imagine, see, that they had something to do with me getting out of the ghetto—but even the guys I ran around with, the tough hoodlums, if one of their parents were to be seen in the street drunk or something like that, I mean, this was unheard of. The kid would be ostracized and criticized and everything else. He'd be so embarrassed he couldn't hold his head up.

"Things have changed entirely now, though. Kids today don't even—I mean, this don't mean nothing to them. It's an accepted thing to see your father or mother drunk or whatever. When I was in school, sure, we had kids drop out, but those who stayed in weren't so bad. They didn't *learn* much, but the teachers didn't have the headaches of today. Now the kids'll beat up the teachers, or the parents go over to the school and threaten or even hit the teachers.

"It's the same with policemen. When I was a teen-ager, we didn't particularly *like* the policeman, but we had a lot more respect for him than the teen-agers do now. I mean, police brutality couldn't be defined the same way. Today you might see some beatnik sitting on the corner and you tell him to move off the street or something, and he'll start hollering police brutality. Well, this doesn't make sense, not even to me.

"See, when I was a teen-ager and the man came up and

told me to get off the corner and go home or whatever, if you didn't go home he'd crack you across the rump with his nightstick. Well, this was the accepted thing. And when you got home, when I went home and told my mother, I'd get *another* crack. Today if this happens, in addition to the cry of police brutality which goes up immediately, when that kid goes home and tells his mother or whoever, she'll come back and join in the chorus!

"But see, this is different days in a different age. When I was coming up, this so-called social revolution wasn't going on. Now the police officer has come into the position of almost the enemy in the ghetto. Now he represents the establishment, which allegedly had denied us long, so long, of our just due. So if a guy goes into the ghetto with a tie on, they think that either you're a policeman or you're trying to sell something. They think you're trying to victimize somebody. Either you're trying to make somebody buy something, or you're the law.

"I think the way it was before was better, because you got a taste of corporal punishment. I don't mean to say that a policeman should be given authority to go around beating people with his nightstick or anything, but I mean, well, how much did it hurt? You know, a little crack on the rump? It didn't even make a mark. This was an act that, well, you're bad kids, you're doing wrong, stop, desist, go home . . . and this didn't make us *hate* policemen. We had a lot of respect for them. At least *I* didn't hate them, and none of the kids I ran around with hated policemen. But on the other hand, at that time there weren't nearly as *many* policemen. You might go all day in my neighborhood at that time and you wouldn't see a police car. I mean, you wasn't exposed to as many police as are around today. So it's a hard determination to make, to compare the way things are now and how they were then.

"Maybe the cops *were* brutal in those days but none ever brutalized me. I got cracked on the behind when I was standing on the corner, being out late at night, and I'd be afraid to tell my mother when I went home. Sometimes now,

as I say, if a policeman just barely *pushes* somebody there'll
be a half-dozen people at the station house hollering about
police brutality. It's a different time, a different society, different attitudes, and the laws are different."

Over coffee, Ernie and Roy decided that their best lead
in the Rudolph James case was Leroy Williams. "First," Ernie
said, "I'm gonna call that ice-cream woman."

In a phone booth, Ernie checked the number and dialed.
The woman answered and said, "You're in luck. My lady
friend came in just after you left. She told me again that it
were a woman and a man beating up on another man."

"Did she describe them to you?"

"She said the woman was a bull dagger, a stud broad."

"Uh-hunh."

"A lesbian, with a yellow wig. Wears short dresses."

"Anything else?"

"No, 'cept it were a little man with her, beating on a
tall man."

"Okay. Listen, now, there's something in this for you if
we get a little closer. Call me if you hear anything else, hear?"

"Mmmm."

In the car again, Ernie said, "I'm pretty sure we're on
the right track, now. Not much to go on. We don't even know
whether it was Rudolph James or another man they was beating, but it sounds like it might be the same incident. So that's
where we are right now."

"Hey—" Roy shouted, pointing. "There's a pair of vice
dicks."

Ernie pushed the gas pedal down and we pulled up
alongside another pair of Negro detectives in an unmarked
car. Kidding, Ernie shouted at them, "Hey, brother, you call
for dicks?"

"Well, what do you know? It's Officer Cox."

"What's happening, man?"

"Same ol' okeydoke."

"You check on that thing I told you 'bout?"

"Yeah. It's true. I got that sawed-off shotgun they got the woman with. We found it last night."

"Good!" Ernie shouted.

"And we got the boy, a bit later."

"Man, you guys better stick to vice. You're showing us up."

"What can we do for you this time?"

"We're looking for a broad," Ernie said. "A stud broad with a yellow wig. She and a little man was doing some boxing under the el Monday night. We don't want nothing heated up—just a witness. Or maybe you can get us her name, hunh?"

"We'll try."

"Good. Listen, now, I don't want the word to go out who we're looking for—not yet, anyway. Let it lay."

"Okay, man. We'll see what we can do."

"Thanks."

Driving uptown, Ernie outlined his thoughts to me. "I told 'em to let the word lay because something might develop, you know? I mean, even if they get us a name for the broad, and even though an idea of what she looks like, we still don't know *what* she is. We can probably find out, but at the price of heating everything up. It's more important to me that we find a good witness. Because we could pick her up, and if she didn't tell us anything, then we'd just be standing there, you know, looking at each other. And we'd eventually have to turn her loose. It might have been more than one guy doing the beating, because Rudolph was really worked over. And on the street back there a guy might knock another guy down and kick him a few times, and that's it. In this case, either the guy had a weapon, like a baseball bat, or it was more than one guy."

"Or else Rudolph got walked, kicked, pretty damn bad," Roy offered.

"That could be what happened, you're right."

"Let's find Leroy Williams, okay?" Roy insisted.

"That's what we're doing, man. He's probably been arrested before, for something. We can check his record," Ernie
told me, "and see if he's got another address, aside from the
hotel, and it might possibly be where he's living at now. We'll
put a name check on him in Records and see if we can come
up with anything—a picture, preferably. Actually, addresses
don't mean too much, 'cause guys like Williams don't stay
nowhere too long. And a lot of times, when they get arrested,
no matter where they live, they give the same damn address.
They might not have lived there for two, three, four years.
But they use the address out of habit."

"Maybe Williams uses grass," Roy said.

"If he does, I hope we can catch him dirty. Damn, that'd
be beautiful, wouldn't it? If we catch him dirty," Ernie advised me, "with some reefers in his pocket or something, we'd
really have him. He'd tell us anything we want to know. Then
if he tells us that he saw Joe Jones or somebody fighting with
Rudolph James, we'll go over to Joe Jones and throw him
a bone: 'Hey, Joe, I understand that somebody tried to jump
on you.' He'll say, 'Hey, yeah! Yeah, that's right! He jumped
on me!' Then we got him admitting something, rather than
giving us a straight denial to a question."

"I'll never forget the time," said Roy, "that Ernie lied to
a guy and fooled him into 'fessing up, and a policewoman
chewed him out."

"Yeah, she lit into me! She cursed me up and down for
fooling the guy. And yet the same broad probably uses all
kinds of trickery in her own life, you know?"

In the modern, well-scrubbed Records Room at headquarters, Ernie asked a girl behind the counter for a check
on all past arrests of anyone named Leroy Williams. There
were six separate files under that name. Ernie sifted through
them, checking the general areas of the city in which the
arrests took place. He also checked the ages and physical
descriptions of the six men, finally pulling one card which

appeared most appropriate. This Leroy Williams had a long list of narcotics arrests, abruptly ending in 1953. The detectives obtained his photograph, which showed a dark-complexioned, mouselike face.

"Nothing much else to go on," Ernie said. "I hope we don't have to spend more time locating a witness than finding the actual perpetrator."

"Well," Roy said, "as far as I'm concerned, it's usually *harder* to get the witness."

"And harder to get the *witness* to talk than to get the *offender* to 'fess up."

Ernie and Roy decided to drive back to the Acco Hotel, where they would ask Robert Dagger to look at the photograph of Leroy Williams. "We might also ask the desk clerk if he left a forwarding address," Roy said.

"Don't count on it."

"Maybe we should also go back to Wilton," Roy suggested, "and get a photograph of Rudolph James. It would be helpful if we find Leroy Williams, so he could identify the victim."

"No," Ernie replied, "I don't want to go back to the brother. If we tell him we think it happened outside the hotel, he'll think we were paid off or something."

"Guess you're right."

At the Acco Hotel again, Ernie leaned against the window in the hallway, waiting for the desk clerk. At last the woman appeared. Recognizing Ernie, she let him in.

"Hello, ma'am, Officer Cox again. I'd like to see Robert Dagger."

"He ain't here, now."

"Oh. Listen, did Leroy Williams ever leave a forwarding address?"

"Nope."

"Oh."

As Ernie started to leave, the woman said, "But Mr. Williams just moved back into the hotel."

"He did?"

"Yep."

"Just between the time we were here and now?"

"Uh-hunh."

"What room is he in?"

"He took his old room back."

"The dead man's room?"

"Nothing happened in this hotel!"

"Don't worry 'bout nothing, ma'am."

Ernie started up the stairs to find Leroy Williams. The woman watched him reach the first landing, then said, "He ain't up there now."

Glaring at her, Ernie asked, "Why didn't you say so?" The woman shrugged. "Do you know where he is?"

"Mmmm."

Ernie waited for the woman to speak further. After a moment, he said, "Well, where *is* he?"

"He's next door. He's in the cellar next door, cooking his meat."

"Cooking?"

"He got a friend down there, with a grill."

Ernie mumbled, "Thank you" and walked quickly out of the hotel. I was surprised at what seemed like a great coincidence, but there was Leroy Williams, looking exactly like the photograph. He was sitting on the steps leading down to the cellar of the building next door. Seeing him, Ernie first gestured to Roy, who got out of the car and sauntered over. Leroy wore a loose T-shirt hanging over baggy, green pants. He balanced a plate on his lap, stabbing and cutting a piece of steak.

"Yessir, gentlemen!" Leroy's voice came out in a raspy, good-natured manner.

"We're police."

"I'd offer you some steak, but—"

"That's okay. Is your name John Sylvester?"

"No, you got the wrong fella. I'm Leroy Williams."

"How're you doing, Leroy?"

"Well, I'm doing fair—sociable."

"You drunk, man?"

"No, no."

"Well, listen Leroy, come over in the car and we'll just talk a little bit, okay?"

"Sure, sure. I'm sociable, like I said." Leroy put his plate on the steps and stood up. As we walked to the car, he asked, "What'cha wanna know, gentlemen?"

"Just sit in there in the back seat, Leroy . . . Good . . . we want to know about that fight you saw under the el, where those dudes were boxing."

"Oh. You mean where the dude that had my room got his jaws boxed?" Leroy sat next to me, apparently assuming I was a cop.

"That's right," Ernie said.

"I was standing under the el and I seen it. A tall fella and a short, dark fella—they got to fighting on the sidewalk. Now, the big fella wasn't hittin' the little fella at all! The big fella slipped, fell on the ground—I seen it all from across the street—and no po-leece or nothing came in sight. I seen the big fella fall and the little fella was kicking him. He was kicking the hell out of him, yessir."

"Was there a gal involved?"

"The little dude had his woman with him."

"Did she have on a blond wig?"

"I think so. I won't swear to this, now."

"What color hair?"

"She had on an orange suit. I don't know if she had blond hair on or not. But the fella, he was about your complexion, a little lighter. Because you know, when you're messin' around with that stuff, the junk, you lose your color to a certain extent. But if he hadn't lost his color, he would have been your complexion."

"You think he was a dope addict?"

"Oh, certainly he was a dope addict."

"How many times had you seen him before?"

"I never seen him before in my life."

"What about the broad?"

"I never seen her before, neither. I just happened to be right there, just got off the el, and I was coming over to hotel here, to cook a piece of meat next door. I was just standing by the fruit stand and in front of the pawn shop, when the fight took place. I had a piece of meat like usual, and my buddy puts it on the grill for me. Now, that was Monday. And this afternoon I saw Mr. Dagger on the street, and he told me that the dude who had my old room was stomped on. So I figured I could get the room back."

"You do some time, man, in 1952—somewhere back there?"

"In '53."

"For burglary or something?"

"Mmmm. Mmmm. You must have been looking at my sheets."

"Well, we been looking for *you*."

"But why you looking in my chart like that? That's *past* stuff, man."

"You been clean, though."

"I know! I ain't *gonna* do nothing, either. Nothing but drink and get drunk, and go to work. And miss a few days there, and argue with my boss."

"Listen, tell me this. When you first saw this occurrence, were they talking or fighting?"

"When I first seen 'em they was fighting, 'cause I'm on one side of the street, helping Herman put his fruit stand up, and I turn around and seen a crowd out there, and I seen 'em trading blows. And so I told Herman, 'Lookie here!' And I seen this little cat just hitting the big cat. But the big cat was jes' sort of *holding* him, to try to push him away. And the little cat's shooting his fist down here, up here, down here, up here; while the big cat was just kind of holding him as if he didn't want to fight. After a while, the little one swung him and he fell down between the cars. And after that, all I could see was the little cat doing this: [kicking his legs] walk-

ing him. If anybody ever walked *me* like that, y'all would
have to come get me, because I'd make it as rough on him as
I could."

"Yeah, I don't blame you, neither."

"I ain't never hurt nobody like that. You wup me fair
and that's all right."

"Well, listen—this little dude, did he look like he knew
what he was doing when he was fighting? Did he look like a
professional or something, or was he just swinging?"

"No, he knew how to carry his fists, man. Because he
was going in and coming up, going in and coming up; and
now, if you jes' fighting, and don't know how to fight, you ain't
gonna be as *scientific* as this. But if you know how to go to
the gut and come to the head, in the gut, to the head, in the
gut, to the head . . ."

"How old a guy do you think he was?"

"Yessir, well, I'm forty-three, so now maybe he was
thirty-seven or thirty-eight."

"How was he wearing his hair?"

"He had had a process, I could tell."

"A regular process?"

"Mmmm. Mmmm."

"Well, where was the broad at this time?"

"She was just standing right there. She picked his hat up
off the ground. Actually, she was trying to break the fight up.
But after they acted like they didn't want to break it up, she
just stood with her little dude's hat. And after he walked on
the big cat, they walked away together."

"In other words, you think the broad was his lady?"

"She *had* to be his lady, because she was trying to pull
him away . . ."

"What kind of build did she have—medium, slender, or
stacked? Nice legs?"

"I didn't search her good."

"You had a better look at the dude, then?"

"I could see him, but I didn't get his face too good."

"Listen," Ernie said, "what are you doing right now?"

"Right now I'm gonna go back and finish my piece of steak that I had cooked on the grill, there."

"We, we wanna go and take a little statement from you."

"What kind of statement?"

"Just the same as we asked you here in the car."

"Well, go ahead. Make your run, man."

"Won't take but a half-hour."

"Make your run. I'm sociable."

As we rode to the station house, Ernie commented, "You were a pretty swift dude in your younger days, weren't you?"

Laughing, Leroy said, "Yeah, but I was always by myself. Every time I ran with somebody, I got in trouble, so I stopped running with people. I started staying with Leroy. Leroy stays with Leroy, and Leroy stays out of trouble."

"Well, you done a pretty good job of it in the last few years."

"That's because I been trying to be a nice cat, man. I got me a nice young baby for an old lady. And my mother and father, sister, and brothers—they is all in my corner. And everybody I meets likes me, so therefore I feel good. Only thing is, the hotel won't let me bring the old lady inside any more."

"Whoo, man, you're paying your rent and they won't let you have no old ladies up there? Man, that's pretty strong, ain't it?"

Roy broke in, "Sounds like you're living at the Y, Leroy."

"It does," Leroy said. "I don't like being in no place where I can't have no fraternizing, you know?"

"I used to go in that hotel when I was younger," Ernie said, "but the cockroaches run me out of there one night."

"I woke up one morning in that hotel," Leroy confided, "and the girl I was with done left me. She left me fifteen cents to catch a cab."

"She gotcha, hunh?"

"Got me," Leroy said. "She took fifty, sixty dollars, and that was from a loan I had made from my boss."

"Well, everybody gets beat. Happens to the best of 'em Leroy."

"Yeah, that's life, but I'm still sociable."

In a small room at the station house, Leroy relaxed in a chair, his thin legs crossed, and repeated his testimony to Ernie, who used his two forefingers at the typewriter. "Typing was completely new to me when I became a detective," he told Leroy. "Now it's part of a dick's training. I had to buy one of them self-teaching booklets. I still only use two fingers, or sometimes four." Leroy nodded in sympathy.

I wandered down the hall, where Roy was speaking with another detective about a different case. "I asked the crime lab to check the slugs from the gun," he was saying. "They'll make a test fire for me, but of course that's only to cover myself in court."

In the main office, three white detectives stood over a teen-age black gang member who had been picked up on a theft charge. The boy had offered to give information about his gang activities in exchange for having the charges dropped. "I want to get out of the gang, anyway," he said.

'Why did you join in the first place? the detective asked.

"I just didn't wanna get hurt, man," he mumbled. "About ten days ago, they ordered me to shoot another guy." The boy folded his arms and stared out the window.

"Who ordered you?"

"That's none of your business."

"Did you shoot the other boy?"

"I shot at him, but I missed."

"Well, you're lucky."

The boy went on to tell the detectives that his gang had been picking up between $4,000 and $5,000 a week from white storeowners who paid for protection. He said the gang also collected about $7,000 per week in dues. "And the University of Chicago was paying us to keep off students."

"How do you know all these amounts?"

"I watched 'em count the money in a church office."

"How old are you, son?"

"I'm fourteen."

"Does the gang have weapons?"

"You know they do, don't you?"

"I want you to tell me."

"They got a stockpile of machine guns and rifles. I used to own a .22-caliber automatic pistol."

"Now, tell us the truth—why are you giving us this information, aside from that little theft we got you on?"

"Because the leaders have kept all the cars and the TVs that we stole."

"Would you be willing to tell us this in court?"

"Hell, no."

"Why not?"

"Because I want to live."

I rode with Ernie in the front seat of the car as we drove Leroy back to the hotel. After letting him off, we went for some ice cream and coffee. I told Ernie about the conversation I had heard between the young gang member and the detectives. He repeated how he had been able, as a boy, "to split the scene when big trouble came up." He said that none of the other boys questioned him, since he was the leader and therefore beyond reproach.

"Another way I avoided a lot of devilment," he said, "was going on fishing trips with my father. We'd always argue, but that was part of the fun. We'd leave on Friday nights and go to some lake and come back to Chicago on Sunday. I used to love those fishing trips. See, they got me out of the ghetto for a while and kept me from getting into more trouble than I did get into. But my father started gambling and drinking quite a bit.

"One Friday night I waited on the porch for him and he didn't show up. He was out drinking, I guess, but I kept waiting. My mother kept coming out and saying, 'Forget it, Ernie, he's not coming home.' But I waited until the sun came up. He never came home that weekend, and so I went out and got into a whole *mess* of trouble.

"So one day my mother got fed up and just walked right out of the house. She didn't have nothing but the clothes she was wearing. She had no money, nowhere to go, nothing. She got a small room in a basement, and she stayed in that basement for seven years. I kept living with my father, and my sister, too.

"My mother went to work in a factory. For seven years she worked day and night, saving her money. Wouldn't buy no clothes, wouldn't go out, nothing. Very strong-willed. I tried to make her move, because I didn't want my mother in any basement, but she said she was going to stay there until she got enough money to buy her own building. And after seven years, she had enough to make a down payment.

"She bought a six-flat building that she owns completely now. It's the building where I have my apartment. At the time, she was the first Negro owner of a building on the block. She took a lot of grief from people, like an inspector who said, 'Pay me $300 or I'll have your building condemned,' even though none of the white owners had inspections. She stood up to him and held on to her building. It was an all-white neighborhood, but the whites got scared and eventually it changed over to the way it is now, all-Negro.

"One way or another, my old lady went through a lot of hell. I was still living with my father and when it came time to graduate from high school, we got into our biggest argument of all. He wanted me to go to college. He said he'd work, selling insurance, to pay the tuition. But I wanted to go into the Army instead and he never forgave me. Never, never got over it, and he died without forgiving me.

"I just couldn't see no college. I wanted to be slick, get out on the street and be a hustler. Have fun, you know—a lot of women and all that. Which I did get a little taste of. See, when I was a teen-ager getting out of high school, the opportunities were nothing like they are now. No comparison at all. If a Negro went to college at that time, he had an idea that he *might* be able to do something with it afterward, but there was always that little sneaking suspicion that he wouldn't.

"I mean, I knew of colored guys that had been to college, some of 'em had degrees, and they wound up working as clerks in the goddamn post office. The colored fellows used to call the post office 'the graveyard of dreams.' That's one big reason why I wasn't interested in college.

"So I graduated from high school and three days later found myself in Fort Jackson, South Carolina, taking basic training. My father was angry as hell. I was a peacetime soldier in the south for eighteen months.

"But here's the point, see—I think the Army saved me. When I got out and came back to the ghetto here, I was amazed at all the guys who had gone to jail or who got killed. Or something terrible had happened to them. One guy I knew —he lived next door to me, we were good friends—I went back to see him after the Army. I asked his mother, 'How's Jack?' She said, 'You didn't know? He's dead.' I said, 'What happened to him?' She said, 'He died of an overdose of narcotics.' That was really a shock, you know? Another friend of mine had stuck up a drugstore and killed the druggist. They found him guilty and he died in the electric chair. In that brief period while I was away in the Army, mostly all my friends had ended up in the penitentiary or dead."

The next day, Ernie and Roy decided to pursue the Rudolph James case in the afternoon hours before work. Their objective was "to find Herman, the guy that's got the fruit stand under the el station, who was looking at the fight with Leroy."

"He's a good bet," said Ernie, "because here's a guy

who's out there on the street every day. He's stationary, so he should know the regulars."

Finding Herman was not difficult. He was arranging his fruits and vegetables when Ernie sauntered up to him and asked about "a little ol' fight" that took place the previous Monday.

Herman, an elderly black man, eyed us with suspicion and replied, "Well, I don't know . . ." Although his voice trailed off, there was a note of finality in his tone.

"You know, Herman," Ernie said casually, "some of the guys told me that this fruitstand of yours, being out here on the sidewalk, might be a little violation of the law. Now, I don't know if what they say is true, but—"

"I ain't bothered nobody, and nobody bothers me," Herman said.

"That's just what *I* was gonna say, Herman. Nobody *bothers* you 'round here. All the guys know you, and nobody wants to cause you no grief or nothing."

"I can't afford no more fines," Herman protested.

"Now listen, Brother Herman, for this nonattention that you're getting, it seems to me that you could, you know, just give me a little hint. That's all, and nobody's gonna bother you."

So, Herman began to describe the fight. Reluctantly, he offered details similar to those given by Leroy Williams, but nothing more of value. Ernie thanked him and we strolled about for a while, looking in the windows of the stores and standing for periods of time to watch the people. Then he crossed the street and went into the pawn shop (Herman had said, "They was boxing right across the street, in front of the pawn shop").

The pawnbroker, a well-dressed man with a thin mustache, greeted Ernie and motioned for us to come to the rear of the store. Ernie told me later, "The pawnbroker consorts with criminals on one hand and police on the other, so it can't be known that he gives information. He wouldn't dare let it be known. I can use him for information, but not as a witness in court." As it turned out, the pawnbroker had not seen the fight, but he assured Ernie that within a short time he would dig up some helpful data.

"Just don't front me off," the pawnbroker said with intensity. "If you know that everybody knows you're a dick, don't come 'round here. That's all I ask of you, man."

"You know I wouldn't put no stigma on you, brother."

"I know you wouldn't try to do that, but jes' the same I feel the strain, you dig? I been jumped on pretty fast when I helped out those vice dicks, about a year ago. The word got out that I was an informant, so I got beat on. I almost went to Florida or some place like that."

"Don't you worry, man," said Ernie. "And you know I got some bread for you, too."

The pawnbroker did not respond. Ernie strolled outside and mingled with the crowd, while I walked back to the car where Roy was waiting. The car had been parked, deliberately, three blocks away. From the car we continued to watch the comings and goings of ghetto residents, hoping to find a girl with a blond wig and orange dress.

"A lot of waiting in this kind of thing," Ernie mused when he returned. "If we don't have an exact location of a person, but like we know that he or she frequents this vicinity, we just wait."

"Think she'll have the wig on?" Roy asked.

"More than likely. If she's a prostitute. Of course, we don't know yet how implicated she is in the murder. Supposedly she just stood by and watched, but she may have initiated the whole thing. If we spot someone who we think is this broad, let's just watch her for a few hours and see what she does. She might go to her little man. Keep her in sight, see where she's coming from, where she's going. I'd rather find the man, actually. *Eventually*, though, we'll pick her up. Take her for a little ride and just get her name and address. Then, we can pull her sheet and find out who she's been getting arrested with. Our man's name might be on it."

For most of the afternoon we waited in the car. Ernie

left the car on occasion to buy Life Savers and chewing gum. "Too bad we can't do more of this kind of thing," he complained to me. "I'd like to do more of it, but during regular hours there's always other work. We'd have to drop our surveillance, run and do something else, and then come back. Now, I *know* that broad hangs around here, because of the kind of broad she is. And I know that sooner or later, she's gonna come by here. But how much *time* is at stake, for waiting, is kind of an uncertain thing. We got the wig to go by and Herman said she had a light complexion. And if she's the type of broad we think she is, she'll have on that orange dress, too. Because they don't have extensive wardrobes.

"If we were in a big hurry, we could get the broad's identity from the prostitutes. Very easily. We could put the squeeze on 'em by threatening to shut down one of their houses here. Or we could just take one whore aside and get her uptight. That would be risky, though, because we wouldn't know if she knows this broad or not. We could go for the play—one of us—and after she makes the deal, then arrest her and then take her back here and threaten to lock her up if she didn't give us the information. But after all that, she might not know anything. And that could work against us, because if we did lock her up and then she got back out on the street, she'd put the word out as to who we're looking for. I don't see nothing the matter, though, with putting a little squeeze here and a little squeeze there. You might say that I'm glad that there's vice going on, because it's helpful to some degree. It's like playing chess. Whoever's got the strongest piece wins."

"Maybe the vice dicks have the broad's name by now," Roy offered. "After all, they sometimes have much better contacts in the neighborhood than we do. Because they stay right around here, don't go nowhere else."

"I hope they do," Ernie said. "Those dicks are another source of information. With their own informants. To me, a detective is only as good as his sources of information, because this ain't no Sherlock Holmes thing out here. No little magnifying glass and looking all over the ground, measuring off a whole lot of stuff and all that. Just a lot of routine questioning and digging around in the neighborhood for a witness. Soliciting information from people in the most underhanded and inconspicuous way possible."

"I try to make an informant out of everyone I talk to," said Roy.

"Same here. Even if I help somebody by performing a menial task, I make it sound like a big deal. Like the other day, some woman called me and asked where she could find something. I told her to hold on and I went and looked in the phone book. I got back on the phone and said, 'Hey, listen, we got lucky.' And she thought I pulled some big strings for her or something."

"In general," Roy said, "I try to make friends with as many people as I possibly can, when I'm out here working."

"And these are people we ordinarily wouldn't want to be friends *with*," Ernie explained to me. "I make 'em *think* I want to be friends with 'em, because the more that I'm accepted, the better it is for getting information, down the line. Every once in a while I like to go get a whore out of jail. If some broad gets locked up and it's a minor offense, I'll go ask the arresting officer to turn her loose. Give her a break. I try to obligate her to me, so that just when such an instance as this comes up, we could go to that broad for the information. On the other hand, she feels that if she gets into some little scrap, she can call me and I'll get her out of it. And in turn, she knows that she don't get nothing for nothing. She's gotta give *me* a little something, too."

"Many people," said Roy, "have a mistaken concept of informant. They think it's done only for money. In some cases it is, but the average cop can't afford to keep any worthwhile informant on his payroll. The main basis for an informant, in the modern situation, is the fact that he *likes* a particular policeman for one reason or another. He'll *accept* money, but that's never the *basis* of it. A good informant is like a good woman. He'll only have a relationship with that one cop."

"I used to have one that would tell only me," Ernie said, laughing, "but he went to California."

"Now, I'm speaking about a really *good* informant, which is based on friendship. Then there are the borderline cases where we'll buy somebody some wine or give him a buck, or pay his cab fare. That kind of thing goes on all the time, but I wouldn't put that guy in a class with one who we *know* will tell us something. I got some that I *think* will tell me what I want to know. But that other little stuff—buying 'em drinks and all—that's just public relations."

"A lot of dicks won't do that," Ernie said. "They say, 'The hell with that. I ain't putting *my* money out.' But those are the dicks that can't solve that case when it comes up."

"There's a guy over in Hyde Park . . . Every time I see him I get ready to run, because he's always asking me for a quarter. That don't hurt much, though. A quarter here and there. Someday, something's gonna happen that I want to know, and that guy with all my quarters will know about it. Now, I'm *hoping* he'll come through, but there's no guarantee. In spite of all my quarters."

"Remember that night I gave a broad about fifteen dollars?" Ernie asked. Roy nodded and I asked Ernie to elaborate. "That was on a homicide. The whore gave me some bullshit. Sent me on a wild goose chase. You know, I never did get that money back. I see her once in a while, now, but what am I going to do to her? Grab her up and *rob* her? Or go back to her and curse at her? That wouldn't bother her in the least. And there's no damn fund down at headquarters that's gonna pay me back. I could go down there and say, 'Well, listen, chief. Uh—I put out fifteen dollars for some information that didn't pan out. I'd like to get reimbursed.' The chief would look at me like I was a damn fool. If it *did* pan out, I suppose I could get it. More than likely. Otherwise, I wouldn't even tell the boss. I feel that it's all part of the game —part of being out here. Nothing ventured, nothing gained. I'm very aware of using all sorts of people who are doing illegal things. Using a lot of trickery to get information. It's a constant matching of wits with criminals. Everybody's defensive when you approach 'em as a cop, but you have to get 'em on your side. Sometimes, for me, it just gets too personal. Like one time I promised to marry a whore. I thought she could help me with a case. She hounded me for two years. Another time I got a broad to rat on her own boyfriend. She gave me the information and left him. I arrested him but then I was stuck with her. Her name was Martha. She carried a knife and a big razor. Wow, she wouldn't let me alone. Finally she went back to Little Rock."

After nearly four hours and several packs of Life Savers and chewing gum, we left the street under the el.

At the office later that Thursday afternoon, a message from the vice detectives was on Ernie's desk: "Broad might be Eloise Hicks. Will try for other name too."

After dinner, I rode with Ernie and Roy up to headquarters, where they ran a name check. There were several files under the name of Eloise Hicks. The most likely one contained a pile of arrest cards two inches thick. From the file room the detectives went two floors below to "pull her sheet" and obtain a photograph. The seven-page file indicated that Eloise had been arrested ninety-one times for prostitution since September 1963. The photograph showed a twenty-four-year-old Negro girl who appeared at least ten years older. Her eyes stared vacantly from the photograph. Her facial expression and posture indicated an overall resignation, a great weariness.

"The only trouble with this," Ernie said, "is that Eloise has absolutely no narcotics arrests. For all this whoring she's done, there are no drugs involved."

"She must really like her line of work," Roy said.

"The trouble is that I'm pretty sure that the broad we want is on drugs. What's worse, I don't see any pimps arrested with this Eloise Hicks. She might not even have one."

"Well," Roy advised, "the easiest way to check it out

is to go down to the Acco Hotel and show this picture to Leroy Williams. Leroy can say 'yes' or 'no' and that'll be that."

When Ernie returned to the car from the Acco Hotel, his face betrayed an exasperation. "Leroy's been kicked out of the hotel," he said. "He didn't leave no forwarding address, either."

"Did we get his mother's address?"

"No."

"A phone number?"

"No. I got a daytime number for his job, but that's all."

The detectives sat quietly in the car in the darkness. Ernie, who was wearing a white turtleneck shirt under his jacket this evening, fiddled with the "love beads" he wears on occasion, "to look more like one of the black-power cats."

"Leroy's having a hard time, isn't he?" I asked.

"Well, people like him are transient. It's hard to keep track of them. They move, change jobs all the time . . ."

"Think we got him in trouble?" Roy said.

"No. The hotel owner came in and said he owed some back rent or something. The woman on the desk hadn't known about that."

"He might still be a dopey."

"Nah. He told me that he kicked the habit when the quality of the stuff became poorer. But he's got a crutch now: he drinks heavy. He had been locked up a lot of times for narcotics and burglary, and for the past fifteen years either he's been clean or, like he half-admitted, hasn't gotten caught. He might smoke a little pot now, but I don't think he's popping. Leroy's got a child by a woman who lives away from here. He's not married to this woman, so she wouldn't be under the name of Williams."

Ernie took out his chewing gum and Roy lit a cigarette. Suddenly Robert Dagger appeared, seemingly out of the bushes beside the car. Poking his curious face into Roy's window, he asked in a mysterious tone: "Was Leroy able to identify the cat?"

Startled, Ernie said, "Brother Dagger! How're you doing?"

"Was Leroy able to identify the stud?"

"No," Roy answered.

Ernie added, "We don't know who this cat *is* yet, Brother Dagger."

"Ooh, you mean you is still in the dark?"

"That's right," Ernie said, scowling.

"Well, let me tell you a little secret. If Leroy saw the fight, he knows the names of who was fighting."

"You think so?"

Dagger smiled, winked, and stole back through the bushes, disappearing finally down an alley. Ernie began to laugh. "I wonder what all *that* means. Does Brother Dagger know more than he's telling?"

"Possibly. Leroy might have told Dagger who the killer was, and neither of them told us."

"Or," said Ernie, "Leroy might have told Dagger that he *knew* who it was. Either way, Dagger don't want to tell us. He wants Leroy to tell. He don't want the stigma on himself, so he puts it on Leroy."

"I'd say this is a low spot," Roy quipped.

"Stagnant," Ernie replied. "Maybe we should spend a few minutes on one of our rape jobs, and then come back and look for Leroy."

Roy sang, "The trouble with Lee-roy . . ."

"Not available, that's the trouble."

The detectives returned to the commercial district under the el, to find that the pawnbroker and Herman, the fruitstand owner, had gone home. For a while they circled in and out of the area, stopping at each corner, watching every movement, looking for a prostitute with a blond wig and an orange dress, or perhaps even Eloise Hicks, who, according to Ernie, was "probably the wrong broad anyway."

Then we drove through the ghetto streets to "gangster park," a crowded playground outside one of Chicago's largest public-housing structures. According to Ernie, this area is a gang-members' meeting place "where four or five shootings take place every weekend, and lots of stabbings."

"When they're not fighting," Ernie observed, "they sit around and drink, smoke some reefers, listen to records, shoot pool. They do a lot of drinking, mostly wine. But there's shooting going on here all the time. We can sit out here for ten or fifteen minutes and I bet we hear a shot. Drugs aren't involved, not too much among the gang-bangers. Naturally they smoke marijuana, but very rarely do you find a gang-banger using heroin, because when he gets to be a drug addict his time is too taken with getting drugs and he has no more time for gang activities. And in the ghetto, if you're a gang-banger, it takes kids in pretty good physical condition, you know? I mean, they're very active in running from somebody; either from the police or from rival gang members. It's just a very busy thing to be a gang-banger in the ghetto."

In his usually philosophic tone, Roy observed, "Each of these gangs reaches a point of development, especially when they achieve a reputation, when they have to ask themselves, 'Well, where do we go from here?' They have to decide whether they're gonna fall apart, or in rare cases whether they'll become constructive, or are they gonna go on to become full-fledged, hard-core criminals? Usually the gangs have a legitimate purpose in forming: for protection against *another* gang. And then, if they overcome this other gang, if they become so feared that they're safe in their own neighborhood, then there's really no need for them to exist. And they got a good thing going. They got prestige in the neighborhood. So then they become idle, shooting pool and drinking wine. So they enter a period where they don't know exactly what to do: are we gonna become stickup men and burglars?

Racketeers? Or are we gonna start marrying, or go into the Army? And some might even go to college."

As if to make sure I would get his point, Ernie injected, "But they're *always* fighting."

"That's what I say—fighting is the reason for bringing the gang into being."

"No matter *what* stage of development they're in," Ernie went on, "they're always gonna be fighting with somebody else, and shooting."

It was dark out when the car pulled up on the edge of the housing-project playground known as gangster park.

"I used to live in a housing project just like this one," Ernie said, pointing to the immense, dirty-yellow structure rising in the night. "It was horrible. Too many people, all bunched up together. Most of 'em were in the same circumstance. They were on ADC, on relief—no husband, no father. I was always sure that in twenty years everybody in the building would be related to each other. The kids run up and down, you know—the mother's gone, father's gone—the kids are running up and down and screwing all over the building. So, sooner or later, they're all going to be related.

"When they first built the projects they was talking about how 'Oh, this is a wonderful thing!' They were pulling down them raggedy hell houses like mine and putting up the high-risers, but the high-risers, to me, are one of the worst monstrosities ever perpetrated on this city. They're just *containing* the Negro in a specific area, building *up* instead of *out*. All them kids, you think you could sleep over there, with all that noise going on until one or two in the morning? You go up in one of those buildings and there's a steady *hum,* like bees. Ooh, brother, I was so glad to get out of there, I didn't know *what* to do. Whoo, boy! There's a *din,* you know? A steady din. Ooh! Of course, I'm a great lover of quiet, of tranquility, when I'm home. But you can't beat that noise.

"Chicago has the largest, most congested public-housing places in the whole world, I think. The people who planned them should have known that when you stack up people on top of each other like that, you can expect a tremendous amount of crime, because of the closeness; and that's what has happened. So a lot of my work is right in the projects. All kinds of violence. Murder . . . And you got to be careful when you go in there as a policeman, because they throw things off the top floor at you. I narrowly missed getting hit with a wine bottle the other day."

"You know those middle-income buildings on the Near South Side?" Roy asked me. "Where they're setting now, ten years ago there was all ghetto there. They displaced the people who were living there. They said they were doing that in order to give the people in that area a place to stay, but *after* they built in that area, the rent was such that the people who were displaced couldn't afford to pay. So now, middle-class Negroes and whites live there, and upper-class Negroes—financially, that is. The ghetto residents, they moved to other ghettos. So on one block you got progress and then one block away, dire poverty. Some people say that the greater the progress, the greater the poverty at the other end, which is true. As progress comes about, poverty also becomes greater, and the two never get together. That's under democracy. So what's the answer?

"See, I'm talking about how do you bring everything onto the same level—and you can't, under a democratic system. So what will eventually happen is that we'll have a different form of government, I think. Say, a hundred years from now, the democracy that we know will no longer exist, just as we're not in the democracy that existed a hundred years ago. Whether they'll call it democracy still, no one knows.

"Now don't get me wrong, I think it's the best form of government, myself, because it offers a certain amount of freedom, which I like. I mean, I like having the incentive to get better, to go higher. You take that away and you're in trouble. But democracy, on the other hand, is like a circle within a circle. The outer rim is the democracy that the whites know, and the inner rim is the restricted area that our people know. And that's the part that needs changing, of course."

Ernie broke in, "The people in the projects, when they see me, they don't know that I come from the projects. Whenever I'm talking to them, especially when I'm trying to solicit information from them, I try to let it come out in the conversation that I used to live in the projects. And they seem to *light up* to that, you know? They say to themselves, 'Yeah, here's somebody who's like us.'"

We left the car and walked through the playground to the housing project. The voices of thousands of people echoed through its concrete caverns. Three small girls boarded the cramped elevator with us. One corner was piled with garbage. Although the girls pressed only the button for the fifth floor, the elevator stopped at each floor. After the girls got off, it continued to stop at every other floor, all the way to the nineteenth. At last, we emerged on a balcony from which I could look down on the playground, at the shadows of people far below.

"I'm always surprised," Ernie commented, "that more kids don't fall off these balconies." As we continued along to apartment 19-F, Ernie took out a police report and muttered, "We got this rape job because the guys on rapes are uptight. This says the woman was made to lie down on the elevator floor . . . at 3:20 in the morning . . . There sure are a lot of rapes in these housing-project elevators."

The detectives were greeted at the door by a young Negro man who pointed to the rear bedroom. I followed Ernie and Roy through the living room, where several young people were holding a record party, to the hallway. "In here," the young man said.

A large, middle-aged Negro woman was sitting on the double bed, breast-feeding a tiny child. Ernie sat in a chair; Roy and I stood next to him. The conversation went on matter-of-factly, in low tones, without any visible embarrassment. She explained how she had walked home from a friend's house, entering her housing-project lobby in the early morning. A Negro man had slipped from behind a pillar and boarded the elevator with her. Between two floors, he suddenly stopped the elevator and produced a knife. "Then," she said, "he told me to take off my underpants. He put his coat down on the floor and told me to lie down."

"How long did he . . .?" Ernie's voice trailed off.

"About twenty minutes."

"Would you remember him if you saw him in a line-up?"

"I'd never forget his face."

"Had you ever seen him before?"

"Never."

"Now, ma'am, we're gonna make every effort to find this guy. You'll hear from us, don't worry."

"Uh-hunh." The woman seemed disinterested, as if nothing the police did could eliminate or even lessen the painful memory of her rape. She turned her full attention back to the baby at her bosom; for a few moments the cops watched in silence.

"Thank you, ma'am," said Ernie, suddenly getting up and leaving the room.

Later, Ernie reflected, "The people in the ghetto don't *expect* good police service. We've had cases where, like they've reported something happened to 'em, like they were stabbed—of course a whole lot of 'em are stabbed, cut or shot or beat up and they never report it—and when a detective gets there, they're *surprised* to see him. They're surprised that you even showed up! They're even *more* surprised when you *catch* the person who victimized them. They can't believe that somebody actually cares enough about their problems."

"Remember that 'fuck-or-die' fellow we caught?" Roy asked.

Laughing, Ernie replied, "Ooh, yeah. He raped a whole *lot* of women. Maybe ten or more. He'd always tell 'em the same thing. After he'd pull his knife out, he'd always give 'em the same warning: 'What do you want to do—fuck or die?' "

Both cops laughed as Ernie told me: "This one little Chinese girl, I was talking to her and I had an idea that the guy who raped her was the same guy, but I wouldn't tell her. I asked her, 'What did he say?' She said, 'Well, he threatened me.' I asked, 'How did he threaten you?' 'Well,' she said, 'he took out a knife and put it to my throat and said he was going to kill me.' I said, 'Well, what *exactly* did he say? Do you remember his exact words?' So she started hemming and hawing, being just a teen-age girl, and I kept trying to pin her down. Finally she said, 'He asked me what did I want to do, fuck or die?' I said, 'Well, what did you tell him?' She said, 'Well, I told him I didn't want to *die*' "—Ernie and Roy laughed for a minute—"So, he screwed her right in the hallway, and her father, who was coming home from work, was the one who interrupted him. He knocked the father down in the hallway and got away. We finally caught him, and that cleared up eight *other* cases. There were a couple of others that I think he did too, but the victims were afraid to identify him, I think. He got thirty to fifty years in prison."

"That guy really picked some attractive victims," Roy added. "Most of the time these rapists, pattern rapists, just pick dogs. They don't pick none that look like nothing, no particular kind of women; just any that happen to be convenient for 'em to grab. But this guy appeared like he was very selective, because every one of the girls was very attractive."

"And *he* looked like a gorilla," Ernie said. "That's one reason why he got caught. I asked one of the girls to give a sketch, and she kept saying to the police artist, 'He looks just like a monkey with a hat on.' " Ernie laughed and continued, "When the artist drew the sketch, when he got through, he drew this little hat on him; and it looked *exactly* like a monkey with a hat on. When some other dicks caught the guy, they brought him in and as soon as he walked in the door, I knew it was him. Man, was he a horrible-looking young boy! Whoo, man, he had long arms, you know? Looked like *extra* long arms. He was very distinctive-looking. That was his downfall. Also, he had his knife in his pocket."

Over coffee and apple pie, plus some spirited flirtatious conversation with a voluptuous waitress, the two detectives decided to resume their search for Eloise Hicks and/or a Negro prostitute with a blond wig. However, before they could pull out of their parking space, the radio dispatcher ordered them to handle a shooting case involving a twenty-two-year-old gang member.

The emergency ward of the hospital was as chaotic as usual. Ernie and Roy waded through the crowd to the nurse behind a desk. Over the almost-deafening noise, Ernie asked, "Where's the guy shot?"

"In the arm."

"That's all?"

"Yeah," the nurse replied, frowning. "Sorry, fellas."

The young man in a torn and blood-stained white shirt was standing proudly in one of the adjacent rooms while a nurse wrapped a bandage around his arm.

"How're you doing, man?" Ernie asked. "I thought we was gonna have us a fresh homicide."

"The bullet's still in my arm," the young man said. "But I'm all right. I been shot in the chest before."

"With all that lead in you, you'll be putting on a lot of weight, man."

"When I find the dude that shot me, I'm gonna kill him. And you can come with me, if you likes."

"You ain't gonna press charges?" Ernie asked.

"Yeah, sure—*after* I kill him. Then you can press all the charges against him that you want."

The doctor came in and gave him a shot. "You go home tonight," he said. "We'll take the bullet out in the morning." Then a nurse entered with a bill for ten dollars, but the young man merely shrugged.

"I'll send it to your home," the nurse said.

"You do that. But ain't nobody at home I know who got ten dollars to give you."

"Who shot you in the chest? Was it a Disciple?" Ernie asked him, referring to another gang.

"Nah, ain't no D shot me. My old-lady cousin did it." Laughing, the young man added, "Ain't that some way to treat a relative?"

"Come on," Ernie said, "we'll take you home."

The young man put on his black beret and accompanied the detectives to their car. He sat in the back seat with me. As they drove into the heart of the South Side ghetto, Ernie turned his head slightly and asked, "You been arrested before?"

"I been picked up on manslaughter and . . . let's see . . . and robbery. But they never hung anything on me."

"You better be careful, man. We got enough homicides on our hands as it is."

"I'm gonna kill that jive dude and then you'll have a hell of a case on your hands."

"I'll get you, too," Ernie replied.

"You'll need a witness, man. The po-leece have picked me up on suspicion before for a little killing. They smacked me around for nothing, too. For *nothing.* One time I was *innocent* and I tried to explain, but the cop says, 'Shut your ass.' The cops stop you for nothing."

"You talking about white cops?"

"No, man, *any* cops."

The detectives let the boy out of the car in front of his house, a dark-brown, wooden building that looked as if it had caved in on one side. The house was set back about twenty yards from the street. Perhaps it had once been a fine home, but now it housed four families, each with several children. The boy walked into the darkness of his cluttered front lawn and began displaying his wound to the youngsters who crowded about him. "He's twenty-two," Ernie said to me, "but he runs with fourteen-year-old kids. Mentally, he's the same age as them, and they look up to him."

The detectives' night might have ended here, but they were summoned by the radio dispatcher again, this time to a district police station to investigate an indecent-liberties case. In a cubicle at the station, a white man sat with a four-year-old girl on his lap. Sitting next to him was another small girl, and standing in the corner, shaking, was a white woman still dressed in her waitress uniform. The couple told Ernie and Roy that the two girls had been put to bed in a motel room on the Near South Side. Both adults had gone out, she to work and he to a tavern. Meanwhile, the desk clerk went to the room, placed a bureau against the door, and proceeded to undress and climb into bed with the two girls. When the woman returned, finding the door blocked, she pushed it open and saw the desk clerk.

"He jumped up from the bed," she said, smoking and looking up at the ceiling, "and I grabbed a champagne bottle. I cracked him over the head. I would have killed him if they hadn't held me down."

Two white patrolmen had arrived on the scene and were able to take control. At the moment, they were with the desk clerk at the hospital, where he was having his head wound stitched.

Approaching the interrogation with as much delicacy, compassion, and tenderness at his command, Ernie said to the four-year-old girl, "Listen, honey, I'm a police officer. I just want the truth . . ." The questioning proceeded slowly, almost painfully, as the little girl responded to Ernie's voice: "Did he touch you here? . . . No? Where did he touch you? . . . How many times?"

In the corridor outside, a seven-year-old Negro girl, wearing pigtails, white blouse, blue shorts, and red knee socks, sat on a chair with wheels underneath it. She held a plastic bag of colorful toys, among them a cluster of lolipops and a music box that periodically went on. A huge patrolman with a belly that protruded over his belt was giving the girl a ride up and down the corridor on the chair. His pink face sweating, the cop said to Roy, "Look at her. We found her wandering around at eleven at night. She's mentally all right, but she never learned to speak. She just grunts like an animal."

The big cop suddenly bent down and shouted at the girl, "How old are you?" The girl's eyes brightened, she smiled, and her head bobbed up and down. "How old? One?" The girl shook her head affirmatively. "Two?" She nodded again. "Three? . . . Four? . . ." The big cop, suddenly immersed in his game, counted all the way up to fifteen, the girl nodding more vigorously each time; and the cop burst into laughter—

"Cut it out!" Roy yelled at him.

"She's enjoying it," the big cop replied after a moment, but Roy's eyes, reflecting his fury, stayed fixed upon the patrolman. The little Negro girl continued to suck on a lolipop, watching the confrontation of the black detective and white patrolman with wonderment.

Then two young white patrolmen brought in the desk clerk, who had had twelve stitches on his forehead. Ernie, having finished his interrogation, emerged from the cubicle and led the desk clerk into another one. Roy followed and sat before a typewriter to record the man's story and vital statistics.

"Are you a lawyer?" the man asked Ernie.

"No, man, I'm on the other side."

The pale, nervous desk clerk, whose yellow shirt was caked with dried blood, raised his eyebrows almost to the bottom edge of the bandage around his head.

"There's the molester," came the voice of a young patrolman. Standing in the doorway next to him were two other white officers with derisive stares on their faces.

"The white cops," Ernie said softly to the suspect, "they hate you more than a colored person."

"I didn't molest anybody. Could I have a cigarette?"

"Any of you guys have a cigarette?" Ernie asked the three patrolmen.

"Ah, he don't get shit," one of the cops yelled, lighting a cigarette for himself.

"I didn't do nothing," the man said to Ernie.

"That woman shoulda cut your throat," the young cop shot back.

"Cool it, will ya?" Ernie asked calmly. Muttering, the cops wandered down the hall. "Now listen, man, you're being charged with indecent liberties."

"Indecent what?"

"Those people from the motel—the woman—said you was in there naked with the two little girls . . ."

"I had my clothes on."

"Well, you gonna need to prove that to a judge, man."

The desk clerk was allowed to call his minister, but during the phone conversation he began to cry. Ernie took the receiver and informed the minister of a court hearing the next morning. Then, setting the phone down, Ernie said, "Come on, man, pull yourself together." The desk clerk, a picture of utter hopelessness, tried to stand up. Helping him to his feet, Ernie observed, "Your nose looks broken."

"I don't know. People have told me it's busted, but I don't know if it was . . ."

"Hunh?"

Roy continued his typing of various forms as Ernie turned the man over to a patrolman. The desk clerk was led away to a jail cell while the couple, with their two girls, stood in the corridor watching.

"Thank you," the woman said to Ernie. "Should I be at court, or . . .?"

Ernie discussed the matter with them, noting that it would be helpful to them to appear at the hearing, "just so the judge knows you're concerned, because if he don't see that concern, he could dismiss the whole case or something."

As Roy joined them, the woman said, "Well, I'm concerned. By God, I'm concerned. If I'd had a gun I would have shot him."

"But Mommy," the four-year-old girl chimed in, startling the group, "you had a gun in your dress pocket!"

Ernie smiled and said to Roy and me in a low, melodic tone, "Out of the mouths of babes."

"Man," said Ernie, "those offenders are in a category all by themself. I felt I could get more out of him with a gentle approach, 'cause I think he was aware, keenly aware, of how repulsive he was." The detectives sat in the front seat of the car, turning occasionally to address me in the back.

"What got to me," Roy recalled, "was interviewing that little girl."

"Well, it's a very delicate thing. Those child-sex cases, that's the only thing where sometimes I use a policewoman."

"What really burns me up, though, is when a judge in court lets a defense lawyer bear down on a kid; and it doesn't take much to shake a kid's testimony."

Ernie replied, "That's because kids are very good observers, but poor interpreters of what they see. They see things we miss, but they fall down later, on interpretation; and lawyers take advantage of that."

"To me," Roy pondered aloud for my sake, "a sex investigation is hard, frustrating; and it takes sometimes years before the offender is run down, like a rapist. It burns the time up. A lot of cops don't like 'em at all. So maybe the broad *was* drunk when the guy had her, but that doesn't mean she wasn't raped. She could be *stupid,* to put herself in a position to be attacked, but *still* she could have been taken against her will."

"Those young patrolmen, the white ones, get all uptight about a sex offender," Ernie said, "but they have a cynical attitude when some colored woman gets raped. They get that attitude from the older patrolmen. Most guys, white or black, when they come on this job, I think, want to do a good job, and they come on and they look up to some of these older guys; but I don't care how strong a man you are, to a certain extent you blow the way the wind blows. And these older patrolmen'll say, 'Ah, these bunch of niggers, they're a pack of animals, so don't get yourself involved, because the more work you do the more trouble you get into.' That's no way to learn your job effectively. So, pretty soon these young guys lose their patience. They see that ignorant colored woman who's been raped—she comes into the station and she can't even express herself. The young white cop, on his part, can't understand her. He sees that maybe she *has* no husband and two or three kids, and many, many cops will say, 'Ah, this bitch is nothing but a whore, anyway. Some trick probably didn't pay her.' And the poor woman stands there and these cops who she's come to for help, they're being rude . . . and she's bewildered. All she knows is that she hasn't got no police service."

"It burns me up," Roy said to me.

"Well, that's why I try to make it a point to let ghetto folks know that we're just as concerned about them as we are about anybody else that gets victimized. I try to sit down and *tell* them this—that the only reason I didn't get there sooner was because I had a lot of other work. I give 'em a card and tell 'em, 'Any time of the day or night if you got a problem, or if you got some information about the guy that bothered you, call me up.' Even if I'm not able to catch the person, they seem to get some satisfaction that they got this kind of treatment."

"A lot of times you can change a person's entire outlook on the police," Roy said.

"It's another source of information, too," Ernie added, glancing at me. "See, I have selfish motives as well. I appreciate the fact that I *can* change a person's outlook, but I'm also thinking about gaining a source of information. It can save weeks of work."

"I hope we can get somewhere on the James case," Roy said, adding, "I'm off tomorrow, so don't catch the offender till I come back."

"Heh, heh."

"I always need to get away from all this," Roy continued.

"I can't sleep at night. I keep going over a case until five in the morning. Dealing with the kind of poverty both of us grew up in, I feel entirely out of touch with the reality that I want for myself, that I worked to get *out of*. It weighs heavy on my mind. I need to relax, to come down off that tense plateau, so to speak."

"I can sleep standing on my head," Ernie injected.

"Mainly I have to avoid bringing problems into my home, to my wife," Roy explained.

Both detectives had been married twice. "Neither of my marriages worked out," Ernie said. "The first one didn't last no time. We were both eighteen. Chaos! Stayed married long enough to make a child. My daughter from the experience is eighteen already, and she had a baby last December. That makes me a grandfather at age thirty-nine. My second marriage lasted seven years. See, home life is the difficult bag for a cop, maybe more so for a dick. For any cop that works hard and gets involved. At home, you got to constantly keep thinking of, 'Why am I acting this way?' You find yourself getting ornery and mean.

"My second wife got fed up with the hours I kept. I'd be messing around with one of these cases and forget about coming home. She got mad one night and attacked me, so I *knew* it was time to go then. Now I go home and put on Tchaikovsky's Fifth, which is always the same, you know? It can't talk back, always pleasant. Or I go to a movie and forget about everything. I doubt that I'll ever try marriage again."

"But in general," Roy broke in, "it's the futility of whatever effort we're making out here as detectives. I mean, where are we going? Things are getting worse, not better. I use my home as an island. I *want* to get involved, but as a detective I really can't help to solve people's problems. Over the last ten years, it's gotten worse in the ghetto. What will happen ten years from now?"

"You need a morbid sense of humor," Ernie said, "for self-defense."

"Sometimes I think of the ghetto as a large mountain of sand, and I'm down there at the bottom with a little shovel. And I look up, and it ain't moving."

"To me," Ernie offered, "it's a real pleasure that people and other cops know that when we're on a case, it'll be solved. They say, 'Look at the dicks—somebody must be in trouble. Well, they'll get him.' I enjoy that."

"But Ernie, does anybody really care about whether we catch the guy who killed Rudolph James? For all we know, James himself should have been in prison."

"Look, I know it's not an exceptional case. But to me, it's like shooting pool: I want to win the game."

Before work the next day, Ernie showed up at Herman's fruit stand under the el with the photograph of Eloise Hicks. Herman shook his head and thus dried up that lead in a few seconds. However, he said he had seen the woman earlier in the day, walking a little black dog.

"What was she wearing?"

"Pink shorts, black blouse. She walked right by here."

"And you're sure she's not the girl in this photograph?"

"Nah, that's not the same trim."

Then Ernie crossed the street and stopped in to visit with the pawnbroker, who seemed excited to see him.

"The man you're looking for," he said with an expression of pride, "is nicknamed Slim."

"You know his real name?"

"No, but I know he's a junk man and that his lady is a whore and an addict. They work together."

"You know her name?" Ernie asked, but the pawnbroker shook his head.

By the time Ernie reported for work he had the name of his prime suspect: Perry Miles. By checking the department's "nickname file" under "Slim" he had found Miles' name and three-page record, plus a photograph. Perry Miles, a thin, craggy-featured Negro, had been in and out of jail continuously for much of his life. "He's beat out the courts lots of times," said Ernie, showing the photograph to John Brice, his other partner.

"That's a strong, brutal face," John noted with a playful touch of melodrama.

"At the moment he's out on bail for armed robbery. He was indicted a few months ago."

For John's sake, Ernie outlined the Rudolph James case, from the original report of his death to the interview with his brother, Wilton; from the Acco Hotel to the interviews with the desk clerk, Robert Dagger, the woman down the hall, and Leroy Williams; and from the fruit-stand owner under the el to the pawnbroker. Ernie reported that after obtaining the photograph of Perry Miles, he had returned to the fruit stand, where Herman, after studying the picture, confirmed that it was in fact Perry Miles who had been fighting under the el.

"Has anybody confirmed the *victim's* identity?" John asked.

"No, but the description they give of the victim is the same as a description of Rudolph James—tall, light-complected."

"Listen," said John, "I think we had this guy Slim in the car once, for something minor, for questioning or something. I know his name was Miles, because I remember that his wife was named Carolyn Miles. She's probably the broad you want."

"Now how the hell do you remember that?"

"I don't know," John replied, laughing. "It wouldn't hurt to check the file for Carolyn Miles, though."

"You'd better be right, Brice. That damn memory bank of yours had better be functioning."

At Ernie's tough-sounding words, John shook with laughter, replying, "Come on, Ernie, don't hold it against me if I'm wrong."

The detectives drove first to headquarters on State Street for Carolyn Miles' records. On the way, Ernie confided to me, "When the time comes, I want to get Leroy Williams to be a witness. He don't know that now, but when the time comes we'll have to convince him that it's safe. That it's his duty and so forth. Naturally, he won't want to."

Of several arrest files under the name of Carolyn Miles, Ernie chose one that appeared appropriate. The full record sheet revealed that this particular Carolyn Miles had been arrested twice with a man named Slim. Her list of arrests included narcotics possession and sale, prostitution, and loitering. The photograph, taken a few years earlier, showed an attractive Negro girl.

"Try to imagine her with a blond wig," Ernie said. "And walking a little black dog. By the way," he told John, "I'm hoping that she and Slim don't know yet that Rudolph James is dead. This way I can get him to talk about the fight and then drop the bomb on him."

Laughing, John said to me, "Yeah, Ernie'll tell this guy Slim, 'Hey, Rudolph James wants to sign a complaint against you.' And Slim'll fall into the trap, he hopes. You know, Ernie, you haven't changed that much."

"Well, listen, I play any game the other guy does. I'll lie to him the way he'll lie to me if he gets the chance. I hope they *don't* know about the murder, because they might leave Illinois. And I don't want the FBI to catch 'em—*I* want to pick 'em up. The stakes are high—very high. I'm playing the game for all it's worth."

"I hope we got a case on Slim," John said. "I mean, I hope this guy Leroy Williams will identify them, or even come to court. By the way, I was in court yesterday morning."

"I thought you were gonna paint the house yesterday."

"Yeah," John said, chuckling again. "But I had to show up on that case where the guy beat up the informant for a state narcotics officer. The informant was a girl, a junkie whore. She had picked out the guy's picture and everything and I even paid her carfare to court yesterday."

"What happened?" I asked.

"The whole case fell apart, that's what. Evidently the guy who beat her up gave her more money than I did, because when we got to court the judge said, 'Well, young lady, what happened?' She says, 'I dunno.' The judge says, 'What did this man do to you?' She yells, 'He didn't do nothing to me.' So the judge turns to me and screams, 'Well, why did you arrest this man?' I said, 'Judge, hold on. She picked his picture out!' The judge looked at her and says, 'Did you pick his picture out for this detective?' She says, 'I don't remember.' I almost crawled under the bench. I said, 'God, judge, she's lying!' The whole case was thrown out on the spot."

Ernie whistled in sympathy.

After a huge dinner of "soul food," half-chicken and bowls of "greens," John took the wheel and drove toward the scene of the fight where Rudolph James apparently had been beaten fatally. After one block, however, John found himself trapped behind a double-parked car.

"You like to pull in behind stopped cars, don't you?" Ernie complained. "You've got a fetish for that, you know?"

"I always say," John said, guffawing, "that if my driving displeases you, I will be only too happy to relinquish the wheel."

"For God's sake," Ernie continued, "we're over on one side of the road, going smoothly, and there's a car stopped way up ahead on the other side of the street; and you'll weave all the way over and pull behind the stopped car like it was a magnet. I don't know why you do that, John."

John squealed with glee as he pulled out and began weaving the car from lane to lane. Then on a serious note he said, "You remember the kid who killed the optometrist and then escaped from the sheriff's office?"

"Uh-hunh."

"Well, the sheriff's office called me and said they got a tip that some kids are holding a party for him tonight, down here near where we are. They gave me the address, so we might check it out around nine o'clock tonight."

"Sounds like bullshit," said Ernie. He explained to me,

"I know damn well that if they had some information that they thought was good, they'd go out here and grab him themselves. I mean, that's a hell of a thing, when a prisoner escapes from the sheriff's police. It's a hell of an affront, so it's *very* incumbent that they be the same ones who apprehend the guy. Why the hell then would they give good leads to us? They wouldn't throw out no goodies unless they don't think too much of the information themselves. We'll turn some ground on it, but the whole idea of someone holding a party for an escaped prisoner doesn't make sense. He *knows* he's wanted for murder, and he knows he escaped from jail, so I don't think he'd attend any party in his honor."

"Well, I agree with you," John said, again trapped behind a double-parked car. "Not to put down the sheriff's office, but they usually don't try as hard as most police."

"Stay in the middle lane," Ernie snapped. "The sheriff's police *do* try hard in the case of an escapee. It's politics. A lot of those men have no professional attitude toward their job whatsoever, and their work shows it. But they *do* take it seriously when someone escapes from them."

"I would hope so," said John, chuckling.

"Look at that," Ernie said, directing my attention to a new supermarket constructed entirely of brick, without windows. "I guess that's a ghetto supermarket."

"The latest style, guaranteed to withstand riots," John added.

Once again the detectives' car pulled into a parking space along the busy commercial section of the ghetto, two blocks from the el. Armed with the photographs of Perry (Slim) Miles and his wife, Carolyn, they watched the passing faces as light-gray evening merged into darkness and neon. Two drunken men wavered outside the car on the sidewalk for a moment and one said to the other, "The police is here."

"Where?"

"Right dere." The two peered through the window at us, then wandered down the block.

A few minutes later, two little Negro boys holding hands

passed by the car. "Hey," said Ernie, and they stopped. Their clothes were filthy and their faces were covered with dirt. The boys, no more than five years old, stared at Ernie for a moment. Then he said, "What are you doing here this late at night?"

"Walking."

"How far away you live, little boy?"

"Up there—" The boy gave his address, which was at least twenty blocks away.

"What are you doing all the way down here?" Ernie demanded.

"We took the el."

"You did?"

"Uh-hunh."

"Well, go home, now, hear? Go on, go home!"

The two little boys, looking as if they were startled by this sudden show of authority directed at them, merely stared back. "Go on," Ernie insisted. "You do as I say!" The boys looked at each other, then back at Ernie. Then they proceeded on their way, still holding hands.

"These streets are home to them," Ernie said, turning to me. "They're out here all the time, all hours of the day and night . . ."

Again the tedious surveillance continued. At one point the detectives saw a well-dressed white man cross the street.

"Man, he's out of place," Ernie said. "Wonder where he's going?"

"He might just disappear halfway down the block," John said, adding, "If he wanders around for any length of time he'll definitely get robbed or beat up."

"We'd better watch him." The two black detectives, unknown to the white man, watched until he wandered up the stairs to the el train and relative safety.

A few seconds later the car radio crackled and the dispatcher said, "A man holding a gun on a policeman . . ."

"I'd say he probably needs help," Ernie commented.

"Yeah," John chuckled, "I imagine he does." Again they

explained to me that detectives only respond if they see something first-hand, or if they are called.

A group of black men came toward the car, glared at Ernie and moved away as he nodded to them. Later, three teen-age boys passed the car, a blanket lying like a sack across their arms.

"Looks like they're carrying a body," Ernie said casually.

"Sho' does," John observed.

"Hey there!" Ernie called. "What's that you got in that blanket?"

"Hunh?"

"What's that y'all got in that blanket, wrapped up there?"

"A man."

Becoming interested, Ernie commanded, "Fold that back there and let me look at it."

"Hunh?"

"Pull it back!"

The Negro boys, looking guilty of something, slowly drew back the blanket. Suddenly another boy jumped out amid a shriek of laughter and they ran away.

Smirking, Ernie said, "Damn, they had me fooled almost."

"When they start carrying bodies through the street," John said in his usual bubbly fashion, "then we got to start worrying."

Incidents on this street seemed to unfold relentlessly before us. Suddenly a man appeared, smiling broadly. "Hey, mister man," he said, "how's every little thing, man? How y'all?"

"Well, if it ain't Sweet Pete," said Ernie, greeting the lively black man. "You remember Pete, don't you John?"

"Oh, yeah. Hi, Pete."

"I been home 'bout seven months now," said Pete. Ernie later told me Pete was thirty-nine years old but looked at least a decade older.

"How much were you in the joint for?" asked Ernie.

"Six years."

"Goddamn! For what? Armed robbery?"

"No, *burglary,* man! You know me better'n that."

"Well . . . Let's see," Ernie said, thinking aloud. "You got a year for a *robbery* we got you on, a long time ago."

"That's right. I did nine months on that."

"You must have gone right back in for the burglary!"

"That's right. I did. I did do that."

"Me and Pete," said John, "we used to live in the same building. Right, Pete?"

"That's right," said Pete, looking at me through a rear window.

"What'choo up to now, Brother Pete?" Ernie asked.

"No more hanky-pank, I'll tell you that. I's tired. I just want my drink, a little woman, and some peace. I'm ready to die."

Eventually Ernie felt compelled to send Pete away from the car, so the detectives could resume surveillance with both eyes. "You wouldn't wanna buy me a drink, would ya?" asked Pete.

"Sure," Ernie said, reaching in his pocket and pulling out a dollar. "Any time for an old friend." With that, Pete crossed the street and went into a tavern.

"Wasn't he some kind of bully at school?" John said.

"Yeah, he sure was. He used to bully me as a kid, but I finally beat him up, and that ended the bullying."

"He used to be a drug addict, too, didn't he?"

"I think so," Ernie replied. "He was an old-school addict, so to speak. He was one of the guys who became addicts in the late '40s or early '50s. Most of those guys are just like he is now, if they ain't in prison or dead. Like he said: 'I'm tired.' He ain't vicious no more. He's been in and out of the big place so often . . . And that's not including shorter stays in the county jail."

"And he's only our age," John said. "You know, Ernie, he has one of the cutest sisters you'd ever want to see. And Sweet Pete, he looks like somebody sat on him."

"How do you know about a cute sister?"

Smiling broadly, John said, "His family lived in the same building as mine. I had one of my first experiences, so to speak, with his sister." With that, John broke into unrestrained laughter.

"Cool down, John," Ernie said lightly. "We're supposed to be grabbing up a murderer."

"Can you imagine," John continued, still holding his sides from his own laughter, "that I was fourteen before I was seduced? I was considered really *behind*. Oh my God, kids teased me in school all the time. I was the laughing stock of the whole school . . . Until Sweet Pete's sister got ahold of me!"

"These little girls in the slum," Ernie said to me, "about eleven or twelve years old, they know more about sex than we do, almost. It's not a rare thing for some of 'em to have babies at that age, in the ghetto."

"Sure," said John. "I see plenty grandmothers in their twenties. They got pregnant at twelve or thirteen, lived on ADC, and they're grandmothers at twenty-six, because *their* daughter got pregnant at age twelve or thirteen."

At this point, a young black man raced past the detectives' unmarked car and dashed into an alley. "What's that?" Ernie yelled, but there seemed to be no one chasing the young man.

"Just a cat running," John offered.

"When I see a guy running, I like to find out what I'd be chasing after him for, *first*. I could shoot him in the back and wind up in hot water."

"Mayor Daley'll back you up," John said, smiling.

"Yeah. Heh, heh, heh. But he'd have a bit of trouble down here. The people here don't need to be told that they can be shot. They know that already. In fact, most of the people in the ghetto think the police will shoot them with *very* little provocation. But it don't stop 'em from committing crime, at least it doesn't *appear* to stop 'em, not to me."

Radio: "Three people shot . . ."

"A lot of people getting shot by *each other* tonight," John observed.

"I shot a guy once," Ernie told me. "I didn't *kill* him, but it was a justified shooting. I see the guy now and he says, 'Hello, officer, how are you?' I don't know how bitter he is about it. Even though he realizes that he was wrong at the time, there's a certain amount of resentment inasmuch as he got shot. Of course, he was trying to shoot *me,* too. I always believe in being fair, in not manhandling people or being abusive; but on the other hand I won't tolerate any abuse from the person I'm dealing with, either. If he becomes the aggressor, then naturally I have to become more aggressive than him, in order to control the situation. But I believe in fairness, in being just. And I *feel good* by doing things this way . . ."

"On this job," John said, "I think it's pretty easy for a man with the best of intentions to shoot someone and then find out later that it should have been handled differently. Guys who like to talk about shooting and hitting people, these are the cops who are most likely to use excessive force when it really isn't necessary."

Suddenly Ernie switched on his spotlight, aiming it through the car window and across the street, where a man stood in the door of a laundromat, a wine bottle in his hand. "Come on over here!" Ernie shouted. Then, to John he said, "He was gonna crack that bottle over another guy's head. Now he's coming over to prove his point." When the stooped-over Negro man reached the car, Ernie yelled, "What'choo gettin' ready to hit him with that bottle for?"

"He was gonna hit *me* with a bottle! So that's why I went and found *me* a bottle."

"You found one all right, man."

The half-drunk man squealed almost hysterically at Ernie's reply, his whole body shaking with laughter. Then he slipped and fell on the sidewalk.

"Get up, man," said Ernie. "I think you better go home."

"Maybe you're right," he replied, getting up.

"I just want to keep you out of trouble, understand?"

"I ain't *in* no trouble," he protested, and started back to the laundromat.

"Come back here!" Ernie demanded.

"Hullo."

"Now, look—don't go back in there, hear?"

"Listen, you got a cigarette?"

"We don't smoke," Ernie said.

"Well, I'm tapped out. You got a quarter?" John gave him a dollar bill. "Thanks, brother. Say, you wouldn't have a little ride home for me . . . ?"

"Hey," said Ernie, "I don't want to *marry* you. I'm just trying to keep you from going to jail. So don't go back in there and mess with that man."

"I'm just trying to keep living, and that's all."

"Fine."

The man slapped his leg, laughing again, and John joined him with his own falsetto giggles.

"Hey, it's about ten o'clock," Ernie said. "Let's check out that party for the kid. If the tip was true, I'd like to see the faces on the sheriff's men when we bring the guy in."

John pulled the car out and turned down a residential street in the darkness. The alleged party was to take place in a large wooden house on the corner of two narrow streets in the South Side. The detectives rode past the building, but there were no lights on. They paused a moment to listen, but no sounds of a gathering could be heard. Suddenly, like an apparition, a Negro prostitute, walking a little black dog, emerged beneath the purple-tinged light of the street lamp. "Creep up next to her," Ernie whispered. "Hi, baby . . ."

"Hi . . ."

"That your little black dog?"

"Mmmm. Mmmm."

"Well, listen, tie him off there to the tree and come into the car a minute. We just wanna talk to you a little bit."

The woman, wearing blue shorts and a white sweater, obeyed, climbing wearily into the back seat next to me. In one arm she clutched a brown paper bag with three wine bottles inside. Her manner was slow and sleepy, and she slurred her words almost without coherence.

"Who was your old man fighting with a few days ago, under the el?"

"Fighting . . . ?"

"Yeah. Just a little scuffle we're checking on."

"Well, we was comin' up the street under the el and they threw a bottle at us. But we didn't pay much mind . . ."

During this conversation, John took out the photograph of Carolyn Miles and quietly checked it with this woman's face. It was not the same person.

"Was it a tall, light dude your man was fighting with?"

"No, the dude was dark and little."

Ernie gradually slipped into the low, lazy tone of the woman, and for a while the detective and the prostitute seemed to be speaking in word-symbols with sexual overtones. "Was you out here today?"

"No, I ain't been out all day."

"What's your phone number, baby?" She told him. "Now, I ain't interested in no vice or nothing like that, you hear, baby? But I don't like people who misuse me, understand?"

"Nat'ch'lly. I know what'cha mean."

"Have we met before?" Ernie asked.

"I seen you in a motel once. I was a clerk."

"Heh, heh, heh. What was I doing?"

"You know better'n me 'bout that," the prostitute answered.

"I brought in a girl, right?"

"You did do that, honey," she said, smiling.

"Well, I guess you're not the one I'm looking for. But you sho' look like her."

"I dunno . . ."

"But I'll find her."

"Heh, heh, heh. You will do that, I'm sure."

Radio: "Car 7144 . . ."

John took the microphone, as the prostitute left the car, and answered the radio dispatcher. The detectives were told to go to a district police station.

"Damn," said Ernie. "Looks like this Slim and his woman are evading us."

"If the gal we're looking for has a little black dog, that was quite a coincidence."

At the district station, two Negro men were being held by patrolmen after they had fought over a woman and then over a gun, which one of the men referred to at different times as "my piece," "my thing," "my roscoe," "my jive," "my cannon," "my shit," "my pipe," and "my heater." Both men were bloody from the fight, which had involved a meat cleaver. "I wasn't afraid to go after him," one man explained, "because I had my shit on me. But he picked up the cleaver and I got my head fat. He took my piece, and if I get it back I won't press charges."

"Why not?" Ernie asked.

" 'Cause we're friends, man," he replied as the other man nodded his head in agreement.

Then the woman involved rushed into the police station, complicating the already indecipherable discussion.

"Is this your husband?" asked Ernie.

"No, he's my man."

"Sorry—I assumed it."

"Well, never assume anything. I was married to my husband for twenty years, got two grown daughters."

"Your husband dead?"

"No, he living at a hotel."

"You live with him there?"

"No, I'm living with this man here."

"Oh, you and your husband are separated."

"That's none of your business. I didn't ask you if you're living with *your* wife or not."

Caught, Ernie grinned. "Heh, heh, heh."

"Heh, heh, heh, shit!"

Later, over coffee, Ernie and John decided to return to the el for one last surveillance of the evening. The confusion at the police station had been straightened out after one of the men promised to return the gun. "They'd never go to court anyway," Ernie explained. "Too much bother. That's a big project, plus it's like *telling* on somebody. After all, they're friends."

"Yeah," John chuckled, "some friends. They'll be back in the alley again tomorrow night, arguing about something else. They're in a twilight of reality, those people. They're high on wine most of the time. Guys like that work at odd jobs, or pick up garbage, or sometimes they're on relief, or disability . . . Just getting along."

"The guy who did the cutting this time," Ernie joined in, "next time he'll be the one getting hurt. This'll go back and forth until one of them is finally killed."

"Same with husband-wife situations. She cuts him one week, he cuts her the next time. Then she knocks him in the head with an iron or something. It goes back and forth until finally one of 'em kills the other."

"I think that sometimes in the ghetto," Ernie said, addressing me, "that the closeness the people are living in— I mean, the frustrations and the suffering—many times are given vent to by all this fighting. Many times the situation is not enough to constitute a real fight, but the guy explodes immediately and beats the woman—not because of what she had done, but because of *his* entire situation."

"Sure," said John, "they get some release in fights."

"In fact," Ernie went on, "you see these guys come out to the tavern and fight, get drunk and all that, well, a lot of times they're just letting off steam, trying to get some relief from home. He might have seven or eight kids there and the best job he can get pays sixty-five, seventy dollars a week. His home is vermin-infested, he don't have hope of anything better. So, even though he's illiterate and slow-witted, he still can have a psychological problem, a mental hang-up. I've read or heard where people that are ignorant usually don't have problems of the modern-day world, like smart people do. That's probably true, but sometimes you don't have to be so smart to get frustrated, especially when you got the oppressive thing on you, no hope . . . Despair takes over, and hell, you see a guy out here, drunk, fighting, and a cop says, 'Look at that asshole.' He probably *is* an asshole, but he's gotta be motivated by *something*. Of course, as a policeman you don't have time to get into all that psychology bag. You gotta hurry up and get this guy under control, get him off the street or whatever you're gonna do with him, and go on to something else. I wish I had time to stop and go into each individual case. I'd say, 'Hey, listen, what's your problem at home? How many kids you got? Are you working? Got a job? How are you and your wife getting along?' I'd ask all that kind of thing. But hell, you wouldn't have no time to do no work if you did that."

"If I didn't like this work," John said, "I'd be on the verge of despair all the time. I'd be a very bitter individual."

"I'll say one thing," Ernie said. "I never met a cop who laughs as much as John does."

"I had an adventurous streak in me," John observed. "I was itching for something exciting. But I never liked to hurt anyone."

"Same here," Ernie said. "I was a fireman for about a year. Boring as hell. I always had this thing in the back of my mind that I wanted to be a cop. It was about the most exciting thing I figured I could get into, on the *right* side of the fence. I drove a bus about five years, just kept going from one job to another until I was about twenty-six years old. That was 1956. I was a motorcycle cop for a while, which was unusual for a colored fellow at the time. The cycle beat was kind of a closed shop, then. The integration bag is pretty new for the Chicago force, in many respects."

"C'mon," said John. "Let's see if we can find Slim and Carolyn."

I asked, "How long do you think it'll take to find them?"

"Look," Ernie said, "we could go back to the station now, type out some forms, and call it a night. But I believe in taking what I call the 'bold step.' In other words, doing just a little bit more than the other guy. And this, to me, will make you a little bit better than that other guy. Most cops don't want to take the bold step. They don't want to spend the time, or put out that money. To be a good dick you can't just spend eight hours."

John said, "What I don't like is the risks. I'm not saying I want praise or anything, but there are inequities . . . I look at another guy who makes the same salary for doing much less work, and I see other dicks who don't want to do better even if they could. I've seen those kind of guys ruin a young detective. They say, 'Ah, take it easy, don't get so wrapped up . . .' And the young guy gets dumped for being inefficient. He's back in uniform and then he doesn't know who to believe."

"And the slackers get the same pay," Ernie echoed. "And these jerks'll invariably be jealous."

Laughing, John said, "I've had a slacker stop speaking to me, more than once, just because we came behind him and solved a case he didn't extend himself on."

"It doesn't bother me," Ernie said, smiling. "I don't give a damn. In fact, I get a kick out of it."

So Ernie and John drove back to the el. It was now past midnight, but the intensity of activity was undiminished. One group of men stood nearby talking loud enough so that the cops could hear them. "How high did you get?" was one phrase that seemed to float through the dark night to the car. "That's nothing-talk," Ernie murmured to me. "Another cry for recognition . . . or just a little improvisation for our benefit. They're all probably doing something illegal, and they think we're watching 'em . . ."

For a half-hour the detectives remained silent, watching everything. At the wheel, Ernie started the car and pulled away. Just then, without fanfare or warning, Perry Miles' face appeared among the shadows. A brief flicker of green light caught the outline of his chin, then his high forehead. John saw him first and calmly whispered, "That's him."

Leaving the car idling in the middle of the street, the two detectives instantly had their guns out and approached Miles from two sides. I stayed in the car and watched. The arrest took place without generating excitement, possibly without the knowledge of anyone else on the street. Slim Miles was ushered to the side of the car. He offered no resistance. His face, far from the "strong, brutal" look of the photograph, seemed at close range to be the visage of a weary, gentle man. The detectives felt their hands rapidly over his body; no weapons were found. Quickly the handcuffs were snapped over his wrists. "Drop your cigarette, man," said Ernie, and Slim opened his lips, allowing the butt to fall to the street. Then he was pushed firmly into the back seat of the car beside me.

For a full minute the detectives drove without speaking. Slim sat still, a bewildered look on his face. Creeping slowly down the street, looking at the crowds, the detectives ignored their prisoner. Then, as they had expected, Carolyn Miles strolled by in a group of people. Ernie leaped from the car, grabbed her arm, and pulled her into the front seat next to John. Carolyn, who was not wearing her blond wig, was drowsy from a recent dose of heroin. Ernie pressed down the gas pedal and we sped away silently through Chicago's crumbling ghetto streets.

It was well past 1 A.M. when Perry and Carolyn Miles were brought into the detectives' office. Slim was ushered into a small room that contained a desk and two chairs. Carolyn was unable to keep her still-pretty figure erect, and she shuffled through the hall dreamily. Then she was led into another room for questioning. She promptly slumped into a suspended position on the edge of a chair.

Ernie rolled up his sleeves and walked into the interrogation room where Slim, sitting in the corner in his rumpled suit, stared up in horror at the face of a 300-pound white detective.

"What's going on?" Ernie said. "Mullin, what are you doing?"

"Nuttin'," the huge detective answered, without taking his eyes from Ernie's cowering prisoner. "Not yet."

"Listen," Ernie said firmly, "get out of here, will you?"

"Let me handle this guy, Ernie. Give me a few minutes alone with him."

"What is this?" Slim cried, trying to find Ernie beyond the towering man in front of him.

"Mullin, this is my case."

"Okay, okay. But if he don't talk, just call me. I'll be next door." Mullin turned his back on Slim, winked at Ernie, and strode out of the room. Ernie shut the door.

"Listen," Ernie said to Slim in a low voice, sitting at the edge of the desk, "don't worry about him. He's a white cop. He ain't on your side, man, but I'll see what I can do for you. All I want is a little information about a fight. Okay?"

"I'll tell you anything, man," said Slim. "Just keep that man outa here."

"Don't pay any attention to him. He's white, so you know what he thinks about all our folks. Now, if there's anything I can do for you, I'll do it. I'll try to help you. But he'll jam you up, you know? He's an asshole from way back, believe me."

"Well, I don't know what you want from me."

"All I want to know is what caused the dude to hit you the other day."

"When was that?"

"Monday evening, under the el ..."

"Oh, yeah. I had to box a dude's jaws pretty bad. See, his wife told him that I had raped her. But I never did do that to her."

"Okay, I understand. Now, what was the guy's name that you was fighting with?"

"Joe Thompson."

"Joe Thompson?"

"Yeah. I've known him for years. I don't know how he could have believed his wife. She's always making up stories."

"What does Joe Thompson look like?"

"Tall, slender . . . light-complected. They call him Robin Hood."

"Now, listen, man, let's go over this once more . . ."

The interrogation continued quietly. Slim repeated his admission that he had been fighting under the el on Monday evening, but not with Rudolph James. However, his description of Joe Thompson was exactly that of James.

"This man you was fighting with," Ernie went on, "this Robin Hood guy . . . When you see him last?"

"I saw him 'bout three o'clock in the afternoon."

"That's about, uh, ten hours ago or so?"

"Yeah, I guess. Look, if she wants to press charges against me, I don't care. You can tell her that for me."

"Never mind," Ernie snapped. For at least a full minute he was silent. Then he asked, "Listen, Slim, was there anybody *else* fighting under the el that day, that you know of?"

"No, I don't think so. Not that I know about."

"Okay . . ." Again Ernie fell silent.

"When I saw Thompson," Slim offered, "he said he was convinced that I didn't go near his wife. We friends again."

"Okay, okay."

"Is he or she pressing a charge against me?"

"No, man, don't worry. Just stay here."

Ernie left him in the small room, shutting the door and walking to the water fountain. In the next room, John was typing while Carolyn Miles continued to hang over her chair, sleeping.

"She say anything?" Ernie asked.

"Nothing coherent. I asked her about the fight and she said something about Robin Hood."

"She did?"

"Yeah. Then she sank off. Look at her—dopey as hell."

"Well, listen. Slim has the same goddamn story. The possibility was dawning on me"—Ernie and John stepped into the hall—"that we been linking this fight up to Rudolph

James when maybe it wasn't even connected to his death. Slim is talking honestly and openly, by appearance. And I gave him a chance to clear himself completely by asking him whether he knew about any *other* fights that day. This could have taken him right off the hook, but he didn't even jump at the chance. He said he didn't know of any other fights."

"Oh, man," whispered John. "You think maybe Wilton James was right? That his brother was killed inside the hotel, after all? Maybe we should have been a little more suspicious of Dagger."

Annoyed with the turn of events, Ernie said, "The trouble is that nobody, none of our witnesses—not Leroy, not Herman, not the pawnbroker—has identified the victim. They've all given the same story, but their description of the victim also fits this guy Joe Thompson, or Robin Hood."

"Can we hold Slim tonight?"

"Damn right we can. But we'll let his old lady go."

"I feel like the whole thing's melting," John said.

Ernie said to me, "We can hold Slim until court the day after tomorrow, because I'm gonna bring charges against him. We'll have to mean business. Either we charge him or they'll release him. If Leroy or Herman—Leroy, preferably —can look at a photograph of Rudolph James and identify him as the victim, and Slim as the offender, we're in. If not, the slate'll be wiped clean. We'll be back at the Acco Hotel."

John said, "Well, let's go see Herman in the morning, with a photograph of Rudolph James."

Ernie opened the door to the tiny room where Slim was hunched over a corner of the desk. Looking up, he asked for a cigarette. The detective left the room and returned with a half-filled pack. Lighting one for Slim, he said, "You know, we picked you up as a suspect for murder."

"Murder!" Slim puffed deeply on his cigarette and shook his head. "Murder," he said softly. "I don't figure it, man."

"Well," Ernie said, "we got information that you was having a fight with a dude under the el on Monday evening, with a tall, light-complected dude. Now, you admit all of that, but you say the dude was Joe Thompson, or Robin Hood."

"That's right. That's *exactly* right."

"I figured you was fightin' with a tall, light-complected dude named Rudolph James."

"Rudolph James?"

"Yeah."

"No, I don't know the cat."

"Sure is a coincidence," Ernie muttered.

"Yeah—one *heck* of a coincidence."

Slim was taken to the city's main jail in a paddy wagon, and the detectives dropped off Carolyn Miles where they had picked her up. Like a fish returning to familiar elements, she seemed to wriggle into the darkness and disappear.

"You should have given Slim the third degree," said John, trying to make light of what appeared to have been a false arrest.

"Well," Ernie said, turning toward me, "that used to be pretty common, to beat out a confession. I used to see police kicking people's asses, trying to get 'em to say something. That goes back about ten years, though. I mean, if getting slapped in the mouth or knocked down . . . well, I saw that. But I've never seen this so-called thing where somebody's tortured by prolonged beating. I've never seen that. But now, even the slapping is out. The way I figure it, if you do your investigation right, you don't need to do it. Confessions are worthless now, anyway, with the court rulings. Mullin and I tried a little version of the race routine back there on Slim . . ."

"Do you think," John asked, "that Slim might have known about James' death and maybe arranged this whole story with Joe Thompson?"

"I don't know, but we better hustle to find out."

Ernie drove me back to my hotel in Chicago. "If you want to come with me tomorrow," he said, "figure about five hours sleep. This job is an irony to me in that respect, because it's given me an interest in college, you know? But how can you work your ass off and study the books at the same time? I'm making a little stab at it by going to school one night a week, but it's not really enough. There's a lot of technical stuff to read.

"Getting to sergeant is the hardest step. That management bag is the toughest bag to get into, but I'm not too broken-hearted about the slow pace, because I like what I'm doing now. I'd *like* to make the additional money, but I also like being able to do what I like to do, because I don't feel like I'm ever going to be rich. When I was a patrolman—and I'd hate to get bumped back into uniform because I studied too much—it was like living in hell if I didn't like what I was doing. You just dread going to work, and that's no way to live.

"See, that extra money I'd make by being a sergeant won't put me on some tremendously higher plateau. Socially, I don't mix with people that well. I just got a very small circle of friends. I think Roy and John are about the only close friends I have. I just don't take to people like, you know, I'm not an outgoing person, really, when you get down to it. I *can* be outgoing when I think it suits my fancy. If I *need* to do it I'll do it—politicking, you know what I mean?

"But normally, I'd just as soon sit home and listen to my records and do a little exercise, and read a magazine; and call up some broad when I feel like being bothered with her. And when I'm through with her, she can go back about her business and let me go back to my records. And I'm satisfied, and I can come to work and do what I want to do. Well, what the hell else is there? What does a rich guy do? He's got a bigger house and a fancier automobile, and more clothing to wear. But when you get down to it, it's the same damn thing.

"I think a man's outlook changes with the years, because when I was younger, all I could think about was being rich. I was money-mad. Now, I'm conscious of money—I want to pay my bills—but it's not an obsession with me like it was then. I always had some scheme I wanted to try, and every time I read about somebody that was rich, you know, and famous, I would start thinking. I would always think it took some kind of odd and unusual thing to make a big buck. You gotta come up with a gimmick, you know, and I would think of these gimmicks I could possibly come up with. I was thinking about a heater one time, an instant heater for automobiles, where like in the wintertime you get in your car and you ride fifteen minutes and freeze, you know? I said, 'Now, if I could only come up with something, I could make a whole lot of money.' And I'd be *serious* about this, but after a while, that all passed—because I thought it was just beyond my reach.

"Now, being a detective, I can't think of anything else I'd rather be doing. I feel like I'm accomplishing something, and a few times I have spoken briefly to law students at college. If somebody had told me, when I was a young gang-banging hoodlum in this ghetto, that I'd be talking to college students, I would have said they was absolutely crazy. First off, we would have had nothing in common, at that time. But now, this ghetto world is not just another world. It's getting closer to everybody . . ."

After the five hours of sleep Ernie had predicted, we drove that morning to the high-rise building to see Wilton James. Ernie obtained a group photograph that included his brother, Rudolph, and then we rode south to Herman's fruit stand. Thrusting the photograph beneath Herman's nose, he said, "Which is the dude that got hisself boxed?"

Herman studied the picture and pointed to Rudolph James. "It could have been this cat. I'm not saying it *was* him, not definitely, but it *could* have been. You get my distinction?"

"I do. Now tell me, Herman, was this dude that got his jaws boxed—this guy here in the picture—is his name Joe Thompson, or Robin Hood?"

"Nah. I know Robin Hood, all right."

"You do?"

"Sure."

"And you say it wasn't him?"

"That's right."

Meanwhile, both Roy and John were also out working on the case, which was headed for a preliminary hearing in felony court the next morning. Roy found Leroy Williams at the restaurant where he worked as a kitchen helper and presented him with a copy of Slim's photograph. Leroy identified him as the one who had done the bulk of the fighting. However, he was unable to recall anyone nicknamed Robin Hood. Ernie met John at the restaurant, showed Leroy the photograph of Rudolph James, and Williams answered, "It could have been him." At the same time, John checked the Records division for a file on Joe Thompson. Finding none that fit the description, he checked the "nickname file" under "Robin Hood," but again found no appropriate file. Later, Ernie went back to the scene under the el and saw the pawnbroker, who confirmed the photograph of Slim Miles and, like Herman, said the victim was definitely not Joe Thompson. The three detectives (and me) met over coffee at about three o'clock in the afternoon. They were satisfied that the case was under control.

"Looks like Slim was lying," Ernie said. Then he added, "All along I felt he was putting me on."

Laughing, John said, "Sure, Ernie, sure."

"Most people lie to us," Roy observed. "Especially a guy like Slim."

"Slim has been a stoolie before, according to the pawnbroker," said Ernie. "The pawnbroker knew that because he's in that life. I can get close, but not as close as he is."

"Now," Roy offered, "we ought to find Robin Hood."

John laughed and said, "That's a hell of an original nickname."

"If push comes to shove," Ernie said, "we'll have the

pawnbroker birddog for us. First, we'll go back to the street and look for Robin Hood on our own, or at least for some people who can finger him. I'm sure the pawnbroker could help us, though. The thing we don't know yet is whether Slim and Robin Hood made up their story together, or whether Slim just ad-libbed it when we picked him up."

"Carolyn had the same story," John said, "so they must have planned it in advance."

"Maybe *without* Robin Hood, though," Ernie added. "In which case, Robin Hood could knock the whole alibi out of the box. But if we catch *him* lying, he'll be an accessory after the fact. He don't know about Herman's testimony, so he might try to fool us."

"You know," I said, "Slim really had me fooled. He had such a straight face. He didn't look vicious at all, either."

"Listen," Ernie said, "Slim has been arrested sixty-five, seventy times, since 1950, so you can bet he learned something. He's a good actor and he's very skilled at fighting. He's been out here all these years, robbing and stealing; and he's working just as hard as us. And he has an advantage: he can throw the rules out the window. He's working hard, because homicide is the end of the line. When a guy has been dealing with police all his life—I mean, Slim started messing with cops when he was twelve, and now he's past forty—well, sometimes he knows more than we do; especially a guy who deals in narcotics. He knows what it takes to beat a case. I know what I have to do to get him, but so does he; and he can skillfully throw blocks in our way. To underestimate a guy like that is the worst thing."

"Maybe," said Roy, "we could find Carolyn and have her lead us to Robin Hood."

"She's real devoted to Slim, isn't she?" I asked.

"Sure. They're legally married, but he's a pimp for her. It's funny, you know? Her laying down with somebody is just a matter of business with him. It never enters his mind that she don't love him. She's not being unfaithful. She's being *very* faithful. She's faithfully giving out trim and bringing back the proceeds. So he says, 'I got me a good woman.' He loves his wife for screwing another man, yet many guys would kill their wives for the same act. What do you call that kind of thing, an irony?"

In the station that evening, Ernie typed out two pages of narrative for the Rudolph James case and marked it "In Custody." Slim Miles was charged with murder and would be held at least until the preliminary hearing the following morning, at which time a trial date and bail would be set. John remained in the office that night to fill out forms for ongoing cases ("status reports"), while Ernie and Roy began surveillance for Joe Thompson alias Robin Hood.

"You know," Ernie said to me when we were in the car, "it's a funny thing, but the people in the ghetto don't have that comradeship when it comes to a guy like Slim. He'll be off the street a couple of weeks and they'll just forget about him. It never dawns on anyone, when they see us, that 'There goes the cops who got him and sent him to the penitentiary.' I mean, they're thinking about their *own* bag. They're thinking, 'I'm glad it wasn't *me.*' "

"Yeah," said Roy, "but the people don't have any opinion about police. I mean, a lot of the opinion expressed about policemen is from folks who have a lot of dealings with them —criminals, lawbreakers. The other people don't seem to know us that well, or have an opinion, because they don't come in contact with us."

"If the average citizen had been taken down to the station, he'd want to know what it was for. He'd be indignant. But a guy like Slim is definitely not the average citizen. He's been arrested so many times that it's just *routine* for him to go to the station. It's just part of his everyday life. He don't even think about whether it's legal or illegal, especially if he's involved in something. He's expecting it's going to happen sooner or later anyway.

"And I think the people on this street have more *respect*

for dicks who try to catch criminals, rather than hate. I think they respect us, because in the first place we've been out here long enough, messing around with the people, so that those who know us know that we don't misuse people or bother them just for the hell of it. But they *also* know that if they do something wrong, and we get on them, they're in big trouble.

"And there are other policemen," Ernie went on, "that they have a different view about. Because some cops'll grab a guy almost for nothing, or slap somebody around . . . I try to make 'em think I'm a gentleman, but also a policeman. It's a fine line. Guys who do the slapping around get respect, but not the same *type* of respect. They just get a *fear*. People are afraid of them, but respect and fear, I think, are two different things. I know one thing: if a guy respected you, he'd talk to you a lot quicker than he would if he feared you. Because with fear comes hate."

The stakeout under the el for Robin Hood was interrupted by a fresh set of instructions from the radio dispatcher. Although the Rudolph James case was "solved," the hardest job ahead was to secure a conviction in the weeks to come. "Meanwhile," Ernie noted, "life goes on."

According to the radio dispatcher, a shooting had taken place in the "gangland" area of the South Side. It was not serious: just a sixteen-year-old boy shooting at a fifteen-year-old boy and missing. The detectives first visited the home of the youth who had been shot at, to see whether charges would be pressed against the older boy. Only the father was at home, with two small children trying to sleep on a mattress in the corner of his filthy living room. Would the father bring charges in his son's behalf? "Nah," said the man as he slumped in a chair in his underwear, his black skin sweating and his face a paradigm of the violent forces whose sounds periodically erupted outside his window. "I can't control it," the man said, pushing aside a spoon on the floor with his bare foot.

"Can't control what?" Ernie asked.

"All that—" He gestured to the window.

"But your son was shot at—with a gun."

"It missed, didn't it?"

"Yeah, but next time it may not."

"Look," said the father, sweeping his arm around in a gesture of annoyance, "if I press some charges or whatever, my son'll *really* be shot at, understand?"

Next, Ernie pulled up the car outside a gloomy, ill-lit row of Victorian mansions that, like the others in the South Side, had turned into slum fortresses for black people. We walked up some concrete steps to a wooden porch and knocked on a screen door. After several minutes we heard the latch opening behind the inside door, and then a frightened Negro woman appeared in the darkness through the screen. "Police officers," said Ernie. "We're looking for Albert Del Rio."

"Yes . . . That's my son."

"Is he in, ma'am?"

"No, he's not."

"Can we come in and talk to you?"

"Uh-hunh."

Albert Del Rio, the sixteen-year-old boy who allegedly did the shooting, was also a suspect in a murder case involving the shotgun slaying of a rival gang member.

"Do you know where Albert is, ma'am?" Ernie asked.

"No, he ain't been home in three weeks. I don't want him to come home, neither."

"Why is that, ma'am?"

"Because he brings trouble, too much trouble."

The woman sat on a couch next to the wall of the living room. Ernie sat near her and Roy and I continued to stand. On the other side of the room, which was lit only by the glow from a streetlight outside on the corner, was a twelve-year-old boy, sleeping on the floor. Beyond the far end of the living room, in what probably was intended as a dining area, several youngsters were trying to sleep on a double bed. Some of them were awake and periodically a curious face appeared over the footboard, followed by giggling and whispering. Mrs. Del Rio, in a bathrobe and hairnet, reached down and grasped her ankles. In that position, she began to cry.

"Ma'am . . . Hey, baby . . ." Ernie leaned closer to her. "You remember me? I'm Ernie Cox. I used to drive a bus, remember?"

"Yeah, I recognized you."

"You're about thirty-five, now, ain't you? Still a young chicken . . ."

"Mmmmm."

"How many kids you got—Ernestine, right?"

"Yeah. Shoot, you got a memory, boy. I got eleven kids. Albert, he's my oldest son."

"Well, listen, Ernestine, we'd like to find Albert, so we can help him stay out of trouble."

"You do that. I'd be glad if you found him—maybe put him away somewhere . . . I don't know where . . . Because even if he gets home I ain't got nothing for him . . . no place for him to sleep . . . And he comes in here and starts in like a wild something. He says some boys want to kill him. So he comes rushing in here, he puts the couch up against the door and takes what I got in the ice box. Then he goes rushing out of here when some rocks come through the window with notes about how they's gonna kill him and burn our house down."

The woman buried her face in her lap and wept, and suddenly Ernie stood up. The woman continued, "As soon as Albert's father started gettin' drunk and staying out, Albert started getting bad . . . and mean . . ."

"Listen, Ernestine, everything'll work out. Don't you worry. Here's my card, and you call us if you need any ol' thing, hear?"

"Yeah, but you catch Albert and put him somewhere, hear me? He can't live here no more and he can't live on the street, so he got to be put somewhere! And school! He needs school, and some clothes . . . He once said he wanted to be a policeman . . ."

"Your husband—is he living here?"

"No . . . He come by once in a while with some money. That's all."

"Well, thanks for your cooperation."

Outside, Ernie shook his head, staring up at the house through his car window. "Sounds like the frontier, the Wild West days, don't it?" he said. "The Injuns are coming! Her son, like a wild animal, barricading the doors . . . She came up here from the south. I used to take her out. Typical family. The husband—the whole situation probably just overpowered him. Now he comes by there, but he don't want to be pinned down to the whole thing. It's got his mind hashed up, so to speak, so he just comes by there once in a while and drops a few dollars in the old lady's pocket, and he feels better. See me get off that couch? You know why I got up, don't you? I spotted something with a whole lot of *legs* crawling by me."

Ernie laughed and then his mood became reflective as he said, "But, man, to me that's a pitiful thing. Believe me, my heart goes out to that woman. If she lives to be fifty, she'll be awful lucky. And you can bet that she don't get the proper medical attention. Probably has no way to know if she's sick, until she just gets so down that she can't move. She's probably got female trouble. I'm sure she does. Discharge, infection, or the womb's out of place—that's common among ghetto women, especially one that's got a lot of kids. But paying a visit to the doctor, making an appointment and going to a pharmacist—to her that's too much of a big deal, there's too much work in that. Too complicated. And who takes care of them kids when she's gone? Hunh?"

The unspoken answer seemed to hang inside the car in the night. I asked, "She doesn't know that you also want Albert on a murder charge, does she?"

"Of course not. She has an *idea* that he's probably in some kind of trouble, but she's got enough of her own. She said her son wanted to be a policeman. Sounds like myself at his age. So ten years from now, Albert will either be dead or in the big place, or he'll be a professional criminal out here in the street. And some of his friends'll be cops."

The next morning, Ernie attended the hearing for Slim Miles in a crowded courtroom. Hundreds of people sat on the folding chairs, most of them poor, most of them Negro. A few dozen patrolmen sat in the jury box or stood against the walls, waiting for their cases to come up. Lawyers, some looking out of place in their silver-gray suits, milled about between the spectators and the judge's chair. Ernie and I waited for more than an hour. Today he wore a green sports jacket, looking more like a lawyer than a cop. We spotted Carolyn Miles in the crowd in a bright yellow dress. At one point she glanced in our direction, saw Ernie, and looked quickly away. When Slim was brought out under guard, she and Ernie approached the bench. Few people paid any attention to Ernie and Slim's lawyer, as they traded information beneath the judge's chair. Slim's story had changed. His lawyer said there had been *two* fights going on under the el, at the same time. No mention was made of Robin Hood. Carolyn was whispering something to Slim and the maneuvering promised to continue as a trial date was set for a month later.

When we had met outside the courtroom Ernie showed me a sheet of paper with the report that at "about 1920 hours" the day before, "five unknown colored youths entered a novelty and candy store" on the South Side and "during a robbery shot the owner." The victim's wife could not identify any of the boys.

Ernie told me that this would be his next "major" investigation and that he would want to start working on it later in that day. Now the judge was calling another case and the detective was pushing through the crowded courtroom to the corridor outside.

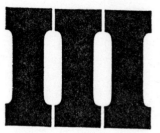

Patrolmen Colin Barker and Gary Cummings
Haight-Ashbury, San Francisco

"You'd better get out of here or they'll kill you."

The young patrolman heard the warning from a sad-eyed, black-haired hippie girl who attempted to smile. Fear and the expectation of violence had permeated Haight-Ashbury by the late summer of 1968. The flower children's "free, hang-loose community" was a shambles of pain, boredom, and suffering. The Summer of Love the year before now seemed a century away. A nightmare of frustration, anger, disillusionment, despair, racial conflict, and disease swirled about Haight Street, turning it into a tension-filled area, simmering with hostility. Fights, holdups, muggings, and rapes were common. Clamorous, raunchy mobs milled about on the sidewalks. Youngsters, many barely out of their teens, emaciated and wild-eyed, stood or sat in doorways alongside sleeping derelicts. Without enthusiasm they whispered their offers of sale to passers-by: "Acid" (LSD) . . . "Speed" (methamphetamine) . . . "Smack" (heroin) . . . "Pot" (marijuana). Violence-prone white hoodlums on motorcycles declared they would beat up any black men they saw with white women. Meanwhile, young Negroes stood on the sidewalk and taunted passing white girls. A scarcity of marijuana had led to an increased use of hard drugs. The "home of the flower children and refuge of youth" had become a magnet for hate.

I followed Patrolman Colin Barker as he moved down the street, becoming at once part of the scene and distinctly outside it. Whatever it was that had brought all these disheveled young people together, whatever they were rebelling against, individually or collectively, now was symbolized by Colin's blue uniform; and they acknowledged the cop as the biggest nonconformist in Haight-Ashbury, a freak show with silver buttons, nightstick, flashlight, walkie-talkie, blue hat, gun. The youthful foot patrolman saw it in their eyes and consoled himself with the thought that their bitterness was too disjointed, too diffused, to gather into a unified rebellion over the sight of one nervous cop.

So he continued on his way into the crowd. To the tune of "Here Comes the Bride," someone sang, "Here comes the pig, here comes the pig, da da da daaaaa, da da daaaaa, da daaaaa . . ."

Two young bearded hippies leaned against a store window and mockingly saluted at the cop as he moved forward slowly, one step after the other. A barefoot girl, her blond hair swung to one side, cocked her head and formed the word "pig" with her lips. Throughout the insulting gesture she tried to keep her face radiant with charm. Another engaged the patrolman in a staring contest—and she won.

"Up against the wall!" shouted a young man acting as a police officer. For Colin Barker's benefit, he and his friend staged a mock frisk. The crowd chanted, "Down with cops!" Others who watched the patrolman coming gave more subtle greetings: a cold, ugly facial expression, a fist, a finger, a defiant yawn.

"Hey, he looks younger than me."

"Gestapo!"

"He's cute."

"I could be his mother."

"You should have had an abortion."

Patrolman Barker, who wore a crew cut beneath his police hat, indeed looked much younger than his twenty-three years. His face had no lines or blemishes and he had a tendency to flush. His blue eyes reflected apprehension but idealism. His uniform appeared a bit stiff, especially where the walkie-talkie hung over his shoulder and rested awkwardly on his chest. Out of self-consciousness he adjusted it from time to time, and occasionally he felt his gun as if to make sure it was still there.

Amid the almost stifling surge of attention directed at him, the young cop seized an opportunity to go on the offensive. To several young men lounging on the hood of a green convertible, he yelled, "Is this your car?"

"No."

"THEN GET OFF IT."

His own sudden authority, plus the chorus of hisses that

followed, brought fresh color to Colin's face. There was no way out of the uniform that entrapped him, no method of disassociating himself from the dark-blue costume, so he assumed the role it signified. Moreover, the crowd seemed determined to make of him what it wished. The young people, strangely grim in their attempts at festivity, would force the cop to shoulder the case for the opposition. Simply by treating him as the enemy they would force him to become it, in manner as well as in appearance.

"Hi, officer," said a pretty young girl. "Want to buy a necklace?"

"No . . . No thanks."

"Awwwww."

Another young girl stepped in front of him, making a fancy bow. "Good evening, officer," she said. "Have a fine night."

"There's a pig in our midst!"

"Want a piece of bread, officer?"

"No, no. No, thank you."

"It's good bread."

The patrolman paused before a doorway, where three unkempt young men were sprawled out. "This isn't your doorway, is it?"

"Nope."

"Then get on your feet."

As they picked themselves up, a wine bottle sheathed in a paper bag rolled off the top step and bounced to the sidewalk. Colin picked it up and went to the curb. He poured out the wine between two parked cars, to a chorus of boos and hisses.

"Hey, he does that real groovy, like he ought to be promoted."

To a young man selling underground newspapers to passing cars, Colin said, "Come on, off the street." Then, looking over his shoulder, he called to the same three young men: "Don't block that doorway!"

"I have a dream," shouted a heckler in the crowd, lost from sight in the chaotic shuffling of bodies, "and I see a picture of a pig with a badge on him."

"Oink, oink! Oink, oink!"

"Officer, do I threaten the security of the United States if I don't take a bath?"

"I don't think so. I don't think what you do matters one way or another."

"Thank you, officer. You're okay."

Colin paused again, this time next to a group of disheveled teen-agers with knapsacks sitting on the sidewalk.

"Come on, get up."

"We're tired."

"Get up!"

"All we're doing is sitting."

"Up!"

A young girl with long pigtails stood up and swung her leg over a motorcycle along the curb. On her blouse was an orange button with the words "Tickle My Fancy." Her breasts were clearly defined beneath a bulging T-shirt.

"All of you—off the cars. Get off the motorcycle, please."

In the window of a store that Colin now paused at, a huge cartoon showed a caricature of Lyndon Baines Johnson urinating on the world.

"Officer, you got any spare change?"

"That's the wrong question to ask a policeman, young lady."

"Gee, officer . . . Just a dime?"

"Look—" Colin Barker clenched his fist and walked past her. For some reason he could not put into words, being asked for money by a middle-class hippie girl, perhaps an ex-college senior, made him furious.

A girl selling beads in the street to tourists was Colin's next objective. "Hey, get off that street, will you?" She jumped back to the curb. Business was poor anyhow; the tourists drove by with doors locked and windows up. From inside their cars they must have heard no sound as they tried to catch glimpses of the frantic scene. Colin looked backward for a moment. Youngsters were already in the street again, panhandling, lounging on the cars, "grooving on the scene," doing their thing.

"Hello, dear," said a new hippie girl, flashing her eyes seductively, challenging the patrolman's veneer of aloofness.

"Hi."

"Hey, officer, are you for real?" asked a bold young man in the crowd.

"You got something to say to me?"

"I mean, dig—are you a *real* police officer?"

"No, it's Halloween."

On the sidewalk ahead, several boys and girls were kneeling over a lovely design in multicolored chalk. A huge set of flowers had been drawn in pink, purple, blue, and white; and a message was printed below the flowers: "I, YOU, WE, ARE GOD." The design, which probably had taken at least an hour to sketch on the damp sidewalk, was about two feet in width and twice that in length.

"All right," said Colin. "Get some water and scrub this off."

"Do we have to?"

"No, I'm just telling you for my goddamn health."

"Aw, come on. We worked hard on this. Is it really against the law?"

"You're blocking the entrance to this man's establishment," said Colin, looking in the window of the laundromat. The middle-aged storekeeper shrugged from behind the glass. A crowd gathered and watched as the youngsters, supplied with buckets of water and heavy brushes from the laundromat, scrubbed the chalk design off the sidewalk. The colors ran together in a blotch before disappearing. Seeing the build-up of the crowd, Colin turned and continued his slow, deliberate stroll through hippieville.

Again a girl with bare feet jumped in front of him. Apparently emboldened by her friends, she held a flower to his face and danced backward as he approached. "Have a flower, officer."

"No thanks, but thanks."

"It's a *nice* flower, sir."

"I can't take it. Really."

"Go on—take it."

"No, really—"

"PLEASE?"

Colin stopped, shaking his head. The girl stared up at him defiantly and shouted, "TAKE THE FLOWER!" Suddenly the patrolman's hand shot out and batted the flower out of her hand. The sound of his hand smacking hers seemed too loud. Red-faced, he turned on his heel and began walking back through the same block. "That wasn't very nice," called the girl. Now the patrolman was walking faster, more rigidly; now he was ready to spring out of his cloak of passivity. His hand gripped the nightstick and his eyes, clear and intense, challenged everything in their field of vision. The images of the young people came into sharper focus. What he saw now was specific. In the beginning he had seen only a large mass of untidy teen-agers and young people; now they were each individuals and he, as an individual, could no longer see the crowd as a whole.

As he walked he heard someone following him, whistling for his benefit. The faces he passed were smiling, expectant; and the whistling came closer to his ear. Still he refused to turn around. He walked through the bodies, sometimes pausing deliberately to wait for someone to move out of his way rather than go around. The whistling grew louder at the back of his head. Colin stopped. The person behind him continued the harsh metallic whistling on one long high note; and then there was a strange silence. Colin heard the person breathing behind him, but still he refused to turn around. Everyone was watching his reaction, waiting.

"ATTENTION!"

The sound made Colin Barker's ears pulsate with pain. Turning abruptly, he faced a tall, thin young man with flowing blond hair, dirty face, and frazzled clothing.

Colin whispered: "What did you say?"

"I said, 'Fuck you, cop!' That's what I said."

In one furious gesture, Colin threw the young man against the wall. He pushed aside a hippie girl and flayed at the young man with his fists. Within seconds the crowd built up and surrounded the fight. From a distance came the sound of a rock smashing through the window of a moving car. The young man screamed and kicked. Colin tried to grab his shirt, but the young man reached up and tore the patrolman's badge off, ripping the uniform. The crowd cheered and Colin smashed his nightstick down, once, twice, a third time. The mob surged in, united, but Colin already was calling for help through his walkie-talkie. He stood back, holding the nightstick over his victim, and waited. Members of the crowd continued to heckle, but the brief show of unified anger seemed to disperse. The young man on the sidewalk, very much aware of his role in the chaos, shouted, "Revolution, now! Kill him!" Colin folded his arms and said nothing.

"I hope," screamed the young man who groveled about like an animal, "that somebody jumps on *you* someday."

"Cool off, fella."

"Hey, you sonofabitch fascist pig! Go ahead, kill me!"

"Shut up, will ya? You make me sick."

"Then puke, you pig! Beat me! Get this pig off my back!" As the young man tried to get up, Colin pushed him back to the ground. "I won't be a slave to you! Hey, somebody shoot this pig!"

"Shut your mouth!" Colin demanded.

"Next time you see me, brother, you'll be behind my gunsight. You pig! You can't face up to a nigger, 'cause he'll put a .22 in your head!"

At last the paddy wagon rolled up and two patrolmen jumped out. They helped Colin drag the screaming young man into the back of the truck.

"What's the trouble, Colin?"

"I think he's on LSD or something. He's out of his head."

Behind the paddy wagon, in an unmarked car, sat four members of the San Francisco tactical patrol. The four husky uniformed cops stared at the crowd with contempt. One of them jumped from the car and stood, legs apart, challenging anyone to provoke him. Most of the crowd seemed to fear him, because the heckling abruptly stopped. Colin hopped into the cab of the paddy wagon as it rolled off down the fog-engulfed street to the station house in Golden Gate Park.

I walked back through Haight Street toward the station to catch up with Patrolman Barker. He had told me that back in 1962 the Park Station had "almost been put out of business." That year, an efficiency expert had looked over the quiet, integrated neighborhood of working people in and around Haight-Ashbury and had recommended removal of the station because of the area's low crime rate. Since that time police business has soared.

Even so, the headquarters building itself, set apart from any residential or commercial areas and isolated from "Hashbury" by lovely trees and bushes, is often deceptively quiet. At times, the station resembles a placid, suburban police headquarters. Its large, square, ground-floor lobby, lined by benches on two sides, at times is entirely empty except for the sergeant and a clerk.

After I'd been with Colin Barker for a few days, I realized that these periods of tranquility usually occur during the eight-to-four-o'clock shift, during the day, when the older patrolmen are out in radio cars or on foot patrol. "The older guys get the day watch," Colin had told me. "It's a choice beat, because most incidents flare up at night."

This evening when I entered the station it was nearly six o'clock, but the atmosphere was still quiet. Colin had booked his prisoner and was upstairs in the locker room with his partner, Gary Cummings, who had been held up because the captain had wanted to speak to him alone. The two patrolmen, both in their early twenties, were having an argument. As I entered the locker room, Gary was saying, "The two boys are pleading self-defense."

"*Self-defense?*" cried Colin Barker. "It was outright murder, with no provocation at all."

"How do *you* know?"

"What do you mean, how do I know? I was there!"

After a silence, Gary said, "I think we'll see a lot more of this thing, where Negroes who shoot at cops make a legal claim to self-defense."

"Well," said Colin, "the day they let a guy off for killing a cop in cold blood—that's the day they can have my resignation."

"You know," Gary argued, "there's always the *possibility* that self-defense might be a valid claim. I mean, people can't get over the idea that . . . Well, they seem to think that policemen are almost infallible."

"Did I say that?"

"No, but establishment people think so," said Gary. "The people who never come in contact with the police, they think that all policemen are nice guys, that the cops are everybody's friend, and all that crap."

"So what? It's plain and simple: Fred was killed by two colored punks, both of whom were known to peddle narcotics in the Haight."

"But there is the *possibility*," Gary pressed him, "that the cop who gets shot by some Negro perhaps *had* threatened the black guy with death. Maybe not at that particular time, but beforehand, on another occasion. You don't know if Fred had stopped those same guys two or three times before that night and told them, 'Niggers, if I ever stop you again, I'm gonna blow your head off.' So when they saw him there, coming at them in the park at night, they might have figured he was gonna make good on his threat. Now, if a cop tells me he's gonna blow *my* head off, I'm gonna believe him. I'm *supposed* to believe him."

"First of all," Colin said, "Fred never shot anybody. Second, there's a law that says you have to go along with anything a policeman says, even if you're innocent. You're supposed to go along with the arrest."

"I can't bitch about that, but what about continual harassment? And I've seen cops lie in court, plant phony evidence, and so on—"

"Look, Gary, what are you trying to say? That Fred Rennie *should* have been shot? What the hell kind of a kick are you on?"

"You know as well as I do! Fred was *famous* for planting phony stuff on his prisoners. And you know that when he got shot in the park they looked through his clothing and found about a dozen needles in his pocket. Now, I'm sure he wasn't using them on *himself*. And the chances are *very* good that those two Negro guys knew this about him, and they maybe figured he was going to plant stuff on them illegally."

"Well, why don't you go to court and testify on their behalf?" Colin shouted, his face red with anger. "Sounds to me like you're on the opposite side."

"Opposite side from what?" Gary asked.

"From what is right! It could just as well have been *me* who got killed. Fred walked one way and I walked the other way. If we had walked different ways, it would have been me."

"Have *you* ever threatened a Negro, or tried to plant stuff on anybody?"

"Of course not," Colin replied.

"Then how do you know they would have shot you?"

"They would have. They would have shot you, too, Cummings."

"Maybe I'm guilty, in some way. Maybe they have a right to shoot at me."

"Maybe you're just paranoiac."

With that the patrolmen stopped arguing and turned to me to explain that Gary, who had been on the force for two years, had just been transferred to Park Station. He was Colin Barker's new partner, replacing Patrolman Fred Rennie, who had been killed the week before.

"I've been sort of nervous since then," Colin told me. He explained that he and Fred Rennie had been walking through the park shortly after eleven o'clock one night, looking in the bushes for drunks or young people with sleeping bags, when they heard footsteps in the darkness beyond the foliage. Colin started to his left and Fred climbed the steps to his right, so that they would approach the person from two sides. For a long half-minute, Colin walked alone. Suddenly there was a shotgun blast. Colin ran to the pathway and around the opposite edge of the bushes to the top of the concrete steps. Shining his flashlight on the ground, he saw Fred Rennie lying dead on his back. The blast had caught him directly in the face. Ten minutes later, the tactical squad picked up two Negro teen-agers as suspects. They also found the shotgun nearby.

"I've been jumping now," Colin said as he finished the story, "every time I hear a strange noise."

Gary handed me a newspaper account of the pretrial hearing for the two boys charged with killing Fred Rennie. The story, printed in one of the daily papers, described how the courtroom had been the scene of violent emotions expressed by black spectators. When the not-guilty plea was entered, they had murmured, "That's right, that's right. You tell 'em, brother!" According to the news story, the two boys were led back to their cells amid angry cries of "Hold it, hold it! How come they ain't getting out on bail?" Outside the packed courtroom, the news story continued, a group had passed out leaflets announcing, "These two black brothers need every black person's support at the pigpen Hall of Justice. Let every black person with a black heart show the pigs that we care about our brothers."

Apparently this news article had triggered the argument between the two patrolmen. Because their views seemed so contradictory, I decided that evening to follow both of them during my stay at Haight-Ashbury.

Gary went downstairs to do some paperwork while Colin unwrapped two ham sandwiches on the bench next to his locker. "I eat dinner here a lot," he said somewhat apologetically. "My wife is a great one for saving money."

I asked Colin for his views of Haight-Ashbury's evolution to its present hostile state. He told me that he had arrived at Park Station, his first and only police post to date, back in early 1967.

"Already," he said, "there was resentment from working people, Negro and white, toward the hippies. The hippies had caused an increase in rents by all their publicity, but at the same time they had caused a decline in property value. They really destroyed the property. You wouldn't believe that wealthy kids could act that way, but I've seen dozens of places that had to be condemned after the hippies moved out. They really did a lot of damage. I mean, they viciously destroyed property.

"If the whole thing hadn't been publicized, the original hippies and the storeowners probably could have gotten along. They weren't really happy about each other, but I think they would have made it all right. If there had never been a word of publicity about Haight Street, other than word of mouth, I don't think they would have had half the trouble.

"It's fantastic, now. It's unbelievable how many strong-arm robberies there are. A guy comes up and says, 'I'm gonna punch you in the nose if you don't give me your wallet.' It's just unbelievable. Before, when we had a robbery suspect it would never be a hippie, never a guy with long hair or a beard. But that's all changed, now that the real hippies are gone. We're getting a lot of shootings, some stabbings—two people killed last week by stabbing—robbery, assault, rape. Of course there are so many things that go unreported. Rapes are hardly ever reported.

"So what are we dealing with out here? There's only a few flower children left. You've got the juveniles now, some of them runaways, maybe fourteen through nineteen years old. Most of the kids I see are really lonely kids. And all I can see is that they don't have any real firm basis at home, no home life. And that's why they're coming here. They're looking for something else. They haven't found anything at home, and I don't know whether they feel rejected by their parents or what, but they're real lonely. I mean, you can see that they're pitiful, really pitiful.

"And look at the street—it's a garbage pit! I just can't understand it, myself, maybe because I'm a cop and I have to look at things like I was a parent. God knows, I'm not that much older than these kids. Lots of them are older than me. And these kids come from a much better background than I came from. Their fathers are wealthy attorneys or, like the other night, I was taking around the vice-president of a big food company who was looking for his seventeen-year-old daughter. All those pictures of runaway kids on the walls here in the station, they have to be cleared out each month to make way for new ones. We find a lot of them here, too. There's a fantastic turnover in runaway juveniles. I mean, it gets so bad that you can't arrest them all. You just don't have the time. It takes too much time to get 'em into the station and book 'em.

"Then, as I said, there's the subhoodlum element, both white and Negro, who have moved into the street, so the place is really rough. The young colored element accounts for a large percentage of the robbery and assaults that we have out here, which is one of the facts that aren't often printed in the papers. And the Negro kids are in conflict with the white motorcycle kids. They have problems with the Negro guys who stand on the street and hassle the Caucasian girls, physically and verbally, and they're frightened of them.

"There are four or five different groups out here. There's also the political activists who are willing to provoke an incident just to defy authority. They want to overthrow the government. Then you've got some of the older guys out here who sell dope and chase the young girls.

"Now, there's another group that's really not brought out too much. There's actually the mentally ill out here. I would say that at least 15 percent of the people I've arrested for one thing or another have either been in a mental institution or were outpatients from some psychiatric clinic. Some of them have problems that aren't too severe, but there are a lot of out-and-out real nuts walking around on the street. And some of these nuts are on drugs! They may have been *halfway* all right before, but the drugs really did 'em in. They don't know whether the drugs caused the mental illness or whether the mental illness led them to take drugs. Sometimes it's a combination of the two.

"The biggest problem of all is the drugs. These Negro kids from the Fillmore, only several blocks away, bring phony drugs onto the street and they'll sell them to these people. They'll take kids off Haight Street and go around the corner like they're going to sell them drugs, and that's where we get all our shootings and knifings. They take 'em around the corner and pull out a gun and say, 'Let's have your money.' So here's a strong-arm robbery that never gets reported because it was illicit in nature to begin with. I'd say that 20 or 30 percent of these armed robberies are never reported.

"The things that people in Haight-Ashbury resent most is the plainclothes operation of the police. They hate the undercover narcotics guys above all else. This is especially true now because drugs are scarce to begin with. When they see a street seller getting hassled they go into a frenzy. Even so, there's a lot of phony stuff. For every piece of legitimate narcotics that's sold up here, I would say there is four or five times as much phony stuff.

"This area, in the not too distant future, will be Skid Row. It could go that way or it might go back to the way it was before, but it's kind of hard to go back. Eventually, even the motorcycle element will leave. So many businesses have closed, reputable businesses . . . Appliance stores, a supermarket, meat stores, all middle-class businesses . . . They can't make it any more. See, all these people who spent twenty-five years out here, for example, building up a little jewelry store, or a little hardware or appliance shop—they've moved out to better areas. They've relocated and taken all they had with them. They tried to hold on. They thought that all this would pass over, but they took a beating. They were losing their shirts, so they got out. And they can't afford to move back here, even if they wanted to. They'll have built up a new clientele by the time this passes over, if it does.

"But now it's fashionable to grow a long beard and wear weird clothes, and to *say* you're a hippie. But all they do is just walk around, and groove on the scene, go to the park, listen to a little banjo music and bongo drums, and make like they're having a big time. I don't think any of 'em really are, though. I mean, they're dirty people, now, that's all. Just dirty. Dirty, poor, sad-looking people. There might have been *something* to the earlier movement. At least they weren't bothering anybody, they were self-supporting. We didn't have trouble with people begging on the streets, but now ..."

Colin Barker studied economics at a California junior college and still attends business school. His brother is a poet who teaches literature at an eastern university.

"You find with a lot of cops," he told me, "that it's a family thing. Their fathers, uncles, or relatives were cops. I wanted to be an auto mechanic at one time. I also wanted to fly airplanes. And being a cop, it's the same thing: you like something if you feel you can do it well. For example, I'm no good at golf or basketball, so I just don't play those sports. But you have to work for a living, so you choose something you can do well and that you like to do. If I had had the money and the education, and the natural ability to go with it, I would have liked to have gone into medicine. However, I don't think I'm bright enough for that. I'm just not that smart.

"It's funny, but I *like* working in Haight-Ashbury. Many cops don't like it at all. There's been a fantastic turnover lately in the station. We've had promotions and guys resigning, and transfers and all that. The station's all changed since I've been here. Just in eighteen months, all the faces seem to have changed.

"Believe it or not, I *asked* to work on Haight Street,

maybe because I'm dealing with my own generation, I don't know. I had worked in the radio car around here for a while —I still do on occasion—and I kind of wanted to see what it was like to walk the beat. And I like it better. I have a more intimate relationship with the people. You can meet the people on the street, talk to them. I've even made friends with guys I've busted for felony charges. Guys say, 'Hey, Colin, what's going on?' and 'Don't bust me again this week, not again,' and that kind of thing. When there's a big crowd, like tonight, you can't have that relationship, but on an individual basis it's different.

"A good many of the kids feel very strongly about their political views and so on. They really hate the cops, but a lot of them change their mind when they deal with you on a personal basis, when they get arrested. Of course, some of them don't change their minds. It depends who they get arrested by. The important thing to realize is that people's opinions are all on an individual basis. A cop can arrest a kid and he'll think, 'Jeez, cops are all right.' And he might be arrested the next night by a different cop and think, 'Fascist pigs.' It's like you can't generalize about humanity. There's just too many personalities involved. You can generalize to a certain degree. You can say, for example, that most policemen are conservative, and you'd be right."

Colin told me about how he had been friends with a family "whose father sort of played a role in my life." The older man was a long-time policeman in San Francisco whose son, Colin's friend, eventually became a patrolman. "I was a bank teller during that time," said Colin. "It was real dull, and here was my friend, really enjoying his police work. I guess I wasn't really cut out for business. Anyhow, I listened to my friend and his father talk about their work—both of them real dedicated cops—and I thought I'd give it a shot. It appealed to me because I was interested in dealing with people and I like to be outside, on the move."

According to Colin, at first he was said to have been accident-prone. On his first day outside a patrol car, he had been assigned to an intersection to direct traffic. After an uneventful hour at this post, a truck turned the corner too fast and a long metal slab flew out, hitting him in the back and confining him to bed for three weeks. He returned to the job as a foot patrolman on Haight Street, and during his fourth tour of duty a young man on "speed" kicked him in the leg. A day later his knee swelled up with calcium deposit and he was confined to the station house as a clerk until it healed. Out on foot patrol again, Colin arrested an unkempt youth for disorderly conduct. While waiting for the paddy wagon he "got into a beef" with his prisoner and punched him in the face. This time, his finger swelled up with calcium deposit.

"Not long after that," the young patrolman remembered, "some hippie girl gave me a batch of frozen food. I thought it was a nice gesture, so I took it home with me. But she didn't know that the food had been defrosted and refrozen, going bad in the process. My stomach was screwed up for a week."

As one of Colin's fellow officers jokingly told me in the station house, "He's already one of the walking wounded around here."

Although his reaction to these mishaps was cheerful, lately he had become more defensive and even hostile while on the job. "I don't pretend to be a good guy so much any more," Colin said. "It just doesn't work. Everyone has a knife or a gun, it seems. I haven't seen a real hippie out here for so long that I don't think I'd recognize one. As a policeman in the Haight now, it's more of a holding action than anything else. Periodically you feel you're losing the battle. You reach the saturation point, and that's what we've reached out here. The pot boils over and you skim the top off, but you still have the whole pot.

"See, you never know when it's gonna get out of hand. On many occasions on Haight Street they've tried a sit-in to block the traffic, and you have to go in and move 'em out. The crowd will gather and you'll go in and move 'em out again, back and forth. Something stupid like that. One time two guys were throwing a football back and forth, and the next thing, they started a football game. So I went in and said, 'Come on, now, get back on the sidewalk.' But the next thing, members of the crowd started the jeers and the bottle throwing. If you've never been caught in a mob, you can't know the feeling, and you have to feel it to understand it. There's a kind of a panic on the part of each individual member of the crowd. They're gonna go wherever the crowd goes and do whatever it does.

"But the cop has to feel it out initially. I try to ask myself, 'Is this crowd hostile enough to create a big disturbance? Are they gonna loot? Are they gonna burn? Am I gonna have to make mass arrests?' These are things you have to consider, prior to taking action. Like sometimes I can walk into a crowd and with one gesture stop something before it starts. Like one time I walked down the street and there was a hundred people in the crowd. There were five or six people sitting in the doorway on Haight Street, playing guitars and so on, and the crowd was out in the middle of the street. I walked into the crowd and didn't say anything, not a word, and I just walked up to the people playing the instruments and put my finger to my lips, like this. They shut off the instruments and everybody left.

"But the next time, I walked in and did the same thing, with the same kind of group, and all hell broke loose. So there's no set rule of thumb. It's spontaneous when it happens, and there's no time to be afraid. I can't say that I'm really afraid after some situation explodes, because it's there and I'm there, and it's just a situation I have to react to. There's no time to do anything but act."

I left Colin to finish his dinner and went downstairs to see Gary Cummings, who was reading the newspaper in a back room. In both appearance and outlook Gary was different from most policemen I had met. He wore his black, curly hair longer than his colleagues and sprinkled his speech with "hip" phrases.

"This could be the grooviest job in the world," he told me, "but in practice it hasn't worked out that way. I became a cop almost on a dare. It was that sort of scene more than anything else. I knew a guy from Boston, a very bright guy, and yet he had this quirk that he couldn't help but exhibit this very sadistic personality. It would come out, you know? And the cat wanted to be a policeman! Eventually he did become one, too. Anyway, he sort of challenged me into the whole thing."

Gary had gone to work as a clerk for a title-insurance company instead of attending college. "Then I met a girl," he recalled, "and, you know, I thought maybe we were going to get married. So I said I'd better stop drifting along. I read a lot of adventure books and thought about how I might leave the country or I might do this or that. My life had been sort of romantic, really. I was twenty-two at the time and once I met this girl and we started going together—she was, you know, very solid Irish Catholic and all that—I figured I'd better get some sort of career going, in something I was going to enjoy. So, I started going to college. And after about eight months or so, the broad decided that she couldn't wait. She went back to one of her ex-college friends who had money. His parents had money, that is. And they got married.

"So, I just kept going to college and working part time for a stock company in San Francisco. When that got too much I quit and started going on unemployment. I was just doing nothing, laying around, collecting unemployment. I worked in a guest house so I didn't have to pay rent, just messing around.

"And then that friend of mine from Boston was trying the police department there. He sent me letters about himself, and I thought about it. I didn't really think I could make it. You know, it was a challenge. Not because of the mental thing, but physically. I thought I was too thin and so on.

"That's funny, though, because most civilians have a funny idea about policemen. They really do. They think cops are some sort of specimen, especially in the physical area, which isn't true. Most civilians think policemen are in the best shape and that they all know karate and judo, and that cops are all marksmen. Of course, that's the biggest joke in the world. Most cops are *out* of shape, more so than the average civilian, because they don't *do* anything. In fact, before I went on the force, I was in downtown San Francisco watching a motorcycle cop wrestle with some guy. I just stood there and I actually thought that if I assisted him he would *resent* me. I really thought he could handle the situation by himself. But now that I'm a cop, I know that he would have been happy as hell if I had lent him a hand.

"But I had this sort of *image,* you know, and I didn't even think I could make the Police Department. I took the test, anyhow, and I went from one phase to another phase, and I just kept passing. Before I knew it, they told me to come down and be sworn in. And once you go through all the phases, it's just like anything else. Your expectations begin getting higher, and you begin to identify with it. And before I knew it I was in the Police Academy.

"Next thing I knew I was out in the car, and the first time I was in the car I was scared to death. There again, most people have a different view. They think policemen are *continually* in danger and subject to getting killed every minute. I just *knew* that the first night I went to work I was gonna get messed up, if not killed at least maimed. And I remember the guy I was with trying to tell me, 'Hey, relax, it's not *that* bad. If it was that bad, I'd quit.'

"And it really *isn't* that bad. Well, there's always that chance, you know, but there's probably more chance of getting killed in a traffic accident. Obviously, insurance clerks don't get killed proportionately to policemen, but I'm a little fatalistic about it now, like if it's your time it's your time. Otherwise, how can you explain the cop who got shot in the head *five times* the other day? He just walked to his hotel and a couple of days later went to the doctor's office. They X-rayed him and found five bullets in his skull. He lived! And yet Robert Kennedy got only one bullet, less caliber, and he's dead. I mean, if you're meant to go, that's it."

Before being transferred to Park Station, Gary Cummings had developed a "reputation" of sorts for criticizing the behavior of fellow police officers. "I think," he said, "that most cops just accept whatever their colleagues do, as if they were in some kind of elite club in which you're never supposed to question the actions of other members. But I saw some things that were beyond my ability to accept without saying something."

One evening, Gary told me, he was in a San Francisco police station when three white patrolmen from the tactical squad brought in a Negro prisoner. The black man kept saying, "Get your hands off me, you filthy white bastards!" The officers paid little direct attention, but among themselves, and to Gary, they expressed a desire to "kick his ass." The prisoner asked to make a call and was allowed to use a public telephone in the corner of the room.

After about five minutes, the sergeant said, "Hey, that guy's been on the phone for a long time."

"Then," Gary recalled, "I saw the cops putting on their lead gloves. A lot of us have lead gloves. But they put these things on and stood there like vultures hanging around the phone booth. They had already made up their minds what was going to happen."

One of the police officers went to the phone booth and said, "Let's go. Get off that phone. Come on, let's go. Hurry up! Hey, hey! Let's go!"

The Negro, startled at the commotion, looked up and said, "Hey, hold it. Wait a minute."

"He went to hang up the phone," Gary said, "but as soon as he had said, 'Wait a minute,' that was enough for the cops. As far as they were concerned, he had crossed the line. They dragged him out of the phone booth and into a little office, where they didn't even have room to kick his ass. And when I say kick I mean *kick*."

One of the cops said, "Drag him out here," and the man was pulled along the floor back to the main room. Then, according to Gary, five policemen jumped on him, punching and kicking him until he could no longer move.

"I just stood there," Gary remembered, "and at first,

while they were beating him, I was so shocked that I couldn't say anything. Then I found myself shouting at the sergeant. I said something like, 'Hey, what's this for? What did that man do?' The sergeant told me to cool down, but I yelled, 'Is there any way you can explain or justify this to me?' But he didn't say anything, just looked at me like I was a traitor or something and walked away. When the tactical guys got through, they just glared at me. I wasn't about to tangle with them, because they seemed ready to take on *anybody*, they were so charged up. They looked like they had just worked out in a gymnasium, you know? Real proud of themselves."

After that, Gary began to be known as a "queer" and a "liberal" who should not be regarded as "one of the boys."

"Gradually," he said, "I became aware of a lot of factions within the Police Department. It really can be broken down pretty far. I learned it sort of piecemeal. Like black policemen who don't trust other black cops. I know black policemen who would trust me, a white man, before they would trust certain other black cops. And the other white cops know how I feel. Just for their own protection, like self-defense, it didn't take them long to tell each other about me. So if I'm around and some cop who doesn't know my views starts kicking a Negro's ass, another cop will tell him to lay off. I've kept cops from beating guys, just by being present."

Almost as if Gary had become "one of them," he was placed with a Negro policeman for a partner, working in a middle-class black neighborhood of San Francisco. Then he was transferred to Park Station and, according to Gary, "The word was already here. Some sort of reputation had preceded me. When the transfer list came out, some other guys told me that in Park Station the cops looking at the list saw my name and said, 'Well, he's an asshole.' They don't say that kind of thing in *front* of me, because maybe I'm some kind of threat to them, I don't know."

Colin came downstairs and the two cops prepared to go out on foot patrol together. The sergeant leaned through the window of his office and explained to me, "We used to have a single man on foot patrol all the time. Then we had to put two guys together, because there are very few guys who want to walk alone."

I asked the sergeant how the police are dealing with the young people on Haight Street and he replied, "We just don't want to rock the boat. I think you'll agree that cops don't like work any more than the next guy. We don't go out there and advertise for business. We just want to keep the trouble low, not let things get out of hand." The sergeant concluded with a chuckle, "We can't *eliminate* it, though, because then we'd be out of a job."

As the two young patrolmen began their first walking tour together, Colin said to Gary, "Let's get this straight. I'm not gonna get killed out there like Fred did. If you want to spout out liberal philosophy, that's fine with me. But I'm doing things my own way out there."

"Sure," said Gary.

The Haight-Ashbury district was shielded from view, not only by the abundant shrubbery of the park, but by a thick, white fog that rolled in great waves across everything in its way. It engulfed the two patrolmen and slid ahead of them up the lawn, where it crawled over streets lined with Victorian homes and "psychedelic" storefronts.

Colin explained to his new partner that a foot patrolman in Hashbury can almost regulate the amount of "business" that he generates and that the lack of activity in the station house during the day reflects "the old-timers' ability to avoid making a large number of arrests."

"For me," Colin continued, "it's an exception to walk through the Haight and not send at least one guy back to the station to get locked up. But I could, if I wanted to, walk through and get *no* prisoners. The old-timers just avoid getting into trouble. A lot of them see something and just look the other way."

"Why don't you look the other way?" Gary asked. "You like putting people in jail?"

"No, but it's a matter of selectivity. Sometimes, like I've

told guys to move off the steps or out of the street and they've gotten angry. And if they get *mean*, I *have* to grab 'em. You have to draw the line someplace. So you might arrest somebody out here when you weren't even planning to."

"Sounds crazy," Gary mumbled.

"It's a personal matter, sometimes," Colin tried to explain. "With each partner I tend to act differently, because each guy has a special kick, you know?"

"I'll let you know when I find my kick."

"Like one guy I walked with had been a bus driver before coming onto the force, so he always gave out tickets to cars parked in bus zones. When I wasn't with him, I'd never bother with that stuff. And some guys have shorter fuses than others, so that one cop is likely to cause an incident more than another."

The two patrolmen and I emerged from the winding path of Golden Gate Park near the bottom of the uphill lawn, where some Navaho Indians were sprawled on the grass near the top of the hill. "Now, see those guys?" Colin asked. "We've had a sudden influx of Indians, plus one drunken Eskimo last week. Now, personally, I don't like to see drunks lying around on my beat, and I like to arrest them."

"Why?"

"First of all, it's against the law to be drunk in the park," said Colin, "and also they piss me off. My father used to get drunk a lot, so maybe you'd say I have a hang-up about it."

With the four Indians was a young Negro man and a girl with long blond hair. Some in the group were sleeping, others were eating bread with peanut butter and french fries that had been dumped on a blanket. Colin and Gary walked up to the group, but no one moved or spoke. Colin pulled back a blanket, revealing a fifth Indian who was embracing a gallon jug of wine. Colin took the bottle and poured out the red liquid on the grass. He poured it slowly while the group of listless, disheveled people watched him. "Get up," he said to the Indian, who had curled up in a fetal position. "I want to see you walk." The Indian adjusted his orange headband, stood up and walked a few steps, but then he stumbled. One by one, Colin made the Indians rise and then take seats on a nearby park bench, where they slumped against each other.

"Look at them," said Colin. "You'd think they're about thirty or forty years old, but they're only around twenty or so. I've locked two of these guys up before."

"I guess this is what we've done to the American Indian," said Gary, who had been watching the ordeal as a spectator. "Jeez, they're screwed up. They got nothing to look forward to."

"A night in a jail cell, that's what."

"But why arrest them? They're not bothering anybody."

"They've helped to ruin this park, for one thing," Colin said, adding, "I hope you noticed back there the way they've shit right on the pathways."

"You know," said Gary, "the Indians are an industrious people. They helped to build this nation. And look what we've done to them."

"What do you mean, what *we've* done to them?" Colin said.

"Us white people, I mean."

"Well, I never met an Indian until I got here. And they're killing *themselves* on that wine. They must identify with the hippies or something."

The two cops searched the Indians, one of whom took a kitten from under his shirt and handed it to the white girl, who was standing to one side with her Negro escort. Another Indian had a knife, which he surrendered to Colin, who then called for the paddy wagon on his walkie-talkie. While they waited, a group of small Negro boys drifted over to observe.

"Look at all that crap," said Colin, pointing to the food. "No wonder there are rats in the park, now. Before the hippies, we never had rats here. The rats have arrived since I came on the job only eighteen months ago."

Then about thirty yards down the pathway, a young man about eighteen years old began shouting, "Pig, pig, pig!" His long, sandy hair curled at the shoulders and he wore an unkempt, bushy beard. Another young man, dressed in a gray windbreaker and blue jeans, was holding him by the shirt. "Get your hands offa me, goddamn narko pig!" The plainclothes narcotics agent slapped the boy. He fell down and the cop picked him up again. "Nark! Pig!" Again the undercover man slapped him and again he went down. Colin rushed over and helped bring the young man over to the bench. The Indians stared impassively as the long-haired youngster struggled and screamed up the asphalt trail.

The blond girl, still holding the kitten, gave a dollar bill to each Indian and then, strolling away with her Negro companion, she remarked to no one in particular, "My Daddy just gave his first donation to the American Indian, although he doesn't know it."

At last the wagon rolled up, stopping at the curb where the grassy hill ended, and the five Indians were hustled through the back door. Colin shouted, "Let's go, come on, boys." To the two uniformed patrolmen seated in the front of the wagon, he yelled, "Five to go!" One of the Indians, wrapped in a faded, pink blanket, began wandering aimlessly away from the truck. "Hey!" shouted Colin, grabbing him and steering him back to the rear of the wagon. "Get in there, Sam Running Drunk."

"What did this cat do?" Gary asked the narcotics agent, who was pushing his prisoner into the wagon with the Indians.

"He offered to sell me some LSD. Some acid."

"Pig!" shouted the long-haired young man as the doors were swung shut. The plainclothes man jumped on the running board as the wagon pulled away.

Then, from out of the bushes came a man whose brown hair was more than two feet long. He was dressed in a bright pink robe, which hung from his shoulders and billowed down around him, brushing the ground as he moved, dreamlike, past the cops.

"He has arisen!" shouted Colin, laughing. He and Gary watched as the Christ-like figure turned down another trail, through the fog, and disappeared beyond the trees. "Now," Colin said, "we have to go back to the station and book the

Indians. They'll sober up in a cell for the night, that's all. We didn't even make it out of the park."

On the way back, they took another pathway near a small pond. Walking toward them was a young Negro, who stopped as if he were waiting for the cops to pass by. Instead of walking past him, however, Colin said, "Hey, what are you doing in here?"

"Walking, man."

"Put your hands out."

"Oh, no, man . . ." He put his arms straight out as if it were a routine he had gone through many times before. "What was I doing just now 'cept standing, hunh?" The black man's voice betrayed a feeling of utter helplessness as Colin frisked him up and down, searching for weapons. "Hey, man, what am I supposed to do when I see you coming? I ain't done nothing, so I stopped and did *absolutely* nothing. And *still* you stop me." He opened his mouth, took a breath, and let the air out in a violent, soundless expression of despair. "You won't find nothing, man."

Concluding his frisk, Colin said, "Now, get out of here!"

"I'm going, man, I'm going. But I don't know what I'm gonna do with you."

As they walked onward, Gary said, "That was uncalled for, man."

"You don't know this area like I do," Colin said. "These young Negro hoods are a big problem around here."

"You just made that guy hate your guts, you know that?"

"So what? That's the same type of guy who killed Fred. I've stopped many guys and found guns on 'em."

"What do you do on Haight Street, man? Do you stop every hippie you see?"

"Of course not," Colin said evenly. "But sometimes, right before the weekend, we'll go around and arrest all the rock throwers, keep 'em in jail for the weekend. As I've said, the love generation is pretty dead around here."

"Well, exactly how long could *you* say, 'I love you,' when you're getting the shit beat out of you by the cops?"

Colin glared at his colleague for a moment, then said,

"Sounds like you're gonna be out there with them next time, throwing the rocks at us."

"Oh, come on, will ya?"

One evening, when I was with Colin and Gary in a patrol car, the radio dispatcher directed them to a second-floor apartment on one of the streets near Haight-Ashbury.

"It's a rape, a couple of days old," the dispatcher said.

Gary, who was driving, replaced the microphone and the car cruised through the Fillmore and onto Masonic Street. The two patrolmen found themselves outside a light-gray, four-story Victorian building that, like many others in San Francisco, seemed to slump to one side because of the steep inclination of the street. Gary pressed the button beneath a nameplate. After a wait of several minutes, they decided that the buzzer was out of order.

They pushed open the front door and walked up a flight of stairs, pausing at the top. "It's probably this one," Gary said, pointing to one of two doors. A heavy-set girl with long, straggly hair appeared. She wore a black-and-red checkered flannel shirt tucked into a snug pair of blue jeans and a wide black belt. Her pale complexion and bare feet completed what was a typical picture of the "hippie" girl in this area. The young woman greeted the patrolmen with a slight smile and gestured for them to enter.

"I'd offer you a seat, but . . ." She smiled again and nodded to her one-room apartment, which was empty except for two uncovered stained mattresses and a sleeping bag on the floor. A pile of clothing and trinkets was heaped in one corner. On the walls were various designs and the words "LOVE" and "FREE." A large poster was on the ceiling, showing the face of a long-haired man on a motorcycle, looking down at the mattresses.

"We have a report," Gary said, "that you were raped."

"The report tells it like it is," the girl said, still smiling and fitting her fingers into the front pockets of her blue jeans.

"Where did it happen?"

"Right here. Two days ago, night before last."

"You get hurt?"

"Nah."

Colin broke in, "Do you know who the guy was? I mean, was he a friend of yours?"

"A friend? Well, if he was a friend I wouldn't call it a rape." She sat down on one of the mattresses. "I don't know the guy's name, but I've seen him on the street before."

"What's he look like?"

"Negro, kind of tall . . . a scar on his forehead."

"Did he hit you, or—?"

"No, no. I grooved on the whole thing. I let it take me where it was going. He had a knife, but I told him to put it away. I figured as long as it was going to happen, we *both* might as well enjoy it. Chalk it up to civil rights."

"Have you been raped before?"

"Oh yeah, several times, but they were friends of mine."

"No wonder you look so tired."

"Well, I've got mononucleosis. That's part of my life trip too, at the moment. You might say, gentlemen, that I'm a wilted flower child."

"Did you report any of the other rapes?"

"No."

"Why'd you report this one?"

"The guy got real dirty. He made me do some things that—well, I was disgusted. But I don't know why the hell I called you, really. I guess I just wanted to meet a couple of groovy cops. Some nice straights. So I've met you. Goodbye."

The two young patrolmen stood there for a moment as if they were unsure of what to do next. Then Gary said to Colin, "I guess we don't need the crime lab. There's nothing in here to take any prints from, no hard surfaces to touch."

Colin asked the young woman, "You're making a charge of rape?"

"Oh, well . . . Why not? Sure. I might as well. I mean, I wouldn't want you to have come here for nothing."

"Thanks," said Gary with a tinge of sarcasm. "We'll

make a report and the detective will get it. One of 'em will be in touch with you."

"Great. A detective! Sounds groovy."

"Listen," Colin said. "This place is kind of dangerous. How come you stay here?"

"I wouldn't trade my experiences at Haight for anybody's, anywhere. Three years ago I was an ugly little girl all ready to get married to a square, a rich square. Then I put an ad in an underground paper: 'Hip Girl Wants to Meet Groovy People.' That was the whole ad. I got about 600 responses, and I've been grooving ever since. Way up high one day, way down the next. Don't knock it."

Colin and Gary returned to their car and Gary called in to report the felony charge. To an inspector he gave the girl's name and address, adding, "I just wanted to make sure you got the report and to say that we don't need the crime lab. There's no chance of any fingerprints. The thing is a couple of days old and there's no furniture anyway."

The inspector on the other end said, "Did it have any class?"

"What's that?"

"Did it have any class?"

"Class?"

"Yeah. Was it a good rape?"

"Well," Gary said, "yeah, I think the girl is telling the truth. I think she was really raped. She's bringing the charge of rape, so as far as I'm concerned, it's bona fide."

"Well ... uh ..." The inspector stuttered for a moment, but then he said, "What I mean is, was she white?"

"Hunh?"

"Was the girl white?"

"Yeah. The girl is white. Why?"

"What about the suspect? Is he white, too?"

"No. He's Negro."

"Well, hey, hey, wait a minute. We'll get the crime lab."

"I already told you," Gary replied. "We don't need the crime lab. All I'm doing is giving you a report."

"Well, do you have her number?"

"I think so. Wait a minute, now. No, she doesn't have a telephone."

"Well, go back and tell her that we're gonna send the crime lab out there. Tell her they'll be out there in a few hours. You can never tell when some prints might be left around."

Gary drove in silence for a few blocks. Stopping the car, he said, "Have you ever heard that expression before?"

"What expression?" Colin asked.

"What he asked me: 'Did it have any class?' "

"Yeah, I heard of it. In fact, you embarrassed that inspector. You made him explain in plain language what he was talking about."

"I don't see any big joke in it," Gary said after his partner chuckled to himself. "Doesn't that make you angry?"

"I don't know. Not really."

"Christ! If that had been a Negro girl—! That guy must figure that a black woman can't be raped or something. Class? Man! Do you think that broad back there has class?"

"Look, don't make a big deal about it, will you? So the old man is a little prejudiced. He's not gonna make you or me act any differently."

"Well, it ticks me off," Gary said. "Did you know that I'm living with a Negro woman in the Haight?"

"Yeah, I knew that."

"From who?"

"Never mind, Gary. Every guy in the station knows that you run around with colored people, in the colored bars and so on."

"So what do they say about me?"

"Nothing. Nothing at all."

"Well," Gary went on, "my point is that I'm getting closer to people who have good reason to hate cops, ironically because I'm a cop myself. Now, if some white guy, or *any* guy had raped my woman, we probably would *not* have sent the crime lab. Not if that inspector had his say."

"Gary, you're the one who said you didn't want the crime lab on this case. Any time you ask for it, you get it. You know that. Color makes no damn difference."

"Ha! I've had cops in the car with me that have treated black girls on the street, ones that I know personally—these guys have made remarks like 'She's probably a hustler,' and so forth. They think that the same way that some guys automatically assume that if a black man has a hair process and drives a Cadillac, he's gotta be a pimp. And *automatically* they make these judgments. Yet I know black guys who have processes and drive Cadillacs who work for the government or are Post Office employees or presidents of social clubs and so on. The end result, anyway, is that these stereotypes that cops have in their minds really get in the way of their effectiveness as policemen."

"Well, the stereotypes don't come from nowhere," Colin replied. "Most cops think like they do after a million experiences of the same kind. If it becomes a stereotype, well, then that's what it is."

"What burns me up is that these cops, I've seen them go into a black house—and I don't care what it is, a family fight, a burglary, or whatever—and they just kiss it off, disregard it. Yet if you go to Pacific Heights among the rich whites you take your hat off and say, 'Yes sir,' and 'Yes ma'am.' And you're lucky if they don't make you go through the servants' entrance. When you go up in those mansions, brother, that's the way it is."

"Maybe so, but that's just a natural reaction to the place you're in. As a cop taking official action, you don't end up doing anything any differently."

"I'm not saying it's a deliberate thing," Gary returned. "It's a reflection of the society, like you said. But still, I've seen guys make reports in certain instances where if they were in a black community they'd no more make out a report than do nothing. They'll go into certain areas, white neighborhoods, and make a report about some stupid thing like ball playing or a ball going over the fence. But they'll go in on a cutting or stabbing in a black area and maybe not even make out a report. If you go to Pacific Heights—"

"No, no. I treat everybody the same."

"Well, Colin, you're lying to yourself. I've been up in those places, and you go up there, where the guy's grandmother was one of the original Rockefellers—and you're gonna go up there and be John Law and play *policeman* with those people? I've found out about all they own—what they call property—from the maid in the kitchen, not from them. And in Los Angeles they have a general order that in a certain area, a white area, when you go to their homes you go through the servants' entrance, the *side* entrance. In those places, the police department is nothing but a servant. Now, I don't know if you're kidding yourself or kidding me, but—"

"All I'm saying is that the *end result* is the same thing!"

"Hey, listen, down in my old car section, in a middle-class Negro neighborhood, if somebody kills somebody you *know* he's going to jail. And in Pacific Heights where a broad killed her husband, she was out on bail! Now, murder is supposed to be *no* bail. Her family had money and all that, so there's your end result."

Toward the end of their extremely quiet tour that evening, the two cops were assigned to investigate a complaint that a "noisy party" was going on.

"Man," Gary exclaimed, "what kind of police call is that?"

"Where is it?" I asked.

"In the Fillmore. It's an all-black street, I know that much."

"A noisy party could be just about anything," Colin said. "It could be anything from a family fight to a riot."

"Well, don't get uptight before we even get there," Gary snapped. "There's nothing, there's not a thing we can do about a noisy party. Not legally. We can tell them to cool down, but that's *all* we do. Then we leave. We go up there and protect our dignity, and leave."

"Dignity?" echoed Colin.

"Yeah, dignity. You think we'd be sent into a rich white area on a 'noisy party' complaint? I doubt it. I mean, what are we gonna do, call the goddamn wagon and lock everybody up? Hell, no. The main thing we're doing on a call like this is placating the complainant."

The young patrolmen parked outside a tiny, two-story building. The wooden structure was wedged in between two larger buildings near the middle of a tree-shaded, apparently quiet block.

"Did you know," Gary said to me, "that at this hour, at 11:30 P.M., you can't get a taxi anywhere in this area?"

"That's because of these hoodlums," Colin replied. "Look here!"

Dozens of young black men, their average age about nineteen, were milling about on the dark lawn and sitting on the small wooden porch, drinking wine and beer. Some wore Africa-style dress and several wore black berets.

"The party is supposed to be upstairs," Gary said.

"You know what I think?" Colin said.

"No. What?"

"I think we shouldn't even get out of the car. That's one helluva lot of black faces out there."

"Keep cool, man," Gary urged. "Did you ever think of something like this as an opportunity?"

"An opportunity for what? To get killed?"

"Calm down, man. You're gonna be an old man by the time you retire from this job, and you got a long way to go. I mean an opportunity to give these cats a feeling that maybe all cops aren't so bad, you know? Just act friendly to them."

"For how long? Listen, we're just gonna walk into trouble. Nothing but black militants out there. It doesn't take any wizard to look and tell that most of these guys are really militant. There's too many of 'em, Gary."

"Come on," Gary replied evenly. "We've got to go talk to the complainant."

The two young policemen got out of their car while the youngsters in the yard watched stoically. "Don't walk on the grass," Gary commanded in an almost whispered tone. "You wouldn't do that in a white neighborhood." We walked slowly toward the house on the narrow sidewalk. As Gary later recalled, "It was an eerie scene." There were no hostile remarks uttered, no catcalls of "Pigs" or "Honkies" from the staring spectators. I followed Gary and Colin up the four gray steps to the porch and stopped at the screen door. Then they pushed open the door and entered a dark, cramped hallway. A flight of stairs at the far end led up to the apartment where the party obviously was being held. A James Brown "soul" record reverberated through the wood-frame building. Gary knocked on the door to the left as we came in, and an elderly Negro woman opened it as far as the chain would allow.

"Police, ma'am. May we come inside?"

"Yes, just a second." She undid the door chain and we entered her small living room. Colin closed the door behind him and the three of them stood in a huddle to talk over the situation. "My husband is in the other room," the woman said, "and he can't sleep but for the noise upstairs. He has to be up at four o'clock in the morning for his job. They been having these parties up there every week, it seems to me. They don't make no trouble, but they're just too noisy. Me and my husband are too old to be having all this commotion all night long, 'specially with him having to be up, and—"

"Okay, okay," Gary interrupted. "Look, I'll go up there and talk to whoever is giving the party, and I'll *ask* him if he'll turn the noise down a little bit. But there's nothing else we can do about it."

"You do what you have to, officer. We just can't sleep at all, and every week they—"

"As far as your solving this thing about parties every week," Gary broke in, "you're either going to have to go to the district attorney, or probably the best thing is to talk to the landlord. If it's recurrent, tell the landlord and he'll tell the kids to move out."

"Okay, I'll do that."

"Now," Gary said, "do you know the name of the guy who lives up there? I mean, the guy's name who's having the party?"

"His name is Robert Ellis."

"Bobby Ellis?"

"Yeah, I know 'cause I seen his mail."

Gary turned to Colin and said, "Bobby Ellis is head of that black student union. Shit, he's militant as hell." Colin said nothing, but his pale face seemed a shade whiter in the dim glow of the only lamp in the living room. Gary repeated his advice to the elderly woman and returned to the hallway. Starting for the stairs at the far end, he called, "Come on, will ya?" Colin followed as they went up to find Bobby Ellis.

When we reached a small stair landing as we climbed up, Gary paused to look out the side window. Down in the darkness he saw two young black men leaning against the patrol car. One of them was wiping the side of the car with his shirttail.

"Oh, man," Gary said to his nervous partner. "You know what? I left the car doors unlocked."

"Can you see what's going on down there?"

"Not really. I just hope to hell they haven't taken the shotgun out of the car."

"Boy, you *are* an idiot, you know that?" Colin felt his gun. "Why the hell didn't you lock the car?"

"I forgot, man. I don't usually lock the car. Will you please calm down?"

"If I see one of these guys with that shotgun . . ."

"What will you do? Start a shoot-out like the wild west? Blow up the whole place? Come on, we'll just go down to the car and check it. I'll lock it up and then we'll come back up to talk to Ellis."

We descended the stairs, went out on the porch, where

some of the youngsters were clapping to the rhythmic thumping of bongo drums, and walked to the car. Perhaps twenty-five young men were outside, watching to see how the cops were behaving. Gary looked in the back seat; the shotgun was still there.

"Okay," he said. "I'll lock the doors and then we'll go back up there."

"Forget it," said Colin, his voice beginning to shake. "I'm not going back up there. For Chrissakes, if something breaks out we wouldn't have a chance. They've got us outnumbered by 50 to 1. I just don't think it's sensible police action to go up there."

"Okay, buddy, I'll tell you what. Get in the car, get on the air, put in a call, and ask for one more car to come by, to back us up. We'll have them come by and they can watch our car while we go upstairs and talk to the kid giving the party. And they'll see that nothing happens to our car."

Colin hesitated a moment and then slipped into the driver's seat. He reached for the microphone, feeling his hand in the darkness under the dashboard. After a moment he discovered the wire, but without the microphone. "They've cut it out of the car! They've cut the goddamn microphone! It's gone!"

"Okay, man, okay," Gary answered. "Don't get excited."

"What the hell do you mean? We can't even call for help!"

"Colin, buddy, we don't *need* any help—not yet, anyway. So relax a minute, will ya?"

"Let's get out of here."

"Hey, man, hey! So they cut out the microphone, what's the big deal? It was done in a Halloween spirit."

"You must be kidding," Colin said from inside the car. "This ain't Halloween. And seriously, this is—"

"Hey, hey! Before I was a policeman, when I was a kid? And when I saw an empty police car? Listen, I had to resist myself like hell so as not to take that car for a ride or something. You know, I wanted to drive the police car a block away and park it. Same with these guys here. So just stop gettin' so nervous. It was a practical joke."

Colin got out of the car and looked at the Negro youngsters, who seemed unconcerned about the presence of the police car. They even seemed unaware that the microphone had been stolen.

Turning to me, Gary said, "Goddamn, now when we go back to the station tonight I'll have to make a report explaining why that microphone got cut out of the car, and why I didn't lock it up. I guess that was my mistake."

"Well, let's just get out of here," Colin urged.

"Look, man, we're gonna carry through and do what we had intended to do." Gary reached inside his pocket and pulled out a dime. Thrusting it toward Colin, he said, "Go across the street to that funky little bar over there and call Communications. Ask them to send us one car. To back us up."

"All right," Colin muttered, taking the dime and running across the street to the tiny neighborhood tavern. Gary and I remained standing next to the patrol car. He folded his arms, listening to the bongo music, and waited for Colin to return.

Suddenly the car radio crackled and the dispatcher was saying, "Attention all units, all units, we got a 904 Code Two, all units . . ." Gary, unable to transmit from his radio, stood in shock as he heard his location being described as a major trouble spot.

As Colin emerged from the saloon, sirens were approaching from almost every direction. Then the whirling red lights and sirens came into the block, first one car and then two, three, four cars, until a total of five cars filled the block.

"What the hell's going on?" Gary screamed to his partner as a sixth and seventh car rolled up. "What the hell did you tell them?"

"I just said we needed help right away."

"Well, damn! These guys are coming from everywhere! Man, oh, man, I feel like a first-class asshole!"

The small street by now was jammed with patrol cars,

their lights turning wildly round and round, flashing red beams across trees and houses in the night; their sirens screamed and moaned in wild and uneven pitch. For at least a block in each direction, we could see nothing but police cars, parked and idling, unable to move.

Almost crying with the pain of his embarrassment, Gary said, "All these cars—and nothing has happened!" For a moment he almost lunged at Colin as if to grab ahold of his neck, but then he turned and saw the huge crowd of young black men standing on the lawn. They, also, were watching as the policemen moved out of their cars, nightsticks in hand. For a moment Gary seemed unsure of which way to turn, to the black youths on the lawn or to his colleagues. Then, from the house came Bobby Ellis, a slightly built, clear-eyed young man whose spotless yellow windbreaker seemed to glow in the dark. Gary walked up to him and began to apologize, but Ellis, with great composure, shook his head.

"Nobody talks to nobody," he said. "Not with all this pig out here. Man, you got the sergeant out here and everybody else. What is all this?"

Gary Cummings swallowed and tried to look Ellis directly in the eye. "Well, uh . . ." he stumbled. "Uh, you got a noisy party up there."

After a pause, Bobby Ellis said, "Well, goddamn, you didn't have to call out the whole police force, did you?"

Gary tried to find the right words, but none came forth. Ellis lifted his head up and surveyed the line of cops standing at the curb. Behind the student-union leader, the other black youngsters began yelling, "Honkies! Pigs! Hey, motherfuckers!"

Almost whispering, Gary said, "Listen, man, this was a mistake. I apologize."

The heckling from behind Bobby Ellis grew more angry in tone, but the militant leader seemed in complete control. "What do you want?" he asked.

"Nothing," said Gary. "Just a little less noise. This ain't a bust or anything."

"Okay. I'll quiet the party down if you get all these cops out of here. Can you do that?"

Gary turned his head for a moment to look at the phalanx of policemen. Later he told me what went through his mind during those tense moments: "Getting those cops out of there was asking a lot. Because they're policemen just like me, and I knew what was on their minds. I could see that all they wanted to do was just, you know—zam!—right now! They wanted to go in there and start clubbing. But each cop was afraid to take the initiative on his own and to start it."

After a moment's pause, Gary replied to Bobby Ellis, "Yeah, I'll get 'em out of here." He walked back to the car where Colin was talking to the sergeant. "Goddamn it, sergeant," yelled Gary, "get these policemen out of here!"

"You sure everything's okay?"

"It won't be okay if these guys stay here much longer."

The sergeant returned to his car, went on the air and told all the units to return to wherever they had come from. The patrolmen, almost reluctantly, walked away from the scene and went back to their cars, a chorus of jeers at their backs.

The next day, Gary called Bobby Ellis on the phone, to apologize for the entire incident. "Ellis told me," Gary reported, "that there were still a couple of those patrol cars riding around the area for hours, harassing every goddamn kid who left that party. They got called a lot of names by the kids. I guess their ego was involved, I don't know."

There was at least one thing upon which Gary and Colin could agree: Compared to the members of the tactical patrol force, they felt like ultrasensitive social workers in police uniforms. Unlike the two young patrolmen, who are both under 160 pounds, the tactical police in San Francisco are above average in height and weight. They wear black leather jackets, white crash helmets, and big gun belts with equipment that jangles as they stride in and out of the station house. Though their physiques are huge, their faces seemed to me clean and blank, as if they were in some kind of occupational limbo, waiting for something to happen so that their big, restless bodies could go into motion again. Outside, they cruise in and out of streets in unmarked cars, two men in front and two in back; even in the station house they seem to stay together, aware of their unique status as the elite group within the patrol force.

Early one evening after roll call, I sat with Gary and Colin in a corner of the station house while they filled out forms and did their paperwork. We watched a group of tactical cops who looked as if they were getting ready to charge outside for the beginning of a shift. "Those guys make me nervous," said Gary, smiling.

Even Colin had to agree: "If more of us get killed on the beat, they'll probably put the tactical squad out there. Can you imagine their reaction to all the hecklers on just one stroll through the Haight?"

"They'd close the street like the Gestapo."

Three of the burly tactical men were waiting impatiently for their fourth partner to come down from the locker room. They seemed unable to stand still. One of them impulsively clapped his hands together and occasionally whistled and shouted, "Hey!" At the same time, he was constantly rising and falling on the balls of his feet. One of his partners suddenly threw him a black leather glove and barked, "Think fast!" The cop caught the glove, shouted, "Hey," and tossed it back.

"They have so much damn energy," Colin remarked. "I went to a house call with that guy," he said, calling my attention to the cop who was rising and falling on the balls of his feet. "He doesn't *walk* upstairs; he *runs*. We stopped for coffee later in the night and he ate enough for three people and this was only a few hours after a big dinner."

The fourth member of the squadron, which was dubbed the "goon platoon" by youngsters in Haight-Ashbury, nimbly descended the stairs and shouted, "Ready?"

"Right!"

The foursome put on their white helmets and strode outside.

"They have automatic rifles," Gary commented to me after they were beyond earshot. "They just float around, sticking pretty close to the street, so to speak. Whatever they want to take on, they can do it. To me, they act like they think they're constantly on riot duty. It must carry over, in their minds. That real tall one is a brute."

"I always see a few units out there," Colin noted. "They're called in when there's trouble, and they sort of go on their own. They can on-view something. I must admit, though, that they're a different breed of cop. Like overgrown, dangerous kids. I don't really like them."

"They responded to our 'noisy party' the other night, along with the other ten million units," Gary added. "Boy, were they hungry for action! Their training, I think, is a little too much in one direction—the physical—and it kind of makes their brains lopsided. I think there's only one Negro guy on the 'tac' squad. They probably don't want *any* black guys, because otherwise they wouldn't be able to talk to each other in their usual language."

"They're great for riots, though," said Colin. "The department took a bunch of its biggest, meanest, gung-ho types and put 'em on the riot squad. Now, if you want a display of *force,* I mean if you *need* that display, they're *it*. But I have to agree—they're just kind of like animals. They don't know how—I mean, it's almost impossible to talk to them on any intelligent level. And they really don't know how to deal with people, or relate to them."

"Well," Gary observed, "they probably do serve a need. Obviously in certain tough situations you don't need a bunch of policemen who are as disorganized as the rioters, because cops can be rioters themselves. You do need an organized force. My only complaint about the 'tac' squad is that they don't have enough emphasis upon restraint. There's too much of that image there. Maybe they begin reading their own press. You know: 'The tough tactical unit.' It has a nice sound. Now, I don't know if there's any correlation between size and ability—I guess that's a stupid thought. But I think most cats who have any sort of sensitivity would turn away from that type of position. There's no service involved. They don't really help people—I mean, they're not involved in family fights, or they're not advising people in civil matters, which I consider to be a service. They don't get down and deal with the little kids and so on . . ."

"Well, whenever I'm in trouble I'm glad to see them around," said Colin. "That Chemical Mace we used last year was beautiful. Instant! Out of commission! I wish we had something like that now. Supposedly it damages the eyes, but they ought to develop something else like it."

"You ought to quit thinking about how you can put people out of commission and start trying to communicate with them more," Gary countered.

"I know that," said Colin. "On foot patrol I used to brush off guys who wanted to talk. I used to say, 'I gotta get going,' and then walk away from them. But then I suddenly realized: 'Where am I going? I've got all night.' "

As they did their office work, Gary said wryly, "This has to be the only job in the world where you have to fill out six forms to go on vacation."

But before the young patrolmen had finished with their paperwork, the tactical patrol returned. The thick front door of the station house slammed open and a young Negro man, his arms handcuffed behind his back, sailed headfirst into the room, landing on the floor. His friend, also handcuffed, was escorted briskly through the door and shoved down on the dark-green bench, causing his head to snap back and smash against the wall. His dark glasses fell from one ear and dangled on his face. A huge tactical cop took one stride and kicked the young man on the floor in the stomach, as he tried to get on his feet. "Take these cuffs offa me!" he screamed. "I'll fight!"

The tactical police, full of energy, smiled at each other

as their wild, contemptuous prisoner managed to stand up. "Why don't you shoot me!" he pleaded. "If *I* had a gun I'd shoot *you*." With that he was thrown toward the desk clerk's window and held rigidly while another cop felt through his clothing. "The white man never did this to me," he sobbed, "until this guy used me like a punching bag! Go on, break my arm! Rip it off!" The cop nearly complied with his request.

"How old are you?" asked the sergeant from behind the window.

"I'm eighteen! And never in my life—! White man! Knocking me down, for nothing! Just nothing! If you gonna kill me, why don't you just kill me!"

Then he was thrown toward the bench. He fell, still shouting, and was slammed into the bench alongside his partner. Immediately he stood up, struggling with the handcuffs behind him, and charged at the tactical police.

"SIT OVER HERE!" Again he was hurled against the bench. "YOU'RE A PRISONER! YOU DO WHAT YOU'RE TOLD!"

"MOTHERFUCKER WHITE MAN!"

Smiling, Colin said to me, "I've learned never to stand in front of that door. They're always coming in headfirst."

By this time, however, Gary was on his feet and walking casually over to the group of tactical police. "What's going on, fellas?" he asked, a note of bitterness in his voice.

"What's it to you?"

"Hey, man, I'm a policeman like you. I just thought I'd find out why you're kicking this guy's ass." The glare from the tactical cops was ferocious. Gary added, "I just want to find out which side I'm on."

"Listen, Cummings," yelled the sergeant, "there's only *one* side of the story—*our* side."

Then the fourth tactical cop entered with a long-haired white youngster who was told to sit down on another bench. The "tac" men explained to me that the white youngster had been lured into the Panhandle, a block-long extension of Golden Gate Park, under the impression that the two Negroes would sell him some marijuana. When he got to the Panhandle, they pulled out a gun and tried to rob him. At that moment, the tactical squad happened to cruise by. As they approached, one of the Negroes attempted to throw his gun away while the other one swallowed several "speed," or methedrine tablets to avoid being caught with them. Thus the wild antagonism from the one Negro youngster was attributed to the effect of the pills.

"Can I go to the bathroom?" he called.

"No! Stay where you are!"

"Can I make a phone call?"

"SIT DOWN."

Added to this commotion was the entrance of a plainclothes man with four white "hippie" prisoners: a boy and girl handcuffed together and two young men, also handcuffed to each other. They were seated next to the two black youngsters, who by contrast were clean and well-dressed.

"Hey, what'cha busted for, brother?" said a white boy to the Negro prisoner next to him, in a gesture apparently aimed at solidarity.

"None of your fucking white-ass business" was the reply.

"Okay," the plainclothes man announced, "dump everything out of your pockets and onto the table." He released the handcuffs from his four white prisoners and, with some reluctance, they dumped out several bags of pink and blue capsules, which Colin said were LSD, along with a jumble of keys and trinkets and wallets.

Suddenly the tactical police looked around the room and discovered that their white prisoner was missing. "Hey, hey, hey! Where's our guy? Where's the guy that was almost robbed? He's escaped! Hey, hey, hey!" The response was sudden and swift. The desk sergeant, Colin, Gary, and three other patrolmen dashed out of the station with the tactical cops, who, inexplicably to me, had grins on their faces in the midst of crisis. The cops scurried in every direction in the early-evening fog around the building. "Which way? Which way?" came the shouts of frenzied police officers. Meanwhile, unaware of the panic he had caused, the youngster wandered out of the men's room and returned to his place on the bench.

The desk clerk looked up and shouted: "He's right here!"

The crisis subsided, but not the churned-up energy within the cops. "You! Sit over there and don't move!" came the sergeant's loud bark.

"I had to puke," said the young man.

Hearing all the commotion, the jacketless, white-haired lieutenant came from the rear office, snapping his suspenders. "What's all the racket?" he said, as if he had been thrown out of a comfortable hammock. "The hippies rioting again? How're you doing, men?" He addressed the tactical police, who grinned and nodded. "What'cha got here? Same old stuff, hunh? I see, I see: beads, barefoot, dirty, filthy. What's their problem, police brutality? All they have to do is shout or sneeze and there'll be a TV camera in here, but if I go out and get killed by some punk-communist kid, after being a policeman since before they were born, I'd be lucky to have an obituary on the back page! Ain't that right? Look at 'em —prize packages!"

Gary and Colin were about to leave the station house at this point when an older policeman, Sam, announced that he would take a stroll with them, "just to keep in touch with things." Sam had had a foot beat for at least a dozen years, but had long since retreated to the station house from the havoc of the new generation on Haight Street. "When I walked the beat," he told me, "it was a routine security check of buildings and friendly drunks. You could have shot a cannon down the street and hit nobody, it was so nice and peaceful. I've seen this area evolve to where it is today, and if you ask me it's gone the way the whole country's gonna go if we don't hold the line. These boys, you know, are the only thing that stands between the community and chaos. It was even integrated, here, *Niggra* and white."

"The hippie thing had a lot of appeal for the straights, so to speak," said Colin.

"Hippies! What is that? No responsibility, for one thing. They're on their own, with no boss, do what they want, be a bum, have free love. I know all that. Supposedly the art and the creativity was the big thing, although there are few artists out here that are any damn good, if you ask me. I think the sex angle attracted most of 'em."

"The thing that knocked 'em out of the saddle," Colin added as they walked into the park, "was the narcotics."

"That's correct, because you bring in narcotics and you bring in crime. This'll be an area for urban renewal in a few years. I mean, this is a ghetto over here now, plain and simple. As I say, it used to be a good beat. This would have been a nice place to have spent my declining years as a policeman, but the place attracted everybody—retarded people and dirty, disrespectful kids . . . people who believed what they read in the papers about love and sex and all that. They come in here and take advantage of it all, and how can we do a job? No backing from the courts, and the place is a nursery. A real nursery!

"I told my wife, 'We brought up three kids and sent them to college. They don't grow their hair long and spit at policemen and throw bricks at them. So why do I have to play nursemaid to everybody else's kid?' That's when I left the beat and became a clerk. I mean, you lock up one juvenile and there are fifteen more on the street. I got stacks of sheets for runaway kids in the station, just for this month! Hundreds! And it takes time to process a juvenile. They won't give information out; they're from out of town and won't say where they're from. And they change their names, give false identification papers. And when you do finally find out who they are, they go to Youth Guidance and they're set free. They go home and run away a week later, right back here. Our service is fine for the parent, but the kid doesn't give a damn about his parents. So the kid looks on the policeman as almost his father and mother. They feel like we're here so they can rebel against authority. A cop is close by, so he scratches easily. You crash a pad and then almost anything can happen. I'm no spring chicken, either. No, no, I'll leave it all to you younger guys. I didn't become a cop to run a nursery school."

"It may be a nursery school," said Colin, "but the kids are pretty dangerous. Knives, guns . . ."

Shortly before 6:30 P.M., I strolled with Sam and the two young policemen through a section of the park with picnic tables, where elderly men were hunched over card games. Summer evenings like this one are chilly in San Francisco, and a breeze tossed litter and leaves about in tiny swirls on the concrete-patio section beneath the patrolmen's feet. The smell of urine carried into our nostrils.

"These old guys," said Colin, "are afraid to go to the public men's room. The kids have made it a horror for old people, what with the muggings and robberies. So these older fellows just urinate and defecate all over the park."

As we passed by the small pond, a Negro man was whispering to a Negro girl. She continued on up the path and the man uttered, "Bitch!"

"Hey!" called Colin. "Hold on." Walking up to him, Colin ordered, "Put your hands out."

"What for, man?"

"Just put those hands out."

Wearily, the black man held out his arms and Colin frisked him up and down. "I don't know why you do this," he said to the young cop.

"You've been drinking, haven't you?" said Colin.

"A little. Just a little."

"What were you harassing that girl for?"

"What girl?"

"The one that just passed by here."

"I wasn't harassing her, man! That's my cousin!"

"I heard you call her a bitch. Now that wasn't very nice, was it?"

"Man, she's my *cousin*. I just asked her for a little spare change, that's all."

Colin did not respond. He completed his frisk and said, "I think a night in jail would do you good."

"Oh, no! That's impossible!"

"You behave, now," said Sam. To Colin and Gary he said, "I'll take him back to the station. Thanks for the exercise, fellas."

"Don't hold me, man," said the prisoner, struggling to disengage his arm from Sam's grip. "Don't hold me!"

Sam took out his handcuffs and snapped them across the black man's wrists. "Okay," he said. "That'll hold you. Come along now. I've got to get you booked so I can have my dinner."

"How long am I gonna be in jail? What about my job?"

"Come on," said the elder policeman, escorting him down the path toward the station house.

For half a minute, Gary and Colin said nothing. Then Gary shouted, "What the hell are we doing—arresting guys for almost nothing?"

"What do you mean? If these guys get arrested a few times, they'll stay out of the park."

"It's sickening to me. Sickening! He didn't do a damn thing against the law."

"He was loitering in the park, leering at girls and what-not, and half-drunk at that. You don't believe that story about how that girl was his cousin, do you?"

"No, I don't believe that. But there's a *chance* he was telling the truth. Anyhow, it just wasn't *necessary* to arrest him."

"It depends on what you mean by 'necessary.' If we hadn't come along, he might have molested that girl. What do you think he's doing in the park, taking a stroll for the hell of it?"

"Let's put it this way," Gary said. "I don't *know* any different."

A moment later, the cops stopped before a bench where two drunken Indians were leaning against each other. Colin put the walkie-talkie to his lips and said, "Two to go."

This time, Gary merely turned his back as Colin made the Indians stand up to be frisked. Colin poured out a bottle of wine and led the Indians up to the street to wait for the wagon. A tall, bespectacled man with a notebook and pen, who had been watching from a distance, came over and benignly inquired, "Pardon me, but in all due respect, do you have a warrant for this kind of thing?"

"No," answered Colin. "I don't have a warrant. It's an onsight arrest."

"Well—"

"And I don't need a warrant to arrest *you* for interfering, either, so beat it!"

Colin, fist clenched at his side, stared at the man as he backed off a few steps and began jotting something down in his notebook, shaking his head.

"What are you—a reporter?" asked Colin.

"That, kind sir, is none of your business."

Gary walked up to the stranger but Colin, suddenly red-faced and almost losing control, shouted, "Cummings! Don't talk to that guy. It's against rules to talk to reporters. Look at him, the bastard."

The man smiled, eagerly transcribing everything that was being said, and walked away.

One of the Indians, wearing a headband and medallion in hippie style, said, "The white man got me drunk."

"Is that so?" Colin responded. "You're blaming us for you getting yourself drunk, hunh?"

The Indian nodded but explained no further. After the paddy wagon had come and taken them away, Colin and Gary began their walk into Haight Street. "That guy was with one of the underground papers," Colin explained to me.

"So what?" Gary replied.

We took the left side of Haight Street, along which, curiously, about 90 percent of the young people congregated. Then, we stopped to chat with the manager of a large supermarket, who told me that his hired store detectives were catching an average of 200 shoplifters, mostly young people, per week, and that another supermarket in Haight-Ashbury had been forced to close recently after losing $5,400 worth of merchandise to shoplifters in a three-month period.

The cops continued toward the main intersections of the Haight-Ashbury area, stopping occasionally to talk to storeowners, bartenders, and abandoned-looking youngsters. The daylight was giving way to a gray-white fog that came in almost as a daily forerunner of nighttime. The fog made the street like an arena filled with fragments of human forms; nothing complete, no "whole" person could be seen. The patrolmen decided to stop for dinner at a Mexican cafe. We paused to watch a bearded, bushy-haired man who had dropped a round, white onion on the street. It rolled beneath a car. The man got down on his hands and knees to reach it. At last, with half of his body beneath the car, he grabbed it. Standing up, he rubbed it on his thigh and returned it to the pocket of his long, green coat. Then four motorcycle riders with black leather jackets roared through the street, bodies deep in their saddles and arms stretched upward and out to the handle bars. Their image seemed to offer some kind of community counterpart to the tactical squad. A man with a blanket wrapped about himself played a flute as he walked by. A girl stood gazing into space with a sign in one hand: "Buy Free Things." Another girl, with long red hair falling over an Army jacket, squatted next to a little Negro boy, who reached inside the brown paper bag she held, pulling out a french-fried potato. The cops went inside for their meal.

A sign in the restaurant announced: "Credit extended to those over 79 years of age, when accompanied by their parents." Next to this sign another one read: "Those not eating, wait outside for your friends." As if in response, a button worn by a young man hunched over a bowl of soup at the counter declared: "Jesus wore long hair."

The middle-aged proprietress seemed glad to see the cops. She had been held up a few nights before "by three Mexican-Indian types."

"How much did they get?" asked Gary.

"About ninety dollars. If you boys had come in here, they would have killed you. You wouldn't have had a chance."

"Well," said Colin, "they might come back and shoot *you* if we don't get 'em."

"All I could think of," the woman went on, "was 'Thank God that I've got my burial plot paid for.' "

"Did all three have guns?"

"Two of 'em did for sure. Thank God you fellas didn't come in when they were here. I thought of what happened to little Freddie in the park. I saw the guns and got that dog feeling."

"Dog feeling?"

"My back bristled up, just like a dog."

The two patrolmen and I quietly ate a large, inexpensive dinner of chicken and rice. Once outside again, they sauntered through the crowd and within minutes Colin stopped a young man with a black walking stick. As a group of spectators gathered, Colin took the cane and asked, "Wouldn't be anything inside this, would there?"

"No."

"Promise?"

"Yes."

Colin started to unscrew the silver top of the cane and paused. "You wouldn't lie to me, would you?"

"No."

The top came off and Colin pulled out a long sword. The young man, as if surprised at the existence of the blade, whistled.

"Hands up the pole," Colin ordered, giving the cane to Gary and then frisking the young man. The crowd hissed as Colin called for the paddy wagon.

One youngster held a knife blade up and defiantly challenged, "This is legal, right?"

"That's right," Colin said. "It's legal to carry an unexposed knife. But if it's concealed, like in a cane, it's a misdemeanor."

"What does that mean?" asked the young prisoner who was now being handcuffed by Colin.

"It means you can get up to a year in the county jail."

"Oh, no!"

The paddy wagon made its appearance and the prisoner was swiftly taken off the street and forgotten. "You know," Colin said to me as he and Gary continued their strolling, "their was one cop in the Haight who supposedly made too many arrests, and the hippies allegedly had a plot to kill him."

"What happened?" I asked.

"He was transferred. His wife came down to the station and demanded it."

On the corner, a group of long-haired residents of Hashbury had surrounded a charter bus full of tourists. Gary and Colin pushed through the street and dispersed the crowd with no trouble. As the bus pulled away, an eager lady aimed her camera out of the window at a bearded man who threatened to drop his pants. Colin ordered him back to the sidewalk.

A girl then came up to the cops and informed them that a man in a parked car was "exposing himself." She led them to a small red car along the side of Haight Street. Colin rapped on the window and motioned for the man, a well-dressed executive type, to step out. "He's the kind who make speeches about young people being sick," said the girl. "And look at him! He's perverted!" Colin politely asked the man what he was doing in hippieville. The reply was a sophisticated, innocent, embarrassed shrug. "Arrest him!" called the girl.

"Do you want to press charges?" asked Gary.

"Yes! Yes, I do! Dirty old man!"

Colin said, "The girl says you were exposing yourself."

"No, I didn't do that."

"Liar!" the girl yelled.

"I think you'd better leave this area," Colin said, and the man jumped back into his car. He struggled to maneuver his car out of the parking space as the hippies taunted and jeered at him.

"We could have arrested that guy," Gary said.

"For what? It would be his word over the girl's."

"Well, I'll bet she was telling the truth. What else would a guy like that be doing here? If the roles had been reversed somehow, you can bet we'd have arrested *her*."

"I checked his driver's license," Colin said. "His name is Donaldson. Lots of credit cards and so on. He might be a big shot. A perverted big shot. He'd be out on bail and we'd be in hot water."

Gary muttered an obscenity. We continued walking to the end of the block, where a crowd of hippies watched the tactical police escort a young man with a banjo into their car. The scene was strangely silent, as if the young people had no way to express their frustration.

"Pardon me, officer," a large man with shoulder-length hair said, his voice betraying the frustration. "Could you kindly tell me what that fellow is being arrested for?"

"I don't know," Gary said. "We just got here."

"Disturbing the peace," Colin answered.

A few minutes later, Gary asked almost to himself, "What's worse, a kid playing a banjo or a guy exposing himself?" Colin did not answer.

It was almost dark when the cops crossed to the other side of Haight Street at Masonic Street and began walking back. They stopped to chat with a young girl who told us her kitten was being eaten up by worms, and moments later they halted a man carrying a croquet mallet.

"What's this for?" Colin asked.

"Protection, man."

"I suggest you don't carry it around. It could get you into more trouble than it would get you out of."

"Sure, man. I found it this afternoon, anyway."

The cops crossed the street and we went into the Straight Theater, an old auditorium used for psychedelic dance parties. Colin, Gary, and I walked up to the balcony and looked down on the wood floor below. Some youngsters were squatting around the edges and others danced without partners to the amplified, ear-breaking sounds of electric guitars. "You can smell the marijuana in here," Colin noted. Red, green, purple, yellow, blue, and white lights swirled in chaotic fashion about the auditorium while the kids on the floor swayed dreamily to the high-decibel music. A black-and-white movie was being run on a small screen to one side of the dance floor. The film strip, showing a naked woman writhing on her back and drinking from a bottle of wine, was repeated without beginning or end; and the viewer could anticipate each of the woman's movements as they occurred over and over like suspended reality in the midst of pounding music and pulsating color.

The cops went down to the lobby, brushing past a group of youngsters to the outside. The girl behind the ticket window called, "How'd you like the show?"

"Real groovy," said Colin, chuckling to himself.

"Next time," the girl said with a smile, "I'll charge you the normal rate."

Gary and Colin were soon stopped by a middle-aged Negro man who asked if they had heard about an off-duty white policeman being assaulted and robbed in the Fillmore district.

"The way I hear it," said Gary, "the cop was drunk. Why he was in the black neighborhood, off-duty, is what you might call 'a subject of conjecture' by quite a few other policemen."

The Negro man, himself under the influence of a few drinks, changed the subject to "little black boys harassing white girls." He urged the cops to "stand up to those little punks."

"Sounds like you're Uncle Tomming," said Gary.

"I tell my own people," the man went on, "that we don't even understand *ourselves*. We don't know why we do what we do! We need communication, that's what. And I'm a hundred percent behind you boys, hear? Now, it's up to you cops to stand up to the little punks. Lemme show you—" He made a move for Colin's gun and the patrolman jumped back.

"I'm not gonna take your gun, man. I'm just demonstrating."
He pretended to take Colin's gun, adding, "Now, don't you
back off, hear? Don't give up!"

"I think you'd better go home, fella," said Colin.

"No, wait! Wait, man. I'm not gonna mess with you,
don't worry. You don't hafta be afraid of me."

His face red, Colin replied, "I'm not afraid."

"Then what you backing off for, man? I want to say that
I'm *with* you, not against you. One hundred percent! Now,
let's say you go to the Grand Canyon, right? And you look
down over the cliff and there's a guy hanging down there on
a little ol' twig, okay?"

"Yeah, yeah," Colin said impatiently.

"So you look down and he says, 'Hey, brother, give me
a hand up there, will you?' And you think about that a while
and then you say, 'Okay, sure.' So you gives him a hand and
he climbs to the top of the cliff. Now, you give somebody
something and they're gonna want a little more, right? So he
says to you, 'Hey, brother, you got a cigarette?' And you give
him a cigarette. Then he says, 'Hey, brother, you got a lift
into town?' So you drives him into town and he says, 'Hey,
brother, I could use a new set of clothes, after hanging on the
branch all that time.' So you give him some money for new
clothes and he says, 'Hey, brother, I could use me a little
woman. It's been a long time.' And you show him where the
whore house is, but he says, 'Hey, brother, I want *your* little
woman.' Now, by this time you're getting a bit uptight, am I
on the track? You feel like you're gonna kick his ass good,
right?"

"That's right," Colin echoed with impatience.

"Well, that's what I mean! So don't let these little black
boys go around harassing the white girls. It ain't good for
nobody."

Later, the cops approached an old laundry truck parked
around a corner from Haight Street. Gary went to the front

and Colin started toward the back, saying to me, "Ever since Fred got killed, I hate taking on bushes or cars. You never know what the hell's gonna pop out." Through a rear window, Colin aimed the beam of his flashlight on a group of boys and girls, who were embracing each other in the darkness. One of the boys crawled to the rear and opened the doors. At Colin's request, he handed over his crumpled driver's license. "I'd advise you to take this bus away from here," said Colin. "I don't want to find you here when I get back later tonight."

"Where should I go?"

"Where do you live?"

"New York."

"Well, go to a hotel."

The boy laughed and said, "Okay, we'll get out of here."

When they had walked another block away, Colin said, "There's probably at least one runaway in that laundry truck. I'm glad we didn't bring 'em all into the station, though. Too much trouble."

A minute later we heard, "Officer? Officer!" From a side street ran a squat, middle-aged woman. She was out of breath and for a minute could not speak.

"Take your time," Gary said.

"I live down five blocks," she said, "but I get off the number 7 bus right down there. I just got off it now, and"— she caught her breath—"I heard a girl yelling. I am back from work, got off just a block down there."

"On the street, was she?"

"No, no." The woman gestured with her head. "Up in the house. The girl was yelling for help and something about a man was holding a gun on her."

"Okay, okay," said Colin with an air of authoritative calm. "We'll follow you and you can point out the house." The woman nodded her head, still breathing heavily, and walked down the side street. "One thing I've learned," Colin said to me, "is never to run anywhere, if you can help it. Too much panic sets in."

Standing in the darkness, the woman pointed up to the second floor of a Victorian home with tiny porticoes and steeples, a remnant of a past generation. Colin and Gary heard no screams, but the woman insisted, "Up there," and turned away toward her home.

The cops went in and up to the second floor. It was quiet and almost entirely dark. Then we heard a girl's voice from one of the rooms: "I see my mother. Hello, Mom! Don't let the bad men take me away. La, la, la." Colin knocked on the door and the girl screamed, "They're coming!"

In the silence that followed, Colin tried to push open the door but it was locked from the inside. "Open up. Police!"

After a moment the door was unlocked. A bearded man with his shirt off and a medallion hung around his neck greeted them. Inside, the girl began screaming again.

"You'd better not come in here."

"Why not?" Colin asked.

"What's going on?" Gary echoed.

"She's high, man. Real high. I don't advise that you go inside. She's not harming anyone." Again the girl screamed. Gary asked the man to come out to the hallway to explain, but Colin tried to push past him. "Don't go in there, man! You have no legal right!"

The girl, white and naked, was dancing about the room, apparently having drug-induced hallucinations. "Don't go near her," the man pleaded.

"Shut up," Colin returned. "Hey," he called to the girl. "Are you all right?" He stepped into the room.

The girl stopped dancing—there was no music—and stared at Colin. A few seconds passed, but it seemed as long as a minute. Then, without warning, she turned away, looked back at the uniform a moment, and rushed straight into the window, splashing the glass over the sparsely furnished room.

Instantly Colin was behind her, pulling her by the legs back over the broken glass as she writhed and screamed, "Don't touch me! Don't touch me!" She fell onto the floor in a heap, seemingly without pain. Gary placed a shirt he picked up from a chair over her bloody skin and helped her to stand up. His walkie-talkie shaking in his hands, Colin called for a patrol car and an ambulance.

"You shouldn't have gone in there," said the bearded man in a hoarse whisper. "You had no right to just barge in. She wasn't harming anybody."

"Not much," Colin snapped, brushing off his uniform.

"You had no—"

"Shut your fat head!"

Somehow the girl managed to wriggle into a sacklike dress by the time the ambulance had arrived. She swayed about the floor, blood dripping down her legs. Colin exchanged information with the radio-car men and the bearded man demanded to be taken with the girl in the ambulance.

"You're going to the station," Colin angrily retorted.

"What for? You won't find any acid on me, man!"

"Then get the hell out of here!" Colin said. "No, stay here!"

The radio-car cops followed the ambulance to the hospital and the two foot patrolmen held the bearded man while they searched the apartment. Finding no drugs, they left the scene.

Colin angrily kicked the sidewalk. "These kids," he said to me, "they take any kind of pills at all. They shoot any damn thing at all into their veins. Speed, LSD—right down into their stomachs. They even shoot up salt—anything! That girl probably took a pill from some guy on the street. Or from the guy she was with. Sometimes they don't even *know* what it is they've put inside themselves. I asked a kid once and he said, 'No, I don't know what I shot up with. If it kills me, so what? I never died before, so why should I be afraid of something I don't know about? Dying might be a good trip.' The kids here are crazy—just crazy."

"Maybe we should have listened to that guy before barging in there," Gary said. "We frightened her."

"Oh, come *on* now! These kids are killing *themselves.* How old was she? Eighteen? And goddamn, the VD rate here is ten times that of the rest of the city, and hepatitis is at least five times as great. And you could walk down Haight Street and hand out anything—poison, aspirin, anything—and the kids would take 'em and pop 'em into their mouths. They'll take anything for a change of reality."

"A thousand hippies can't be wrong," said Gary, attempting to be humorous.

On Haight Street a little Negro boy looked up at the cops and asked, "Can I go to jail?"

Smiling, Colin answered, "In a few more years." Continuing his previous line of thought, he said, "What bothers me is that our being around stops drug sales from taking place, but not as soon as we move on down the block. I used to gawk at the girls around here. I was tripping over ash cans and walking into parking meters all the time. Couldn't get my eyes off the girls. Now, I'm just disgusted."

Later on in the evening, at the far edge of Haight Street's commercial section, the patrolmen passed by four young men who were sitting on some stairs, almost hidden by shadow. Colin stopped and splashed his flashlight beam across their faces. "How're you doing, fellas?" came the young cop's high-pitched voice. There was no immediate answer, so the patrolman added, "I'd like to see your IDs." Three of the young men immediately reached for their wallets, while the fourth, wearing a bright-gold blouse and shoulder-length hair, seemed upset. Gary checked the identification cards of the other three and the nervous boy walked to the sidewalk, fishing a crumpled pink paper from his pocket.

Colin trained his flashlight on the pink sheet and the boy said, "You can't arrest me."

Although Colin had no intention of arresting him, he asked, "Why not?"

"Because I'm a juvenile."

Without warning the boy sprinted away from Colin and across the street. Instantly Colin was on his heels. They looked like football players, the frontrunner with the ball and Colin in pursuit, trying to tackle him. Within a period of no more than three seconds, Gary made up his mind to stay with the group of three young men on the steps. I stayed with him. He shouted for them to get off the steps and to stand with "faces against the wall," as he watched Colin's pursuit over his shoulder. The fleeing boy had reached a small grass embankment diagonally across the street, where he tripped and fell. Colin drew his gun as the boy wheeled around.

"I was going to shoot him right then," Colin said later. "We had two murders in the week and for all I knew, this was the kid that did it. When he turned around he could have had a gun. How would I know? Kids think we're pursuing them even when we're not. They'll see us coming and start shooting. They get paranoiac."

Luckily for himself, the boy made no erratic movements when he turned around to face his captor. He lay rigidly, arms out, as the patrolman's gun came directly toward his face.

The other three young men were leaning against a garage door, palms stretched up against it, when Colin returned with his fingers clutching the boy's silk shirt. He handcuffed the boy and shoved him alongside the others.

"Hey," said Gary with admiration, "you really moved out on him."

"I had my gun drawn and I was all set to use it, too," Colin said, panting. "I'm not in the mood to chase these cats around too much longer. Bad for the ticker. The goddamn walkie-talkie was getting in my way, too."

After Colin had called for the wagon, the handcuffed boy said, "You can't arrest me! I just got out of juvenile court!"

"Where do you live?"

"Anywhere."

"This pink paper ain't worth shit. What's your name?"

"Jingle Bells."

"Occupation?"

"I'm a tourist attraction."

"Cut the crap!" Colin shouted. "Are you a student?"

"No! I'm a juvenile!" Colin pushed his hand against the

back of the boy's head, smashing his face into the garage door. "And on the side," the boy said bravely, "I keep a look-out for police brutality."

"I should have shot your face off over there," Colin replied.

Colin and Gary rode back to the station with their prisoners. I walked. When I arrived, at about eleven o'clock, the station was in a state of near pandemonium. Three Indians and several hippie types sat next to a clean-cut but drunken young man accused of having deserted the Navy.

"How long have you been out?" an officer was asking him.

"I've been stoned for three days," he replied, looking out of place among the dirty-haired residents of Hashbury with whom he had been arrested.

The station house was filled with youngsters and cops. Along the wall were dozens of photographs of young people who were missing from homes across the country. Most of the pictures showed either young men in jackets and ties or girls posing in pretty dresses—appearances that had changed drastically between then and now.

"My knife was exposed," a young man cried out. "It was exposed over my boot! But the cop pressed it down and busted me for having a concealed weapon!"

"You—shut up!"

"Somebody stole my bus," came another youthful voice, referring to a stolen car.

"Call the auto-theft detail."

A youngster struggled with a police officer who shouted, "Just sit down and don't argue!"

"Then get your hands away. Don't touch me, pig! I'm contagious."

"Hey," came still another angry voice. "How do these narcotics guys get paid for these arrests? By the head? By the bounty?"

One after another, youngsters were dragged up to the desk clerk's window and the officers went through their pockets. At the same time, the sergeant recorded the necessary data.

"Pig!" shouted a wild-eyed youngster dressed as a cowboy.

"What do you have a sock in your pocket for?" the cop asked.

"What's it to you? Is it a crime?"

The young man wheeled around and spit in the cop's face. The officer wiped the saliva off and pushed the boy back against the window. Meanwhile, three tactical men paced back and forth, glaring at the disheveled kids all over the room and particularly at the one who had done the spitting. They smiled at each other and shook their heads. One of the tactical cops walked over to the disrespectful young man and, as the boy yelled several obscenities, grabbed his face and squeezed it with one hand. He shook the boy's face furiously, making it go red and then pale.

"Punishment!" cried a Negro man in the crowd of hippie-type prisoners. "The white man's always talking about justice, but you pigs don't see that. This police department ain't no part of justice, it's part of *punishment*. Punishment, not justice!"

Ironically, the single Negro officer in the station was the one who held on to this black man. He pushed him toward the clerk's window and said, "Here's another one for you."

Without looking up, the sergeant said, "What is he— hippie, Yippie, Indian, or nigger?"

"A nigger!" shouted the black policeman. "Like me!"

"Oh," said the sergeant, surprised but not apologetic. The black officer was angry, but he seemed satisfied that he had made his point.

Marijuana leaves and speed pills, along with an assortment of knives and wallets and other personal belongings, were spread out on the long table. Patrolmen were at typewriters, attempting to fill out forms in order to book their prisoners. Colin and Gary went through the procedure with the desk clerk. The passive threesome was cleared, but the young man with the gold shirt was held for resisting an officer.

Colin explained to me, "I found this envelope on him. It has what looks like the remains of some marijuana leaves. I'm gonna stick him for it. If he hadn't run, I never would book him for this."

"I'm a juvenile," cried the young man for what seemed the thousandth time.

"Well," said Colin wearily, "you're going downtown and they'll print you and find out who the hell you are. We'll see how old you really are."

"I'm seventeen years old!"

"I don't care if you're ten years old, you're going to city prison."

"City prison! No! Last time there they just *kept* me there for twenty days!"

"They should have kept you there longer."

"Listen, I'll go home if you let me free," the boy yelled in desperation, almost crying. "I'm a juvenile! You're trying to hassle my mind!"

After almost two hours at the station, during which time the young man called his parents and verified that he was in fact a juvenile and deserving of less harsh treatment, the two young cops went off duty, to their separate private lives. Colin lived in an apartment in San Francisco with a wife who was expecting her first child. Gary stopped in a "colored bar" until closing time, then went home to the Negro girl, and her four children, with whom he was living.

Next evening, I met the cops at the Mexican cafe, where we ordered the same meal of chicken and rice. They commented that the mood of Haight-Ashbury seemed desperate, and they were right.

Later that night, at the station house, I learned how desperate the evening had been. We were told that an undercover narcotics agent had been out walking through the crowd unnoticed. As one of the police officers later explained, "This cop was well known in the Haight, but he could still make narcotics arrests. People just associated him with the uniform, you know? Once a cop is out of that uniform, his face doesn't mean anything. For some reason, when he's in uniform and makes an arrest, most of the time he doesn't get any trouble. The minute he gets out of the monkey suit, even showing 'em the badge, or the star, doesn't mean anything. The kids want to punch him right in the eye and knock him down. It just infuriates these kids, because they don't believe that narcotics should be against the law. And it infuriates them to be arrested for it or to see one of their friends being busted. They'll riot against the 'narkos' if they get the opportunity. They'll literally come down and drag that guy away from the cop, even if they have to kick him in the head to do it. They'll go right ahead and start slugging, with no compunction whatsoever. Among these kids, the laws against narcotics are a direct threat to a way of life, which is just what drug taking is for them."

On this evening, according to several cops I spoke to, the plainclothes "nark" moved among the young people who whispered, "Acid? Lids? Mescaline? Speed?" He paused casually next to a pair of black dealers from Oakland. After a minute he nodded to the two men and they motioned for him to follow them around the corner. The undercover man said, "Do you have any lids?" referring to marijuana.

"Acid," was the reply.

"Yes."

The transaction was made and then came the words, "You're under arrest." The agent moved quickly, handcuffing the men together and calling for a patrol car in the callbox nearby. As they waited for the car, the dealers began shouting to the crowd on Haight Street. Together they broke loose and ran around the corner, ducking into a saloon. They screamed at the Negro owner to protect them, that they were being arrested illegally, but the owner told them to leave. Just then, the radio car pulled up and two officers, plus the undercover man, attempted to drag the prisoners out of the bar.

"The kids on the street hate the 'narkos' so much," said one police officer who had been on the scene, "that right away they responded to the shouting. In thirty seconds everybody on that street knew there was something big on—the word spread like wildfire. Then the bottles and rocks started coming; glass was being smashed all over. It was as if they had been waiting all the time for something to happen, and as if they were ready for it when it came."

The patrol car was surrounded by a mass of angry, shouting people. Within minutes, the Haight-Ashbury district was shattered by surges of street violence and flaming Molotov cocktails. Colin and Gary and I were still in the restaurant when we heard the sirens and dashed toward the crowd, leaving their dinners of chicken and rice behind them on the table. I followed, but stayed a block away from the melee so as not to become involved.

Colin later described his initial feelings this way: "I don't mind an actual confrontation breaking out around me, but the thing that scares me is like knowing that the crowd was gathering for a real riot. I mean, at first you're on the outside and you have to go in there. You can think for a minute, and that gives you time to get scared. You know there are snipers, you know there are Molotov cocktails—you know all these things, but you're not yet in the middle of them. You become apprehensive, like, 'Hey, I can get hurt over there.' And then you start worrying yourself to death. It's that time for rationalizing that's bad."

When Colin pushed his way into the crowd he saw that the patrol car had no way of leaving the scene. "They were completely surrounded," he said. "They asked for a unit to respond and one did. No overresponse, just one unit. But they were trapped, so they called for more units."

One of the cops in a radio car responding to the scene

recalled later, "The psychology behind it was 'Okay, you're there, the red lights are on, you got a lot of spectators coming around, so we'll leave! And if we do that, the crowd will go away.' Well, this didn't occur. Not in this particular instance. Good Lord knows why not. We left, the crowd stayed—even after the two dope sellers were taken out of there. Members of the crowd, the hard-core kids who come up to the street looking for narcotics and just to raise hell, they started picking up bottles and sticks and things like that, and they threw 'em at passing automobiles and buses.

"The crowd became unruly, and so that necessitated all the cops to return. This all took maybe five minutes. The first couple of units came back in and they took 'em on pretty heavy. So they brought in more units, and again they had to disperse the crowd. They dispersed it to a degree and left the area again. The crowd then moved to another location, half-way down the block. And the same thing began all over again. This occurred periodically. It was word of mouth, you know: 'Come down to Haight Street,' and so everybody was throwing bottles. Well, we put as many units as we had in the station up on Haight Street. And the crowds began to gather on this one corner, and they gathered and gathered and gathered. They just built up, so to speak, and it looked like a Mexican stand-off. You know—a policeman on each corner and the crowd milling about, back and forth. So once again we said, 'Let's leave the area. We'll try it again.' Of course, in the process of leaving the area, and of building up a substantial force, we were pretty disorganized. But we all left and the cops gathered in the station house to prepare themselves. One of the prime things, of course, is having enough power to put something down as soon as possible, and having wagons available, because if you have a prisoner, what are you gonna do with him once you got him? You gotta get rid of him somehow. So they called for wagons from outside districts. So while the crowd was gathering, we were preparing our next move."

Meanwhile, Colin had gone to a rooftop in order to

prevent people from throwing things off it. I remained on the fringe of the disturbance. "I'm up there watching the action," he said, "and as soon as the cops left, the crowd started throwing more bottles, bricks, sticks—every kind of thing—at cars . . . and jeez, they hit a couple of buses real good. Busted the windows right out of them. And I could see it all going on down there. The most frustrating thing is to be in a position where you can see people doing things, things that are absolutely wrong, and being totally helpless to do anything about it.

"I spotted one particular individual," Colin went on, "who was actually acting like the commander of a rat pack. The kids were just following him around. You could see these little sporadic groups forming, away from the crowd itself, and then the bottles again. Many people in the crowd were spectators; not all, but a percentage of them were. Then, one group started smashing windows in the store directly underneath me! They were looting right below me, and I could hear the windows breaking and alarms going off. So I'm standing on the roof and what was I gonna do? Shoot ten people standing down below because they're burglarizing a store? I *could* have done it. I could have done it easily, no problem at all. It probably would have put a stop to it for quite a while —as a deterrent, you know . . ."

Gary, meanwhile, had been mingling with the crowd, trying to talk the participants out of being violent; but to little avail. At one point he saw me and threw up his hands despairingly.

The *Berkeley Barb*, a local underground newspaper, had a somewhat different version of the outbreak: "Ask any cop just what he was doing out there tonight, what it was all about, and the ones who answer you at all will probably say that they were defending the community against a riot by the hippies. It's no secret any more WHO starts riots, is it? When a cop speaks about defending society, what he means is defending one way of life by destroying those who would lead their lives another way."

The underground press has never been popular, to say the least, with policemen. However, Gary Cummings regularly combed the various papers for allegations of police brutality. After the "hippie riot," which ended with a "sweep" of thirty tactical cops through the street, Gary brought the following allegation in the underground press to Colin's attention: "The cops who had arrested us took us into the interrogation room, closed the door and proceeded to methodically, carefully and skillfully beat us up. They used a small sap or blackjack, their fists, elbows and boots. They worked us over for about 15 minutes, it seemed. I could see very little, because I was protecting my face. . . . The cops concentrated on my kidneys, chest and groin. I found myself pleading with them to stop. They would not."

"The other side to that story," Colin said, "is that the kids wanted the police to beat them up. Not all of them, maybe, but a great many of them. This wasn't a riot in the same sense as Watts, for example. The kids—and many of them are much older than kids—tried their best to make the *police* break the law by beating them up. So maybe they succeeded, I don't know."

Gary, who had tried to calm the crowd through "establishing a dialogue," had not succeeded. "The sight of those cops in riot gear charging down the street," he said, "waving their clubs and using them on those fleeing kids, was enough to even frighten me." Gary told me he had witnessed one scene where an officer was rousting a young man off the street. "He told the kid to get going and started whacking him on the back with his stick. The kid started running and crying, 'I'm going, I'm going, I'm sorry, I'm sorry.' But the cop chased after him, clubbing him. He jabbed his stick into the kid's stomach, and when the guy fell, the cop kicked him in the ribs."

"That was a bad scene," said Gary, "and I'm inclined to think that it's society to blame, not so much the police or the kids. I mean, the whole thing boils down to a confrontation and anything can happen. It's really a minor battle in a big civil war, I think. But it's as if Haight-Ashbury was an arena, with the kids on one side and the cops on the other, each going wild, while the rest of society just sits back and chooses sides.

"These white kids, the hippies, have made police brutality a part of their lives by going against society. They're just beginning to catch up with the Negroes, and I think it helps them to identify with black people. Myself, I don't think I ever even thought about police brutality, because cops just weren't an important part of my life. For the average white person, the policeman never enters his life. They never even *talk* to a policeman. But you show me a black person and I can guarantee you—and I don't care who he is, a doctor or a lawyer or what—that he's had some kind of dealings with the police. And you show me the *average* black person and he's had *more* than one dealing with police. Now, I'm not saying that it's always been unfavorable. Sometimes it *is* favorable. But he's had dealings, while the average white person has never come into contact with a cop. The closest he's come to a policeman is the guy standing on the corner directing traffic. Or worse, the rich whites have had contact with cops because they get special favors.

"I know this one Negro civil rights leader named Lassiter, who went to jail for demonstrations. I heard on the car radio two days after he had gotten out of jail that the police had stopped him on the street. And they ran a check on him over the air. The guy in Communications said, 'Is that *the* Mr. Lassiter?' And the cop in the car chuckled and said, 'Yeah, it's him.' Well, the guy had just gotten out of jail two days before, and you *know* they didn't have any warrants for him. They just wanted to harass the guy.

"And here we get into the personality of the cop, which is something that's not supposed to matter insofar as keeping the peace and enforcing the law. But some guys, they don't care if it's a Negro or not. Some guys are just so prejudiced that they just like to whip a guy's head. They don't care—

I mean, they use any excuse. The cat's a liberal, or his hair is that way, or he may wear a certain type of clothing. Wham!"

"It's hard to stay liberal on this job," said Colin. "It'll swing most anyone over."

"Like yourself?" I asked.

"Sure, like me. One of those kids yelled at me, 'You're causing the riot.' I told them to go home and some guy three rows back threw a bottle, and everybody was standing around, laughing, egging on the doers. It pisses me off. It's *impossible* to stay liberal as a cop, I think."

"But it shouldn't be that way," Gary joined in. "I mean, they have to put caliber people in these kinds of areas, who are willing to accept some sort of a challenge, who can go into an area and take a situation—even if the people he's dealing with are wrong—and take whatever crap is flying and try to apply some imagination to it—and just turn it around.

"This goes back to something I believe about the whole goddamn Police Department," Gary continued. "There's no psychological screening, as far as applicants go. And as far as assignments, it doesn't make sense to assign your most talented people to certain areas. I mean, it's true that, in general, the worst policemen are assigned to ghetto areas or to big disorders.

"A cat you send to any area that is explodable should be your most talented person, not your most off-balanced. You should send a guy who has less hang-ups than anyone else and who's not gonna get excited about being called a pig and a honkie and so on. I mean, they pay a guy enough so that he should be able to take a little verbal abuse. And he should be able, if something does happen, to turn it around or at least turn it into something less explosive instead of more. And they don't do this. In fact, in San Francisco there isn't any real psychological testing, to see if a guy is prejudiced or not. They teach a guy the law, the regulations, and give him his orders, and he goes outside to judge things as right and wrong. But either the situation is too complex for that or the guy's prejudiced.

"And when I say prejudiced, I don't mean just Negroes. I mean prejudice toward homosexuals, for one thing, and toward any racial group, or hippies . . .

"For example, there's a guy in the station who all the guys think is a homosexual. Now, I don't know if he is or not, and I don't care. All I know about the man is that he's a hell of a nice guy. He has a good mind and so on—but the guys take a real delight in needling him, not to his face but just throwing it out so he can hear it. Now, I just don't understand that—why a policeman gets so goddamn worried about homosexuals and things like that.

"But it's the same old stuff about crimes without victims. For example, prostitution. It's a crime, but there's no victim. No victim at all. Yet the department will tap the energy of any policeman to get whores and pimps and everybody else. Granted, if you have whores and pimps you always have off-shoots—you're always gonna find things like stolen property and so on."

"Well, that's true," Colin said. "With prostitution you almost always have crime. They rob their victims, and —"

"Okay, okay. But once a broad robs a guy, arrest her for robbery! But until she does, leave her alone! It's a business, really. If she finds a customer, she's happy and he's happy. So forget about it! Now, if she robs him and he complains, then bust her for robbery!"

"Do you feel the same way about narcotics?" I asked him.

"Well, I've got nothing against pot at all. Grass, I mean. I don't think anybody needs speed, though. I've got nothing against most of the pills or grass. But anything like heroin, or speed . . . I've seen so many guys on speed, and I've seen what it does. Not only what it makes them capable of doing to other people, but what it does to them. But my feeling about grass is that it should be treated just like alcohol. I don't even think possession should be a misdemeanor. If you smoke so much grass that you get mussed up and can't handle yourself, then they ought to lock you up for the night for your own protection, just like they do with alcoholics. I smoke grass now and then."

"But you bust guys for grass, don't you?" Colin argued.

"It sounds hypocritical, but in unavoidable situations I have busted guys for grass. Yes, I have."

"Well," said Colin, "I'd say you were in conflict, all the way around. Especially with yourself."

"Is that so terrible? Look, I happen to be a cop just like you. I don't go around like our friend Fred did—busting guys for grass and keeping half of it to plant on somebody else he wanted to bust. Or like some guys who keep it to smoke themselves. And when a cop plants some narcotics on a guy, what can the guy do? What's the system gonna do? The system is going to say the cop is innocent. I mean, you think a judge is gonna take a citizen's word over a policeman's? Unless the citizen's got money or prestige? Otherwise the whole goddamn system would break down, if the judge couldn't believe that officer. The whole system would crumble.

"Of course, you're not gonna do that to a guy with money, because most truthfulness is equated with money. You might be the rottenest sonofabitch in the world; but if you've got money our society says, 'You must be righteous or some sort of truthful human being,' and in that case it's the reverse: then the *policeman* must be the bad guy. Then the cop is the bad one, the dishonest one, because he doesn't have that position or that money. That's just the way it is in our country. The guy with prestige can stand up in court and say, 'Well, I didn't do that,' and the court's gonna believe him; but if you're some poor slob, especially from a minority group, well, everybody knows they lie."

"My wife has read so much about police corruption," interrupted Colin, who had been married less than a year, "that she kids me, not too seriously, about not showing her all the money I get from people." Laughing, Colin added,

"I really don't think she believes me that there's very little of that, at least in my experience."

"Well, corruption is hard to prove," Gary said. "But like, I go down to the colored bars after work, you know? And in one bar, all the chairs are hot. They were stolen from one of the big hotels in San Francisco. Now, it never went to court. The cops came in and busted the owner of the bar, but it never went to court. The owner told me, 'It cost me some money downtown.' So that's downtown that got paid off—the higher-ups. But the average cop in blue, like you and me, he's not going around making money."

Two nights later, Haight Street was returning to its normal state of suppressed chaos. Police had arrested more than ninety people in three days of periodic rioting. Forty-five had been injured, including eight cops. On one occasion, several hundred militant youngsters had pulled a large sidewalk trash bin into an intersection to form a barricade. They set it on fire while others dropped flaming Molotov cocktails into the street from rooftops.

Now, on the third night, two dozen helmeted policemen carrying long batons walked back and forth through the grimly quiet street, breaking up any gathering in their path. Squad cars cruised by, undercover men maintained surveillance, and a tactical patrol of fifty men was held in readiness.

The seemingly mindless outbursts of violence had presented an ugly enigma, even for long-time residents of Hashbury. One of them commented, "There are no real hippies here any more, only thugs and pseudo-hippies. I'm getting out."

The San Francisco *Express Times,* an underground paper, acknowledged the victory by the police: "Haight-Ashbury, deep in pain and boredom, suffering from lost dreams, unconsciously reached out for life-giving rebellion last week. It wasn't enough to do the trick. The Haight is still dying." According to this newspaper, the hippies' relationship with the police was humiliating. The cops had shown superior strength and organization while the residents of hippieville were fragmented and unsure of what they wanted. Many thought that this was only the beginning of what was to be a long, drawn-out battle for creation of a "free community" whose values were alien to that of the larger society. The outbreak was viewed as part of the student rebellion, the political rebellion, the social revolution. For the time being, the cops were in control.

To the youngsters who were involved, one of the most frustrating things about the hippie-police confrontation was the way in which they were trapped between two advancing walls of riot cops. As one participant put it to me, "Did you ever try explaining to a riot pig that you would love to get out of his way, but you see, there is this brother of his right behind you who wants you to go the *other* way, and if they would only get together and decide which way they both want you to go that you would be more than happy to go, but you can't go anyplace right now—like you don't have the time to tell them ... ?"

On the other hand, the feeling of solidarity among the police grew stronger during the confrontation and seemed to carry over into the following days. One of the tactical cops told me, "I've been on Haight Street for almost every uprising. I missed the one where they had to use gas. I can't say I was glad to miss it, because you work with these guys, and you know what they're going through, and you feel that just maybe if I'd been out there, somebody wouldn't have gotten hurt, or I would have been able to back up somebody. Like the young cop that got killed out here not long ago. I wish I had been there to help him. And of course I also know that it could have happened to me. It can very easily happen to any one of us at any given time. In jobs like a banker or a store clerk, you have a different thing entirely, because you don't really meet the hostility.

"I get angry. Now, this is the human angle, and you're not gonna be able to get away from this. I don't care what you do, we're not robots, we're people. We have emotions just like anybody else. Like I grabbed a guy one day and he broke my nose. I made the apprehension. I handcuffed him and I was ready to beat hell out of him. I didn't, however. But I think you get angry any time you come close to getting killed. It's just like driving an automobile and some drunk comes by doing eighty miles an hour, and he hits you broadside; and you get out and you'd really like to do that sonofabitch in, you know?

"But I got even more angry after this guy who broke my nose was booked on a felony charge, for forgery—and battery against me, of course—and they dropped the forgery charge because the checks were stolen and the person who owned the checks was subpoenaed and he didn't show up in court. He had to testify, but he refused to show up. Now, this guy who broke my nose was out on bail for two other forgery charges prior to this. And he was allowed to plead guilty to one of the prior forgery charges, a misdemeanor forgery, for which he got six months in county jail. He also went up on the assault against me, which is a felony, and they let him plead guilty to a misdemeanor battery, which was six months. Now, that adds up to *twelve* months, but he served 'em concurrently! So, I was frustrated as hell . . .

"I've enjoyed being a tactical cop. It's a good job. Before joining this squad I was accused of police brutality. As a matter of fact, I received a captain's reprimand on one occasion. They held an investigation and to make everybody happy they reprimanded me. What was I supposed to tell my wife and family?

"It was right after Watts. Now, what sparked Watts? It was a drunk-driver arrest, something real simple like that. And they waited, and they waited, and the cops stayed at the scene; so a disturbance was created and the crowd went into a fit, but the cops didn't leave and it grew and grew and finally blew sky-high. So right after that, I was aware of this chain-reaction kind of thing.

"A kid escaped from a paddy wagon and I chased him.

I was on a relief motorcycle with no radio on it, no red light; and so the wagon guys told me about it and I went off to find him. The patrolman who was chasing the kid caught him and I was right behind him. He caught the kid around the waist, but the kid twisted around and began throwing hands, you know? So I got off the bike and grappled with the kid. We wrestled on the ground and a big crowd gathered around us. Well, the kid ended up with a black eye. Later, he charged police brutality. See, the crowd had gathered. People were coming out of the houses—a Negro district, and the kid was Negro. I was thinking, 'Let's not make the same mistake as Watts.' So we handcuffed the kid but there was no way to transport him away from the crowd, and he was yelling and yelling for his people to help him. I sat him up on the deck of the motorcycle and rode him about a hundred feet, and then I saw the wagon coming and I waved it down. He claimed we had beat him up on the street. None of the people in the crowd substantiated that testimony, however. I was given a reprimand for transporting the kid on the motorcycle. But see, I was trying to avoid another Watts.

"I know one officer who got stabbed in the hand, and he physically took the guy apart. He shot him up."

It was inexplicable to Gary Cummings that Colin Barker would want to join the tactical patrol, but that is what he told us. Gary was a bit stunned, but Colin explained, "The foot-patrol beat is getting too dangerous. Not that I'm afraid, really, but the tactical force would be a good change of pace."

As for Gary, he eventually made friends with one of the few Negro radio-car men and began driving a steady beat with him. One night, Gary expressed some of his most personal thoughts about his job to me.

"My main concern," he said, "is that, well, I have a feeling about what's going to happen. I have a feeling that this country is, within the next five years, going to become a police state. And I think the first person that's going to suffer

is the black man. When I say suffer, I mean physically. I really
believe this.

"I have an emotional hang-up here, because, like everybody else, I've been raised from birth to believe in the free-
enterprise system. The capitalist system and so forth. Now,
I'm not that hip on economics or politics. I'm not like a lot
of guys who fling around words like 'fascist' and 'communist'
and so on. I probably couldn't explain what fascism is, or
bring in the economics of it or anything. I couldn't explain
about communism either. But I see a lot of policemen who
really *act* knowledgeable about it all. They say, 'Oh, there
are communists down here starting riots in Haight-Ashbury.'
And if you ask them to explain what communism is, or different types of communism, they can't.

"So we've been brought up believing in free enterprise
and so on, and you hear the comparisons between our standard of living and Russia's, and you think, 'Hey, this country
is great.' But on the other hand, half the evil in this country
is because of the capitalist system. The slum landlords and
so on. And the police really believe that they're hired to just
go in and keep the peace, to keep order and so on. But they
never ask themselves, 'Well, why aren't the middle-class kids
out in a suburban area rioting?' I mean, why doesn't it ever
occur to them to riot?

"It's the old thing about raising expectations and then
not fulfilling them. I mean, you know you're gonna have
trouble. If you do that to a child, you're in trouble. And
obviously you're gonna have problems on the national level.

"Now, of course, any trouble we may have in San Francisco can be a result also of what may have happened in
Cleveland or Detroit or Oakland. Because, say, if Watts
breaks out, and a kid from there comes here, he's going to
tell a kid up here, 'Man, you guys ain't shit. Because we've
been *doing* it down there.' This is the attitude, you know.
There's a pride about riots.

"And this is another thing I'm sort of afraid of. As far
as riots, it's almost 'the thing to do.' I mean, they wait for

summer. But why wait? Kids on the street will say, 'Man, just wait till the summer.' And you kind of wonder, well, why wait? Even if he has no reason to riot, he's grown up with three or four years of rioting every summer. This has been a real part of the kid's life, see. A seasonal thing, like football season. He figures, you know, that this is *supposed* to happen.

"What I feel, and it might just be an emotional reaction or whatever, is two things: one, that not long ago, twenty-odd years ago, a modern, industrial, supposedly enlightened country put to death six million Jews and three million other Europeans. Just through their concentration camps. All fully justified, as far as *they* were concerned. Killing nine million people. Now, legally, the United States had no right to try those people in Germany for war crimes. It's against our constitution to do that. You can't try anyone for something that was not a crime when he did it. *We* made it a crime, after those acts were committed.

"It's not a crime, for example, for the state of California to put a man to death. The death penalty exists. But if in the future it's eliminated, do we then try the governor or the jury who sent a man to the gas chamber? Of course not, because it was legal to do it at the time. And in Germany, it was perfectly legal—those people were executed through sentencing by the courts. In one way or another, the Germans executed all six or nine million people through legal process. They were either judged undesirable, or whatever. And it was legal! So what are we gonna try them for, murder?

"I'm talking about the way a country can do terrible things under law. Which brings me to the other thing that worries me—that also, in the same period, California locked up an awful lot of Japanese. For—what did we say?—national security. We locked up Japanese. I knew some kids whose families had lost all their property, and really, it's a shame. Everybody else was protected by the Constitution, yet these people weren't. I don't know what we thought they were going to do . . .

"So, the Japanese were put in concentration camps in

California. Now, as far as any rioting, it's possible—and the Negroes think this—that the same thing can happen to the twenty-million or so black people in this country. We've come a long way since the 1940s to now—but the United States has always been an expert at doing the impossible. We suddenly converted from making autos into making battleships and planes—that was a miracle. And I don't think this country would have any trouble getting rid of twenty million people. Especially when they're so identifiable. None, whatsoever. And all this country needs, I think, is the justification. The majority of the white population, I think, already feels that it *does* have the justification, right now. It's frightening.

"So a lot of white liberals, like myself—and especially because I'm a cop—are going to have to choose. And I don't have a lot of encouragement, from reading history, that many white people will have any courage. Let's face it—everybody looks out for himself in the long run. And when it comes down to the point of death, well—you know the story of the guy who fell in love with the girl and they found out he had this fear of rats? So they put the cage up to his face with the rat coming toward him, and what was the guy's reaction? 'Not me, not me, not me! Do it to her!' And this was the one object, the girl, that he loved.

"I know, for myself, that I have a fear of pain and that I'm not ready to die or get killed. But, I don't know. When the thing comes down to a choice, the white liberal can go with his own people or, if the Negro will have him, he can go with the blacks. But how is he gonna move around? The Negro'll be too distrustful.

"One hope, and this is the crazy thing, is a place like Haight-Ashbury. Not so much the young plastic hippies, but the real rebels, the ones who want to defy authority. The hippies aren't the *only* hope or anything like that, but I think we're gonna need them as some kind of bridge, or alliance. I mean, they draw together all kinds of people, and there's some kind of communication between races and so on.

"But the people in control can always find a reason for

something if they want to do it. I don't know if it makes much difference which political party is in power, either; but when Jack Kennedy was in, it seemed there was an attitude that this country had, that now it has lost. There was an enthusiasm. Like the Peace Corps. Here was a guy who got people to give up two and three years of their lives to do something. There was an attitude among the young that I think is missing now.

"I don't think very far ahead, for myself. Certainly not about being a policeman. For most cops, the uniform and the whole experience draws them closer to one side; they merge into a group. With me . . . with me, it has made me look at myself much more critically, as a human being . . ."